Pervez Amirali Hoodbhoy was born in 1950. He obtained a B.Sc. (Electrical Engineering), B.Sc. (Mathematics), M.Sc. (Solid State Physics) and Ph.D. (Nuclear Physics) from MIT. In 1968 he won the Baker Award for Electronics from the British Association of Radio and Electronic Engineers. In 1973 he began teaching at Quaid-e-Azam University, Islamabad, where he also conducts research in nuclear and particle physics. In 1984 he received the Abdus Salam Prize for Mathematics, and in 1990 the Faiz Ahmed Faiz Award for his contribution to education in Pakistan. Dr Hoodbhoy has been a post-doctoral fellow at the University of Washington and a visiting professor at Carnegie Mellon University. He remains a visiting research scientist at MIT, where he spends two months each year. His interest — other than professional — include popular expositions on science, education and social issues.

Islam and Science

Religious Orthodoxy and The Battle for Rationality

Pervez Hoodbhoy

Foreword by Mohammed Abdus Salam

Zed Books Ltd
London and New Jersey

Islam and Science was first published by Zed Books Ltd,
57 Caledonian Road, London N1 9BU, UK and 165 First Avenue,
Atlantic Highlands, New Jersey 07716, USA, in 1991.

Copyright © Pervez Hoodbhoy, 1991.

Cover designed by Andrew Corbett
Typeset by EMS Photosetters, Thorpe Bay, Essex.

Printed and bound by CPI Antony Rowe, Eastbourne

ISBN 1 85649 024 6 Hb
ISBN 1 85649 025 4 Pb

Library of Congress Cataloging-in-Publication Data

Hoodbhoy, Pervez.
    Islam and science : religious orthodoxy and the battle
    for rationality / Pervez Hoodbhoy.
        p.   cm.
    Includes bibliographical references and index.
    ISBN 1-85649-024-6. — ISBN 1-85649-025-4 (pbk.)
    1. Islam and science. I. Title.
BP190.5.S3H66 1991
297'.1975----dc20   91-22885
                                      CIP

Contents

Tables

Foreword

'There is no question but today, of all civilizations on this planet, science is weakest in the lands of Islam. The dangers of this weakness cannot be over-emphasized since honourable survival of a society depends directly on its strength in science and technology in the condition of the present age.'

When Dr Pervez Hoodbhoy asked me to write the preface to his book, he reminded me of a promise I had made to him: 'As you will recall you had agreed to do so, subject to the condition that the point of view expressed in the book is acceptable to you. I do hope that there is no serious disagreement. But even if you should . . . disagree with certain parts of it, I would much prefer that you write a critical essay rather than not write anything at all. I do feel that the book needs to be balanced with a somewhat dissimilar view.'

In fact, I do not disagree with Dr Hoodbhoy on anything he has written in this book. On the contrary, I completely agree with him that the state of science in the Islamic world is abysmal. I stand by the quotation from my writings which appears at the head of this page and with which he opens Chapter Four.

Secondly, I agree with him that religious orthodoxy and the spirit of intolerance are two of the major factors responsible for killing the once flourishing enterprise of science in Islam. Science only prospers provided there are sufficient practitioners to constitute a community which can work with serenity, with fullest support in terms of the necessary experimental and library infrastructure, and with the ability to criticize openly each other's work. These conditions are not satisfied in contemporary Islam.

Thirdly, he is right that Nasr and Sardar are doing a great disservice to science in Muslim countries if they are calling for a religiously and not culturally motivated 'Islamic science', whatever that means. There is only one universal science, its problems and modalities are international and there is no such thing as Islamic science just as there is no Hindu science, no Jewish science, no Confucian science, nor Christian science.

I agree, also, with his contention that Islamic science, as set out by the late President Zia of Pakistan, was a fraud and that its practitioners (whom Professor Hoodbhoy rightly mocks) are (or should be) ashamed of what they have wrought in the name of science.

Finally, I agree that pragmatism may provide the one modality through which real science in Muslim countries may be regenerated — just as is likely to be the case for democracy within Islam. Where I could be critical of Professor Hoodbhoy is that he has not developed this last part of his argument as much as he should have.

One could divide this book into two sections. Section One comprises those chapters which describe the present situation in science and education in the Muslim world. Section Two recounts the history of science within Islam, as well as of the sciences as interpreted in the Zia period in Pakistan.

Let me first stress some of the book's strong points. The chapter on the Catholic Church and its fight with science over the centuries (with ten examples of conflict) is absolutely first-rate. The author's recounting, also, of the story of science in Islam is extremely well done. He also quotes Steven Weinberg's and my research and says that it made no basic difference to our work whether I was an 'avowed believer and Weinberg an avowed atheist'. I can confirm that he is right. We were both 'geographically and ideologically remote from each other' when we conceived the same theory of physics for unifying the weak and electromagnetic forces. If there was any bias towards the unification paradigm in my thinking, it was unconsciously motivated by my background as a Muslim.

As I said, my only criticism is that Hoodbhoy has not been too explicit about what the remedies for our situation are. He does not, for example, come back to the basic question he raises himself: Is science doomed for ever in Islam? Or is it doomed till such time as Muslims take upon themselves a non-fundamentalist attitude?

Personally, I feel that the Islamic world today is not a monolithic structure. It divides naturally into different cultural parts so far as science and technology are concerned. Let me make this point clear. The Gulf Arabs — awash with money — could have taken upon themselves a duty to spend that money to build science within the *whole* Islamic world. They could yet do this, but they have taken no such position — not even towards their fellow Arabs. Secondly there are Egypt, Iran, Pakistan, Nigeria, Turkey, Malaysia and Lebanon — all Muslim countries which, in descending order, have been the largest producers of scientific literature in recent years. Now while it is true that Egypt has the largest community of scientists, Egyptian standards are not uniformly high except for the areas of engineering and low technology. Thirdly, the Iran–Iraq war having come to an end, Iran is now in a good position to resume its age-old supremacy in the sciences in the Islamic world. I find a thirst among its young people — a thirst which is actually being helped by the Shi'ite clergy (the only hierarchically organized clergy in Islam), as I saw for myself when I visited Iran recently. As for Pakistan, it awaits a ruler who will have the same feelings towards science and technology as Jawaharlal Nehru had for Indian science. Indonesia I do not know well enough to be able to make a value judgement. Bangladesh, regrettably, is too poor to do anything for the sciences, notwithstanding the great desire of its young men and women to make the scientific enterprise part of their lives. As for the other countries in Islam, they count for little, except Sudan where the hardest working Arab scientists are to be found, Turkey which may make the grade because of its wish to join Europe, Algeria with its vigorous population, and possibly Morocco and Iraq.

One of the most perceptive sections in this book concerns the position of the ulema in Islam. As the author says, 'Islam had no church, no formal centre of tyrannical religious authority. Paradoxically, a superior moral position — the right of the individual to interpret doctrine without the aid of priests — appears to have led to a systemic organizational weakness which proved to be fatal to Islamic political and economic — not to speak of scientific and technological — power in the long run.'

This, in my opinion, has come about through the wielding of the weapon of excommunication (*takfir*). The list of those who have been excommunicated at some time or other includes such luminaries as Imam Ali — the Kharjites did that — Imam Abu Hanifa and Imam Malik bin Anas, founders of two of the four recognized schools of Islamic theology; Imam Ghazali, Sheikh-ul-Akbar Ibn-i-Arabi, Imam Ibn-i-Taymiyya, Sayyid Muhammad Jonpuri and scientists like Ibn Rushd, Abu Ali Sina, Ibn-ul-Haitham, and others. Often, the verdict of excommunication was a local sectarian aberration. However, sentences of death were carried out; among those actually martyred were mystics like Mansur Al Hallaj, Sheikh-ul-Ashraq Shahabuddin Suhrawardi, Sheikh Alaaee and Sarmad. All this happened despite the absence of an organized clergy within Sunni Islam. In recounting the martyrdom of Sarmad, Abul-Kalam Azad wrote:

During the last 1,300 years, the pens of jurisprudents have always acted like a drawn sword, and the blood of many of the chosen ones of God have stained their persons . . . this martyrdom was not limited to Sufis and the free thinkers — even the greatest Muslim men of orthodox scholarship suffered.

Thus, not having a priesthood in Sunni Islam has not helped us much because of this propensity of the ulema to wield the weapon of excommunication and for our rulers and the general public to listen to them. What, then, is the remedy so that *takfir* does not recur — at least so far as scientific beliefs are concerned?

One remedy would be to try to deal with the two classes of so-called ulema separately. First, there are the lay preachers whose major task is to lead prayers in the rural mosques and who earn their living by performing such functions as officiating at marriage, death and circumcision ceremonies and looking after the upkeep of the mosques. This is a professional class who should have scant interest in fundamentalist persecution once their livelihood is secured. If this can be guaranteed them (like the Christian priests whom they resemble) they would not retard the progress of science and technology.

The second category of ulema is the damaging one. These are men (without spiritual pretensions) who claim to interpret the Holy Quran, issue excommunication *fatwas* — something the Holy Prophet — Peace be upon him — never did — and give their view on *all* subjects — politics, economics, law — in their Friday sermons.

Lest it should be objected that there is no priestly class in (Sunni) Islam, one must state clearly that, in this respect, Islam has had the worst deal of all the great religions of humankind. In most Islamic countries, a class of nearly illiterate men have, in practice, habitually appropriated to themselves the status of a priestly class without possessing even a rudimentary knowledge of their great and tolerant religion. The arrogance, the rapacity, and the low level of commonsense displayed by this class, as well as its intolerance, has been derided by all poets and writers of any consequence in Persia, India, Central Asia and Turkey. This is the class which has been responsible for rabble-rousing throughout the history of Islam and for the repression which matched (fortunately, only sometimes) the systematic persecution perpetrated by the Inquisition in Christian societies. The only *long-term* remedy for the situation is to deprive these persons of their power to make mischief through their Friday sermons which, instead of being spiritually elevating, are usually political tirades. This politicizing should be stopped.

I have been asking the ulema why their sermons should not exhort Muslims to take up the subjects of science and technology, considering that one-eighth of the Holy Book speaks of *taffaqur* and *taskheer* — science and technology. Most have replied that they would like to do so but they do not know enough modern science. They only know the science of the age of Avicenna. The Third World Academy of Sciences (which has the privilege of partly sponsoring Hoodbhoy's book) has been trying to remedy this situation through commissioning books which may be introduced into their religious seminaries.

To summarize, I would say the following are the important considerations for building up science and technology in our Islamic countries:

(1) The number of scientists and technologists to be trained should be pitched at a fairly large figure so as to be 'critical' — and they should be encouraged by the state to make up communities for research and development with their own modalities of operation.

(2) We desperately need basic scientists, at least to teach and serve as reference points for the applied scientists and high technologists.

(3) It must be remembered that, in the conditions of today, applied sciences and high technology are the money spinners. Once this is demonstrated within our societies, there will be less temptation on the part of rulers as well as the ulema to tamper with the scientists' and technologists' work.

(4) Men of science, and women of science, must keep international contact with their peers abroad in order to have the same standards of science and technology as obtain outside the Muslim countries.

(5) Finally, there is hope yet. For example, after 25 years' preaching, for the first time some funds have become available for science from the Gulf. The Trieste Centre this year received a quarter of a million dollars for Arabs from the Kuwait-based Arab Fund for Economic and Social Development. If we can obtain similar funds for Muslims in general, this may make a big difference to the prospects for physics in the Islamic countries.

Mohammed Abdus Salam
1990

Preface

This book was not written to fulfil any long-held plan to write one. Rather, it was force of circumstance that provoked and almost compelled me to write it. The germ of the idea grew from a lecture which the Lahore Education Society invited me to deliver in May 1984 on the subject of Islam and science. Those were bad times for the country in general, and academics in particular. Following the double coup of guns and theology in 1977, dissent from the official line was not tolerated. Many university professors, including some of my colleagues at Quaid-e-Azam University, had been sent to jail and tortured for having expressed views which our new rulers did not like. Meanwhile, numerous charlatans and sycophants, responding to the regime's rhetoric of Islamization, had seized the reins of society and set for themselves the task of 'Islamizing' everything in sight, including science. Highly placed members of the Pakistani scientific establishment were leading advocates of this venture. In seeking to establish their credentials, these 'Islamic scientists' transgressed not only the demands of reason and logic, but also every enlightened interpretation of the Islamic Faith. With breathtaking boldness, they laid claim to various bizarre discoveries which ranged from calculating the speed of heaven using Einstein's Theory of Relativity, to finding the chemical composition of jinns, and even to the extraction of energy from these fiery divine creatures so that Pakistan's energy problems could be solved.

Astonishing though it was, these results of 'Islamic science' were often presented in large-scale, state supported, well funded, national and international conferences, and published in local scientific journals. Indeed, the last section of this book is a reprint entitled 'They Call It Islamic Science'. This is an exposition and critique which was inspired by the First International Conference of Scientific Miracles Of The Holy Quran And Sunnah, organised in Islamabad by the International Islamic University during the time of General Zia. Originally published as an article in the Pakistani monthly magazine *Herald* of January 1988, it drew vituperation and abuse from proponents of the new so-called 'Islamic science'. A heated debate continued for nearly a year after its publication. At the same time, other people made liberal use of it as an exposé of the misuse of Islam by rulers in Islamic countries. It was made part of the official court records in one particular law suit challenging the Islamic credentials of the Zia regime. The reprint published in this book has been slightly revised and references added.

The opportunities provided to me for disputing such attempts to 'Islamize' science encouraged me into thinking and reading further on Islam and science. I soon found that this was a fascinating subject of vast dimensions. That was the beginning of my education in this area, and I discovered that there were numerous important aspects which not only I, but also others with a much deeper knowledge of Islamic history, were quite ignorant of. Therefore, it appeared to me logical, and perhaps useful, to collect together what I had learned and put it in a form appropriate for a book.

I wish to state unequivocally, however, that I have no illusions and make no claims to mastery over the subject of this book, Islam and science, or even of the philosophy of science. It was quite unwillingly, and with considerable trepidation, that I embarked on a project so far removed from my field of professional concern — particle and nuclear physics. But, understanding the relationship of Islam to science is of such immense contemporary importance, and is so pregnant with profound implications for one-fifth of the inhabitants of this globe, that it was a task which simply had to be taken up. I would have preferred someone with a professional interest to have done this job instead, but it seemed unwise to wait indefinitely for it to happen. In any case, for better or worse, the reader holds in his or her hands the results of one attempt to look at science in Islam, both in the past and the present. Whether the attempt was worthwhile is for the reader to decide.

My debt to the people around me is enormous. Colleagues at the Physics Department of Quaid-e-Azam University in Islamabad, where I have spent most of my professional working life, maintained an island of sanity at a time when society at large seemed to be in the throes of a delirium. Among these, I shall mention only three individuals by name. First, my friend Abdul Hameed Nayyar, with whom I have long shared and discussed the ideas contained in this book, and whose clarity of thought, sincerity of purpose, and meticulousness brought about numerous improvements. Secondly, my senior colleague Arifuzzaman, from whose encyclopedic knowledge of history I have gained much, and whose unyielding pessimism provided me a constant challenge to seek the positive. Finally, Khurshid Hasnain, who read various portions with great care and suggested important improvements.

I am grateful to Eqbal Ahmed for his encouragement, suggestions, and careful reading of the manuscript. It would be opportune here for me to acknowledge the powerful influence that he and his writings have had in shaping my ideas and outlook.

From across the oceans, I received numerous pieces of literature, analysis, and some helpful criticism from my friend Zia Mian. I thank Al-Noor Dhanani of the History of Science Department of Harvard University for leading me on to some useful research materials, for a careful reading of the text, and for correcting a number of historical mistakes. I would also like to thank Mr Qudrutallah Fatimi for comments on the original manuscript, some of which have been incorporated into the present text. I gratefully acknowledge a grant from the Third World Academy of Sciences for the purchase of a number of important reference works on the history of thought and science.

I thank the editor of this volume for his meticulousness, attention to detail, and suggestions for improvement. The debt I owe to my parents and family has no measure. And finally, it is for Hajra, Asha, and Alia that I reserve my last and deepest acknowledgement. Their love and support make life happy and meaningful.

Pervez Amirali Hoodbhoy
Islamabad, 1991

1.   Islam and Science: Are They Compatible?

Imagine for a moment a team of Martian anthropologists visiting Earth sometime between the 9th and 13th centuries. Their mission is to study the cultural and social evolution of the human species. Observation reveals that some societies are dynamic and evolving towards higher and more sophisticated forms, while others are static and crippled by traditions and rituals. The visitors file a report with headquarters that the civilization with greatest promise is the Islamic civilization with its *Bait-ul-Hikmah*, astronomical observatories, hospitals and schools. Baghdad, the intellectual centre of the world to which scholars travel from distant lands, appears the brightest spot on earth. To Martian eyes, Ibn Haytham and Omar Khayyam are recognizable as precursors of the modern scientist, a bearer of the universal cosmic intelligence. In contrast, Europe, with its witch-burning popes, appears retrograde and barbaric, sunk in the gloom of the Dark Ages.

Suppose now that the same extra-terrestrial team was to return today. With some embarrassment they would have to report back that their earlier prediction had turned out to be wrong. The part of humanity which once seemed to offer the greatest promise now appears inescapably trapped in a state of frozen medievalism, rejecting the new and clinging desperately to the old. On the other hand, the former retrogrades have climbed the evolutionary ladder and are now aiming for the stars. Was this stunning reversal of roles, ask the visitors, the mere misfortune of one and the good fortune of the other? Was it due to invasions and military defeats? Or was it the result of a fundamental shift in outlook and attitudes? In the study of the rise and fall of civilizations, the academic from Mars would find the Islamic case most interesting.

About 700 years ago, Islamic civilization almost completely lost the will and ability to do science. Since that time, apart from attempts during the Ottoman period and in Mohammed Ali's Egypt, there have been no significant efforts at recovery. Many Muslims acknowledge, and express profound regret at, this fact. Indeed, this is the major preoccupation of the modernist faction in Islam. But most traditionalists feel no regret — in fact, many welcome this loss because, in their view, keeping a distance from science helps preserve Islam from corrupting, secular influences.

Scientific development and ideology are indivisibly linked. Hence the fundamental question: is the Islamic faith in harmonious complementarity with the science of the natural world or is there, rather, an irreconcilable conflict between a metaphysical system based on faith and the demands of reason and empirical enquiry? For over a thousand years philosophers and theologians of Islam have pondered this question which, particularly in this age of space travel and gene splicing, continues to invite intense debate and disagreement. Reformist, modernist, and orthodox Muslims have argued with one another over the compatibility of Islam and science almost to the point of exhaustion. Drawing their ammunition from the same vast storehouse of Islamic tradition, they have chosen different exemplars and scriptural interpretations to arrive at whatever position they considered correct in the first place. At the heart of the dispute is the fundamental issue: science is a secular pursuit, and it is impossible for it to be otherwise. The secular character of science does not mean that it necessarily repudiates the existence of the Divine. But it does mean that the validation of scientific truths does not rely on any form of spiritual authority; observation, experimentation, and logic are the sole arbiters which decide what is true or false. Scientists are free to be as religious as they please, but science recognizes no laws outside its own.

Given that this dispute has been around for so long — and hence that its resolution to the satisfaction of all appears well nigh impossible — it would be wholly pretentious of me to assume that any further discussion, no matter how well reasoned, could put an end to the matter. But, even if there exists a strong temptation to relegate the issue to the backwaters of one's consciousness, its sheer importance permits no easy escape. As the 20th century spins towards the year 2000, the attitude of Islam to science — what it is in theory as well as in actual practice — acquires immense and unprecedented importance for Muslim society. No longer is science, as in the splendid courts of Harun al-Rashid and al-Ma'mun, simply entertainment for enlightened princes or a subject for the exchange of polemics between scholars. Instead, it has become the very means by which, for better or worse, the entire human civilization is being irreversibly transformed. Military strength, political power and economic prosperity have become contingent upon the ability of modern nations to understand, control, and create modern science. The hi-tech war waged by the West against Iraq — televised instantly and watched globally — is one vivid illustration of this.

Historically, the civilization of Islam has paid a heavy price for having failed to acquire science. Indeed, this failure accounts for the retreat of Islamic civilization, and the ascendancy of the West, over the centuries. In medieval times, Islam's relationship to the West had been of a qualitatively different nature. There were times of intimate and fruitful collaboration, as well as times of violence and confrontation. Seven centuries of Muslim rule in Spain gave to the Europeans, among other things, access to the accumulated treasures of Greek and Islamic learning. But, on the other hand, the protracted and bitter confrontation during the Crusades, and later the Ottoman domination of the Balkans, left on both sides a heritage of prejudice and resentment. This feeling of hostility caused the differences between the two civilizations to be magnified. But, as Eqbal Ahmed points out, there had existed an essential commonality of structure between Islamic and Western societies:

> While our cultures were traditional, agrarian and medieval, there existed a structural symmetry between them which accounted for a degree of equality in the exchange of ideas as well as products. Winners and losers manufactured and used the same weapons, traded in comparable goods and debated on familiar intellectual premises. There was a certain congruence of class interests and shared attitudes among aristocrats, craftsmen, traders, scholars.[1]

Then came the Renaissance. The collapse of the medieval feudal economy, the emergence of capitalism on a wide scale, and the ensuing social ferment, gave birth to modern science in Europe some 400 years ago. Experimentation, quantification, prediction, and control became the paradigm of a new culture. Modern science sought, by means of a clearly defined methodology, a rational comprehension of the physical universe. It brought certitude and banished doubt. This methodology derived from a coherent set of rules and criteria independent of the hierarchies of power and wealth; certainty could now be interpretable on the basis of facts that anyone could check. To establish the validity of a truth merely required following the same procedures and did not depend upon the priestly class or temporal authority of an individual. A mysterious and capricious universe could now, for the first time in human history, be understood as mechanical and orderly in which 'number holds sway on the flux'. To its possessors, the scientific method gave undreamed of power. In part this power was used to understand the laws of nature, and subsequently to create new technologies. But, in part, science became the weapon with which less technologically developed peoples around the world were to be systematically subjugated and colonized.

Faced with the brutal onslaught of 18th century mercantile imperialism, traditional Muslim society stood defenceless. Almost all of the Muslim world, ranging from West Africa to East Asia, was rapidly colonized. But the defeat was not in military terms alone, although that was humiliating enough for a civilization hitherto accustomed to conquer. This first contact with modern imperialism — whose strength derived not from numbers but from the analytical methods of modern science — left the Muslims numbed, disoriented, and unsure of themselves. It was an unequal contest. Imperialism was a complex system — an intricate and well oiled machine whose parts seemed to move with clockwork precision. Modern rifles and cannons — as at the battle of Plassey in 1757 — were certainly the most visible manifestations of its strength. But it was the telegraph, steamship, machine produced goods, and modern organizational methods, which were the backbone of the new colossus. These elements were alien to an agrarian and pastoral civilization. Large local armies, untutored in military technique, fought valiantly but were decimated by disciplined British and French regiments a tenth of their size. Gone was the symmetry which had characterized the centuries–old relationship of Islam with the West. In the confrontation of an industrial and capitalist West with a traditional and pre-capitalist society, there could be little doubt of the outcome. Bringing untold miseries in the process, modern imperialism set out in its mission to 'civilize' the 'natives' by destroying their traditional culture. The scars which it inflicted have yet to heal.

The era of decolonization began with the end of the Second World War. With traditional economic, social, cultural, and political relationships already deeply eroded in the encounter with Western imperialism, a fragmented and insecure Muslim polity made its entry into a world which it had had no role in shaping. Even the territorial boundaries of many emergent Muslim states had been defined by the needs or whims of their erstwhile colonial masters. Independence brought euphoria. But the dispossession of the Palestinian people from their native homeland, subsequent Arab defeats on the battlefield, and the failure of Muslim countries in establishing stable democratic institutions, made this short lived. The failures, and eventual demise, of secular nationalist–socialist governments — such as Mossadeq in Iran, Nasser in Egypt, Sukarno in Indonesia, and Zulfiqar Ali Bhutto in Pakistan — led to immense disappointment and frustration, and paved the way for a resurgence of neo-fundamentalist movements.

The rule of military–bureaucratic and tribal–feudal elites, for whom self-perpetuation and preservation are the pre-occupying concerns, has become the dominant mode of government in Muslim countries. Paradoxically, these rulers of modern Islamic states deviate arbitrarily and very far from the social and ethical ideals of Islam, but upon their strength, and thus the strength of the state, has depended the identity and cohesion of the Islamic community. The elites which rule Muslim countries today have shown little ability — or even desire — to address the myriad problems and challenges of a modern world. Of these, the development of science and a rational culture are perhaps the most important. Indeed, compared with non-Muslim countries possessing roughly equivalent resources and a comparable level of cultural development, Muslim states do poorly. This is a major contention of this book which I will later on try to validate quantitatively.

Scientific underdevelopment is certainly one important part of the crisis which envelopes the Muslim world, and it virtually ensures that the political, economic, and intellectual dominance of the West is likely to persist into the foreseeable future. Standing now upon the brink of the 21st century, it is still hard to discern any large-scale movement towards a science-based culture in any Islamic country.

Although it is the crisis of science in these countries that is the principal concern of this book, this is no more than one aspect of a far deeper malaise which arises from the failure of governments in Muslim states to safeguard their national sovereignty and resources, to satisfy the basic needs of their populations, and to establish popular and representative rule. Indeed, at its core, the crisis of Islamic countries is political in nature. Never before, and in no other civilization, have the

links between wealth and weakness, material resources and moral bankruptcy been so tragic. Never before in the history of the Islamic peoples has there been so total a separation of political power and civil society. . . . From Morocco to Syria, from Iraq to Pakistan and Indonesia, Muslims are ruled by armed minorities. Some describe themselves as socialist and democratic; others as Islamic; yet others as Islamic–socialist, and democratic. Nearly all Muslim governments are composed of corrupt and callous elites more adept at repressing the populace than at protecting natural resources or national sovereignty. They are more closely linked to foreign patrons than the domestic polity.[2]

Not to have enough machines and equipment, to lag behind in industrial development, and to be but a spectator as the rest of the world rushes onwards with discoveries and inventions, is bad. But to be denied opportunities for meaningful education, to have governments which are unresponsive to the needs of the people, and to have human dignity regularly flouted — that is truly tragic.

The Task Ahead

To embark on a quest for understanding scientific development, one requires a basic understanding of the scientific enterprise — what the philosophy and *modus operandi* of modern science is, its dependence on the nature and quality of the educational system, and the system of ideas and values which it generates and which in turn are vital if science is to flourish. In this context, it is imperative to realize that Muslim culture is inextricably wedded to the past. Therefore, any serious analysis of the present state of science requires a deep understanding of how science entered the Islamic civilization and flourished in it for nearly five centuries. One is immediately confronted by important and difficult questions: whether the science of the Muslims was specifically Islamic in character, the extent to which it was assimilated into the popular culture, the societal forces which nurtured it, and the nature and extent of the religious opposition to it. In particular, it is important to understand the forces which led to the decline of science and learning in Islamic society after it had reached its peak a millennium ago. These forces continue to be important even today. At another level, one needs to explore the intimate connection of science with technology — with the productive forces in society, the patterns of distribution of political and economic power, and how these in turn affect patterns of technology choice and industrialization.

My account of the dismal state of science in Muslim countries today, my bleak prognosis for it in the years ahead, and the reasons offered in this book for this scientific backwardness, may possibly offend some readers. But the purpose here is to be objective; not necessarily to please. Unless reality is comprehended, there can be no hope of constructive change. Muslims — who comprise one-fifth of all humanity — will continue to suffer an undignified and degraded existence if science, and particularly a rational approach to human problems, is considered alien to Islamic culture. But there is hope for the future as growing numbers of Muslims come to understand the need for attitudinal changes if science is to thrive once more in Muslim lands.

References
1. Eqbal Ahmed, 'Islam and Politics', in *Islam, Politics, and the State*, ed. Mohammad Asghar Khan (London, Zed Press, 1985), p. 14. This essay also contains an excellent discussion of the trauma of Muslim life in the post-colonial era.
2. Ibid., pp. 15–25.

2. Science: Its Nature and Origins

The belief that nature is orderly is not yet universal. Savages, we are told, live in a completely capricious universe, and we still find congregations praying for rain although they would hesitate, probably, to pray that the sun might stand still. That is because astronomy is a more developed science than meteorology.

J. W. N. Sullivan

Science is here to stay — the future of humanity and science are inextricably tied together. Upon science — but guided by universal moral principles — depends the continuation of civilized human existence on earth. The past tells us so. Without science humankind was helpless before wind and storm, ravaged by plague and disease, and terrorized by mindless superstitions. Wasted was the incomparable instrument it possessed: the human mind. Then human beings created science, and science liberated them from superstition.

Nevertheless, it is evident that science in our times is under bitter attack. In a sense this is nothing new; there have always been anti-scientific currents in the course of history and, in particular, religious dogmatists of all persuasions have long excoriated science as a godless pursuit destructive of divinely inspired morality. But disillusion with science is to be found on a much wider scale today. Many of the promises it made for a better world remain unfulfilled. For one, science may have transformed the world into a global village, but it has yet to teach the villagers to learn to talk with and understand each other. We live in a dangerously polluted world whose fragile ecosystems are being irreversibly destroyed by the wastes of industrial civilization. Too often it is militarists with dangerous designs who have learned the value of science. And a kind of reductionist scientific thinking exists which reduces spring blossoms to botany and glorious sunsets to meteorology. It appears also that we will never escape from the atomic shadow of Oppenheimer's sin — the continued existence of humankind is something which can no longer be taken for granted.

Much debate has centred on whether the outstanding problems of humanity usually attributed to science are, in fact, engendered by its misuse of whether they are intrinsic to the very nature of the scientific enterprise. The dispute goes beyond arguments that certain applications of science have created problems for humankind of great, and perhaps even fatal, severity; that is agreed upon by almost everybody. Rather, opponents of science go a step further and insist that scientific epistemology — the very nature of scientific knowledge and its mode of enquiry — is fatally flawed. Hence, it is argued, the time has drawn nigh to seek a liberation of the human spirit from the chains of a stifling ideology, and to create alternatives hitherto unthought of.

But before entering into any discussion concerning alternative science, I shall attempt to define ordinary or conventional science as succinctly as I can. In doing so, I shall present the working scientist's understanding of science, rather than the more esoteric discussions of the philosophers of science.

What Science Is

To address the question 'what is science?' I have set out a convenient glossary of concepts which lie at the heart of modern scientific thinking.

Facts: Science begins with the assumption that there exist facts. A scientist accepts, for example, sense impressions or the pointer readings of his instruments as facts. These facts are considered to be valid provided that different and independent observers agree on the same thing, or if repeated observation at different times and different places leads to identical results. In this manner the subjective opinions and beliefs of individuals are eliminated.

To give but one example of this, suppose that a number of observers equipped with sufficiently powerful telescopes have reached a consensus on the orbital motion, sizes, and shapes of the moons of Jupiter. If so, then their observations are to be accepted as valid facts. That some, or all, of them may be notoriously immoral characters who drink heavily and beat their wives is besides the point. The only thing to guard against is that they must not be allowed to conspire with each other, and should have arrived at their results independently. On the other hand, the dreams and inspirations of a dervish — whose piety and holiness are beyond doubt — cannot be accepted as scientific facts because they are unverifiable, unrepeatable, and personalized.

Laws: Facts are organized into groups, and the relation which holds between facts belonging to the same group is called a law or principle. Laws or principles are merely a systematization of what is observed. To give two examples:

- 'A given quantity of gas will exert pressure on its container in direct proportion to its temperature.' (Boyle's Law)

- 'The inheritance of characteristics must be mediated by units which are transmitted from parent to offspring, and recombined in all possible ways in the sexual process.' (Mendel's Law)

To formulate laws, it is crucial to have facts. But facts by themselves are sterile until there is a mind capable of choosing between them — a mind which under the bare fact can see the soul of the fact. This is what distinguishes a good scientist from a mediocre one.

Hypotheses: These are tentative guesses which represent some preliminary understanding of what is being investigated, and which are to be tested against observation or experiment. Here are two hypotheses:

- 'The probability of lung cancer is directly proportional to the number of cigarettes smoked daily.'

- 'The amount of rainfall in a given place is increased if more people pray for rain.'

To validate either of the above hypotheses, data must be collected in sufficient amount so that chance fluctuations are relatively improbable. Otherwise one could end up with strange conclusions such as increases in human longevity with the number of cigarettes smoked, or a decrease in rainfall with the number of people praying!

Theory: A theory is a grand conceptual scheme that lies at the core of thinking and which provides a complete picture in its domain of validity. But a scientific theory must, in addition, also satisfy certain strict criteria:

- It must be consistent with all known experimental or observational data.

- It must have something new to say, meaning that it should predict facts which are hitherto unknown but which are testable.

For a theory to be more than a narrow hypothesis larded with faith, it must not be merely concocted to explain a narrow set of observations. The hallmark of a true theory is that it applies to a very wide range of phenomena. For example, Newton's theory of gravitation applies equally well to an ant sitting on a cricket ball, to a shell on the way to its target, to the motion of the moon around the earth, to the earth's orbit around the sun, and the sun in relation to the rest of the stars. The key point is universality: one should not need to invoke a different theory to explain each occurrence of a new fact.

One needs to recognize, on the other hand, that there is no completely universal definition of a scientific theory. Sir Karl Popper, a distinguished philosopher of science, asserts that a theory must be falsifiable in principle if it is to qualify as a scientific theory.[1] This means that one must be able clearly to identify a situation where application of the theory leads to a definite answer to the question: is the theory right or wrong? A theory which can explain some things, but can predict nothing, cannot therefore be falsified.

While this falsification criterion is useful and enables us to separate science from non-science, it is not without flaw. To give an example where this criterion is not useful, consider the superstring theory of elementary particles. This theory has, as its ultimate goal, the unification of all the fundamental forces in nature and prediction of every kind of particle in the universe. It is even known as TOE or the Theory Of Everything. Unfortunately, even though the most brilliant minds are struggling to extract testable predictions from superstring theory, they have been unsuccessful to date because the theory is mathematically too difficult. The only predictions of the theory are at the scale of the preposterously large energies which existed at the time of the creation of the universe. There is simply nothing definitive so far that can be tested even in the world's largest particle accelerators. Hence, superstring theory fails the falsification criterion. On the other hand, people are not prepared simply to junk it as unscientific; this is because it is built upon those theoretical principles which have been spectacularly successful in the past, because it is not inconsistent with any known phenomena, and because it at least offers a reasonable hope of unifying all present knowledge and ultimately discovering something completely new. So, although superstring theory is not presently testable, it may be in the future.

Induction and Deduction: Looking at regularities in data allows one to gather knowledge inductively and make simple laws. For example, having seen the sun rise in the east and set in the west every day, we infer by induction that the sun will behave similarly tomorrow as well. Deduction, on the other hand, works differently. Here, we start with some general rules and then derive particular conclusions by applying logical arguments.

The Scientific Method: At last, having defined the necessary concepts, we can define what is called the scientific method. In essence, this is a procedure which comprises of the following sequence of steps:

• Identify a problem. This could be something unknown in terms of its nature, structure, effects, interaction with other things, etc. Or it could be one or more unexplained, or insufficiently explained, relationships between things, events or symbols, etc. Unknown, that is, in terms of known laws and theories.

• Locate and study all existing literature relevant to the problem, and organize and analyse the data according to the existing state of understanding. This will reveal whether those data signal something new, or whether it is something understandable in terms of the existing framework.

• If the problem is genuine in the sense that there is something new and apparently not understandable, then devise a framework of observations or experiments that may yield new significant clues.

• When sufficient clues for the formulation of logical hypotheses have been obtained, select what appears to be the most simple, aesthetic, and satisfying hypothesis.

• Deduce the various implications which follow from the chosen hypothesis and devise observations or experiments to test its validity.

• Even if a series of confirmations is obtained, but one or more exceptions remain unexplained, the hypothesis is suspect and other hypotheses need to be formulated and tested.

- If a hypothesis is successful to the point that there are no apparent exceptions, it is elevated to the status of a law.

- The law will be accepted as correct until such time as some new observation or experiment cannot be explained by use of it. In that event it ceases to have the status of a law, and new hypotheses must be searched for in a renewal of the above procedure.

Actual scientific advance may not occur through such logically balanced procedures; the elements of chance and creativity sometimes defy a simple linear approach. The 'simple' matter of defining the problem, the 'simple' operation of framing hypotheses and devising experiments — these are more of an art than a science. But whatever may be the particular route taken in arriving at a particular theory, the ultimate arbiter of truth is appeal to experiment and observation, and the ultimate usefulness of the theory lies in how many old facts it can explain and how many new things it can tell us.

Science is like a building always in use but in perpetual repair, continuously growing in size and adding to itself new extensions and sections. Criticizing, and sometimes destroying itself, science has steadily grown from primitive observations about nature to the enormously complex structure that it is today. Individual scientists, like a toiling worker ant, are but minions who help in the creation of this giant repository of human knowledge. They take from the stock that exists at any particular moment of history and add to it a little bit of their own. Very soon their work is assimilated, superseded, and lost as happens in individual performance. The results of the great masters of science are incorporated into current science; one almost never needs to study the originals. A graduate student of physics who studied optics from Ibn al-Haytham's *Kitab-al-Manazir* or mechanics from Newton's *Principia* would do so at serious risk to his career and understanding of physics. He would be infinitely better advised to study a modern book which includes the cumulative work of the thousands of workers who, since these great men, have assiduously worked to improve, expand, generalize, and simplify the subject.

Progress in science comes from within science. Thomas Kuhn, whose book *The Structure Of Scientific Revolutions*[2] is a landmark in the study of scientific methodology, distinguishes between normal science, which is practised by the overwhelming majority of scientific workers, and revolutionary science. Normal science is the conduct of science within the framework of an accepted set of beliefs and practices. Kuhn calls this set a paradigm, and scientists working within this paradigm push the frontiers of knowledge to the limit — that is, until the point when the paradigm loses the power of explanation and prediction. For example, Newtonian mechanics worked beautifully as a paradigm for phenomena which involved speeds less than the speed of light, but began to fail when this condition was not met. At this point, a major conceptual jump occurred from normal mechanics to the revolutionary mechanics developed by Einstein. Today, however, the mechanics of Einstein is considered normal science. The lifespan of revolutionary science is short-lived indeed because, once it has demonstrated its superiority by subsuming normal science and going beyond it, it is almost immediately adopted by scientists as the paradigm, and itself becomes part of normal science.

This cumulative and provisional nature of science distinguishes it from other great human institutions such as those of religion, philosophy and art. Religion is based on the existence of eternal, immutable truths which are not to be added to, or taken away, by successive generations. Wisdom is not accumulated, but exists from the outset. The final court of appeal lies not in this world, but in the hereafter. All this does not at all mean that science and religion are in principle mutually incompatible. Rather, it suggests that they belong to separate domains and cannot be mixed.

A Pre-Scientific Theory: Just to make the distinction between scientific and non-scientific modes of thinking absolutely clear, here is an amusing little fable of 'plogglies' by Wendell Johnson which tells the difference admirably well:

> There were once two very perplexing mysteries, over which the wisest men in the land had beat their heads and stroked their beards for years and years . . . Whenever anyone ever wanted to find a lead pencil he couldn't, and whenever anyone wanted to sharpen a lead pencil the sharpener was sure to be filled with lead shavings.
>
> It was a most annoying state of affairs, and after sufficient public agitation a committee of distinguished philosophers was appointed by the government to carry out a searching investigation and, above all, to concoct a suitable explanation of the outrage . . . Their deliberations were carried out under very trying conditions, for the public, impatient and distraught, was clamoring ever more loudly for results. Finally, after what seemed to everyone a very long time, the committee appeared before the Chief of State to deliver a truly brilliant explanation of the twin mysteries.
>
> It was quite simple, after all. Beneath the ground, so the theory went, live a great number of little people. They are called plogglies. At night, when people are asleep, the plogglies come into their houses. They scurry around and gather up all the lead pencils, and then they scamper over to the pencil sharpener and grind them all up. And then they go back into the ground.
>
> The great national unrest subsided. Obviously, this was a brilliant theory. With one stroke it accounted for both mysteries.[3]

Why is the theory of plogglies not a *scientific* theory? The answer is intuitively obvious. The theory was contrived to fit one single set of data; nowhere else can it be applied and it predicts nothing new. Plogglie-like theories in the past are not known to have yielded new knowledge, nor are there any known principles which could tell us when such creatures have to be invoked. Plogglies are, by definition, unobservable — they come out at night when nobody can see them. Moreover, no other habits of plogglies are known and so we don't know what else to expect of them even if they do come out at night. In other words, there is no testable consequence of the plogglie theory, and no one can think of designing one either. Of course, people can continue to believe in plogglies as an article of faith should they so desire.

The Birth of Modern Science

The method of science described in the preceding paragraphs had existed in fragmentary form in various epochs, including the Islamic era. These were, of course, crucial to its subsequent development. But the crystallization of the scientific method occurred in the massive revolution which began in 16th century Europe, and which left in its wake a world transformed both intellectually and physically. Experimentation, quantification, prediction, and control became the paradigm of a new culture. Gone was the old notion of an organic, living, and spiritual universe. Instead of being mysterious and beyond the human ken, it could now be understood as mechanical and orderly: a giant machine run by the laws of physics. After Copernicus, the earth was no longer the centre of the universe but merely one of the many planets circling a rather unremarkable star at the edge of the galaxy. From being the very centrepiece of creation, man suddenly became aware of his cosmic nothingness. But the Age of Reason put him at the very centre of the intellectual universe. Liberated from the prison of medieval Christian theology, pure thought reached out into the immensities of space and the abysses of time. Nothing remained too great or too small for man's intellect to comprehend, and nothing too distant in time or space to assign to it its due weight in the structure of the cosmos. Indeed, mankind was transformed into the self-knowing subject of history and conscious now of 'mankind for itself'.

The new consciousness was, in large measure, brought about by the revolutionary philosophers of the Scientific Revolution. Among these, René Descartes was perhaps the most important.[4] The supreme discovery of his life was a framework of thought — now called the Cartesian framework or method — that would allow a complete science of nature about which there would be absolute certainty; a science based entirely on verifiable first principles. This method was analytic, requiring the dissection of complex thoughts and problems into their elemental parts. Nature is intelligible, said Descartes, and its secrets can be revealed through the discovery of laws by way of experimentation. The subsequent elaboration of mechanistic science — including Newton's grand synthesis — was a development of this central idea, and firmly established that understanding nature required the precise language of mathematics as its prerequisite. Three centuries after Descartes, and notwithstanding far-reaching developments in quantum mechanics, relativity, and the theory of chaos, 20th century science remains solidly wedded to Cartesianism. Without it there would have been no penicillin or antibiotics, and no man could have ventured on the surface of the moon.

With Cartesian reductionism also came the animal–machine. The clock was a privileged model for automatic machines in Descartes' time, and so one finds him comparing animals to a 'clock . . . composed . . . of wheels and springs'. He then extends the comparison to the human body: 'I consider the human body as a machine. . . . My thought . . . compares a sick man and an ill-made clock with my idea of a healthy man and a well-made clock.' The skeleton as a group of levers, the heart as a pump — one discovery followed another. All biology, said the Philosophers of Reason, was chemistry; and all chemistry ultimately physics. Indeed, in the later part of the 20th century, molecular biology and genetic engineering have become the ultimate expression of the Cartesian viewpoint.

Perhaps the most radical elements of Cartesianism was the idea that disease is a malfunctioning of biological mechanisms, a state of the organism stemming from specific causes such as filth, bad food, pests, etc. This flew in the face of what the great fathers and renowned leaders of the Christian Church had preached with great vehemence for centuries, as we shall have a chance to see in the next chapter.

In sweeping away the medieval world order, the Scientific Revolution not only shattered the temporal authority of the Church, but it also altered fundamentally the concept of God in Christian theology.

Paradoxically, this fundamental change was wrought by the founders of modern science and the scientific method who were, for the most part, deeply religious men. Of course, there were some who were not: Laplace, the famous 18th century French mathematician, responding to a question by Napoleon about the motion of the planets remarked: 'God: we have no need for this hypothesis.' But for Descartes, as for Galileo or Newton, the existence of God was essential to a philosophy which recognized the existence of both mind and matter. In fact, the view of the universe as a giant automaton was incomplete and unsatisfactory without a Creator. But this Creator was not the God of Christian theology. Unlike the interventionist God of medieval times who responded to the actions and prayers of his created beings, the role of God in the mechanical universe was to set the universe in place together with the eternal laws which were thenceforth to determine its destiny. As Voltaire put it, God created the universe just as a watch maker assembles a watch. Once made, He has no further concern with it; the law of physics will cause it to function in the precise manner accorded to it by the Divine Plan.

The Philosophers of Reason assiduously denied conscious divine intervention, and hence the occurrence of miracles. This age-old issue stood at the heart of the conflict between the emerging scientific world view and the traditional religious one. Some philosophers sought to resolve the tension by redefining a miracle to mean simply something wonderful. Regarded in this sense everything is miraculous. The precision of planetary orbits, the vastness of the universe, the delicately balanced ecological system of the earth, and the unfathomable complexity of the human mind, are all perpetual miracles. Perhaps the greatest miracle of all, understood in this sense, is that everything in the universe — from the tiniest sub-atomic particles to giant stars and even the universe itself — are guided by the same inexorable physical laws. Science has no explanation for these laws, and cannot refute anyone who says that they are of divine origin.

Compare this with the conventional usage of the term miracle which refers to a violation, or temporary suspension, of the eternal and inexorable laws of physics. As Voltaire said, 'if there is an eclipse of the sun at full moon, if a dead man walks two leagues carrying his head in his arms, we call that a miracle.' Voltaire took an active position against this interpretation of miracles, arguing that God cannot suspend a law established by Himself: 'is it not the most absurd of follies to imagine that the Infinite Being would invert the eternal play of the immense engines which move the entire universe for the sake of three or four hundred ants on this little heap of mud?'

The position that post-Newtonian modern science takes on the issue of miracles has not changed a bit since Voltaire. It certainly does allow a serious physicist to believe in a God who created and ordered the universe. But it does not allow belief in a God who intervenes at will to change the course of a planet, to postpone an eclipse, to alter weather patterns against the dictates of fluid physics, or to change the rules of the cosmic game in any other way. The free changeability of the laws of nature according to His instantaneous desire can reveal to us nothing beyond His immediate, and possibly temporary, intention. The dilemma posed by an interventionist deity is one that scientists are unable to confront, and scientific investigation becomes impossible. What should they do if confronted with an apparently inexplicable phenomenon? suppose they are challenged by a killer disease, or some strange deviation of plantary orbits, or the appearance of a highly unexpected sub-atomic particle. Should they stop looking for physical causes after a certain point and instead attribute it to the Divine Will? If they do, the chances are that some other cleverer colleagues may eventually find the answer, and get credit for it instead.

Science freed us from the capricious forces of nature, and seemed to offer certainty. That was what the whole scientific revolution was about. But could it be that recent developments within science are telling us that the certainties of sciences are but an illusion?

Has Quantum Physics Destroyed Science?

In recent years, there has appeared a growing eagerness to pronounce science — meaning conventional modern science — philosophically, though not yet clinically, dead. The cause of death, it is said, was suicide. The instrument was a device of its own invention called quantum physics.

Here is how the argument goes: modern science started out being based upon common sense and observations of nature. The assumptions were that the same initial conditions in an experiment would always lead to the same result, that the observer did not really matter, and that the physical world had an objective reality. The processes of observation, deduction, and theory-building ultimately gave birth to quantum physics. But, continues the argument, quantum physics says that common sense is to be trusted no more — nature at its most fundamental level is not at all like the nature that we see and experience in our daily lives. Thus, these revelations shatter the concept of reality which underlay the development of physical science and, in particular, nullify the Cartesian assumption that the whole is just the sum of its individual parts. The sequel to this is that the time has drawn nigh to abandon the sinking ship of modern science. Instead, one needs to seek rescue in alternatives provided by Eastern and other philosophies, and to create entities such as Taoist science, Third World science, Islamic science, etc.

Alas, the belief that modern science is on its deathbed is nothing but a flight of wishful imagination. It provides solace to those who regard modern science as the source of evil in the world. But wishing death to the enemy seldom causes him to die. As a matter of fact, far from being a sputtering candle, modern science is today more vigorous, faster expanding, and more secure in its power and scope than it has ever been in the past. The atom — thanks to quantum physics — is so well understood in all its myriad details that its study is almost a closed chapter. Instead, the search for the fundamental constituents of matter has moved off towards gigantic particle accelerators which can examine objects a million times smaller than the atom. At the other end of the scale, we are fairly secure in our knowledge of how the universe began some 15 billion years ago, and of the key events which occurred a few micro-seconds thereafter. This is not to claim that all aspects of cosmic evolution have been understood, but confidence in the correctness of presently known physical laws has grown steadily as more detailed optical, radio, x-ray, and cosmic ray observations become available.

Nevertheless, it cannot be denied that quantum mechanics has indeed led to profoundly disturbing new ideas, some of which appear to be the direct negation of common sense. So we must ask: what is the nature of the challenge this offers to scientific epistemology? Does it require that we abandon the methods of scientific inquiry which have hitherto been the very basis of science? Although the philosophical problems posed by quantum theory are immensely important, they are also very technical and difficult ones. Only a very brief — and therefore unsatisfactory — attempt to address them can be made here.

Quantum physics, born in the first quarter of this century, dominates modern physical science today. It originated from an attempt to explain numerous experimentally observed facts about atoms and radiation — facts which Newtonian physics was spectacularly incapable of accommodating. This success was accompanied, however, by revolutionary conceptual implications for our perception of the physical world. For example, quantum physics predicts that atomic sized (or, for that matter, any size) objects may be thought of either as particles or as waves, the choice depending entirely upon what apparatus or means one employs in order to observe them. Worse, the celebrated Heinsenberg uncertainty principle states that the precise position and velocity of any such object simply cannot be determined together. This is quite disconcerting — before quantum physics the world was thought to be completely predictable, at least in principle. By this was meant that events of the past determine the present, and that the present completely determines the future. The negation of this form of determinism was so upsetting that, for example, it caused Einstein to utter his famous remark: 'God does not play dice with the universe', and to declare his opposition to quantum mechanics. But although he was acknowledged as the leading physicist of his time, Einstein was (justly) ignored by his contemporaries. The evidence against his alternative 'hidden variable' theory — which would have restored determinism — was much too compelling.

There is no doubt that quantum physics has forced us into an acceptance that our present perception of reality is naive. Consider, for example, the implication of a fundamental axiom of quantum mechanics which states that the process of trying to observe a system generally changes it. This fact is readily understandable when the system is an electron or an atom. Until an observation is actually carried out, the electron may be in one of several possible states. Only after a measurement is made can it be definitely known as to which state it actually was in. But in attempting to observe the electron, one has forced the electron to make a choice between different alternatives and, hence, irrevocably altered its state.

Substitute now for the word 'electron' the 'physical universe'. Here lies a dilemma: after its birth, the universe was in a mixture of quantum states. Of the many (infinite) possibilities that existed, only a tiny subset have been actually realized. Has this been because the act of observation has forced certain possibilities to be realized and others excluded? And if so, observation by what or whom? According to the Nobel Prize winning physicist Eugene P. Wigner, this necessarily brings in human consciousness as a determinant in bringing about the present quantum state of the universe. While such an interpretation of quantum physics is disputed, it exemplifies the type of current thinking on problems of existence and reality. (The interested reader may enjoy a recent article entitled 'Is the moon there when nobody looks? Reality and quantum theory', together with other references listed at the end of this chapter.[5])

Still more bizarre is the 'many universes' interpretation of quantum physics. This interpretation, proposed by Hugh Everett in 1957, asserts that every act of observation of a system leads to the creation of a parallel universe occupying the same space–time as the original universe, but incapable of communicating with it. Thus, the universe we currently occupy is only one of the uncountably infinite coexisting universes. This hypothesis solves the problem of measurement in quantum physics but at some cost! Bryce Dewitt, a proponent of the 'many universes' interpretation says:

> Every quantum transition taking place in every star, in every galaxy, in every remote corner of the universe is splitting our local world on Earth into myriads of copies of itself. . . . Here is schizophrenia with a vengeance.[6]

Strange, fascinating, bizarre. Surely quantum physics is a window into an aspect of the universe inaccessible to our common perceptions. To those unfamiliar with its mathematical formulation, it is unsettling and incomprehensible. And to those who would like to be rid of science, disputes over its correct interpretation are like sweet music to the ear.

But let us not lose sight of the wood for the trees. For one, we are firmly anchored to a set of shared experiences — today the vast majority of physicists use quantum mechanics routinely and with complete confidence; not a single experiment or observation out of literally millions has ever yielded anything contradicting it. And, for another, disputes are not the signal of some fatal impending collapse. Indeed, controversies are just part of the normal healthy activity of science. Even if some day quantum mechanics is ultimately replaced by a truer theory bearing a less controversial and more precise interpretation, this would not negate what we know today about the physical world. We have historical precedents for this: Einstein's Relativity did not negate Newton's Mechanics; it enlarged and refined it.

To be sure, the problem of interpretation is not a solved one. But again, the problems are often misunderstood and blown out of proportion. For example, although quantum mechanics is said to be the negation of determinism, one must realize that this is important only for small-scale phenomena pertaining to atoms etc., and utterly irrelevant otherwise (except possibly for the very very early universe). Again, the issue of whether the object under study is disturbed by the process of observation is also pertinent only at the small scale. Even here, one has available the 'Copenhagen interpretation' of quantum physics. What this says basically is that quantum mechanics can meet all situations which relate to concepts that can be connected to some real or hypothetical experiment. One is therefore not permitted to ask questions such as 'what is reality?' or 'what is the state of this or that system?'. Instead, one can ask 'if I do such and such, under such and such conditions, then what will I see?'.

When arguments about what constitutes reality become too complex, it is good to pinch oneself and feel that it is 'real'. So, while flights into metaphysics are all very well, let us not forget that quantum physics stands on the solid bedrock of a million experiments. The scientific method remains intact in its integrity and power, and quantum physics remains very much a product of this method. Should quantum physics ever be replaced by something better, it will be through a Kuhnian type of revolution — through problems generated and understood through its intrinsic structure. Science improves and cleanses itself periodically; but it has never had any meaningful input from various claimed substitutes. These either lie within the boundaries of narrow belief systems, or are so hopelessly vague that even their proponents have no inkling of how they may be effected.

That there is only one science, we can safely conclude. But is it the sole property of the West? That is just as controversial, and even more pertinent a question, to which we must turn.

Is Modern Science Simply Western Science?

In a recently published book, two leading Western scientists, Michael Moravcsik and John Ziman, begin their discourse on the spreading of science to Third World countries with characteristic bluntness:

> With European industrial civilization comes European science. It is a package deal. The question whether a culture thus superseded or repressed had its own form of science has become purely academic: the process of economic growth

and social development is entirely predicated on the 'rational materialism' of post-Renaissance Europe and its North American colonies . . . In the present discussion, it is taken for granted that European science should become a dominant cultural force throughout the world.[7]

I cannot vouch for what other readers of that book — especially those from countries with a colonial past — will have felt upon reading that paragraph. But it certainly left me cold. Something tasted nasty, hurt my self-esteem. I can be more specific. Here are two Western scientists not in the least bit inclined to hide their sense of moral superiority, and in such obvious agreement with the values of their culture that they consider it eminently worthy of export. In an important way they are similar to the missionaries of old, who believed so fervently in Christian salvation. The new missionaries have as their goal, to quote them again, 'that European science should become a dominant cultural force throughout the world'. Hence, so far as this mission is concerned, the cultural and scientific history of the cultures 'superseded or repressed' are worthy only of the trash can.

Many Third World scholars have sworn allegiance to the techniques and philosophy of modern science, and feel gratitude that it found in Europe a fertile soil. But well may they retort: do the vast contributions of the Chinese, Islamic and Hindu civilizations warrant such a peremptory dismissal? Could modern science ever have developed if these great civilizations had not laid the basis for its later development? The tree of science has roots plunging down into diverse cultures. Even the Greeks — who are almost exclusively mentioned as the forefathers of modern science — could not have produced so many innovations and ideas without the contributions, material and intellectual, from various Asiatic and African countries. It is therefore simply false to think that science and technology are essentially and originally Western. And, as for the claimed superiority of European culture, were not Auschwitz and Hiroshima consequences of that same culture? How should we assess a civilization which has created the concepts of megadeaths and mutual assured destruction (MAD)?

One can have no quarrel with the fact that the immediate source of modern science was the cultural upheavals in Europe — the Renaissance and the Scientific Revolution. It is also indubitably correct that these were unprecedented in the scope and nature of the change they wrought. Earlier developments of science had occurred in distant lands and among diverse peoples, and were indeed crucial. But it was not until the birth of an industrial civilization that science became a part of culture and affected in an important way the daily lives of individuals. This is the argument often used to prove that science is an exclusively European phenomenon.

Leaving other arguments aside, it is worthwhile to cast a glance at the history of knowledge — of which the history of science is but a part — and to see how recent a phenomenon it is. Consider the fact that the recorded history of humanity is no more than 10,000 years old, and that consciousness at even a very primitive level is barely a few million years old. But there were countless ages before that during which there was no knowledge, and there may well be countless ages without knowledge in the future. On a cosmic scale, the history of knowledge and science is profoundly irrelevant. It appears to me utterly accidental that science should have developed over the last few thousand years — and in Europe over the last four hundred years. Looked at in this way, parochial pride in the historical cultures which we accidentally happen to be associated with appears quite irrational.

It is highly probable that any species endowed with intelligence will ultimately develop a science of its own, the initial impetus for which would presumably come from reasons of survival. The fact that the human mind is capable of reason and abstraction meant that science pretty much had to develop sooner or later in the course of human progress. So, does it follow that, if science is the result of intelligence, the birth of modern science in Europe was on account of the genetic superiority of the European people? Theorists like Max Weber, among others, would have us believe this. But modern psychology has found no scientific grounds for this in spite of countless tests.

The issue of a universal human intelligence is closely related with one of the most profound questions of modern times, which Bertrand Russell posed in the following words: 'How comes it that human beings, whose contacts with the world are brief and personal and limited, are able to know as much as they do know?' What Russell meant was that the amount of knowledge which each one of us possesses is staggeringly large in spite of the fact that we rarely live beyond 60 or 70 years of age. Anybody who has tried to programme a computer to perform the simplest recognition of patterns, or to make it understand elementary concepts, will understand the full depth of Russell's question.

The modern theory of linguistics suggests that Russell's question may be answerable on the basis of scientific research. This research has underscored the importance of the language faculty as a superb mirror of the mind and our ability to comprehend. Noam Chomsky,[8] the well-known philosopher of linguistics, argues that we know as much as we do essentially because we were born to know. What he says — and with proof that cannot even be touched upon here — is that humans are born with the faculty of language essentially in place. Rational man has emerged from the realms of biological evolution endowed with innate mental structures capable of abstract thought. In essence, he is an intricate 'pre-wired' computer needing only external stimuli to set cognitive and creative processes in operation. The discovery by Chomsky of a universal human grammar brings to us the clear implication that, at the most fundamental level, human thought and behaviour are entirely universal. It demolishes racist theories of development, and establishes the oneness of us all.

Science is indeed the intellectual property of all humankind, and part of the universal cultural heritage. We need pay no heed to those who say it is otherwise.

References

1. K. R. Popper, *Conjectures and Refutations*, (London, Routledge and Kegan Paul, 1963).

2. T. S. Kuhn, *The Structure of Scientific Revolutions*, 2nd edition, (Chicago, University of Chicago Press, 1970).

3. Wendell Johnson, *People in Quandries*, (New York, Harper Brothers, 1946).

4. A good discussion of Cartesianism can be found in P. J. Davis and R. J. Hersh, *Descartes' Dream*, (Boston, Houghton Mifflin, 1986) and Fritjof Capra, *The Turning Point*, (Bantam Books, 1983).

5. N. D. Mermin, 'Is the moon really there when nobody looks? Reality and the quantum theory', in *Physics Today*, April 1985, 38–47.

6. P. C. W. Davies and J. R. Brown, *The Ghost in the Atom*, (Cambridge, Cambridge University Press, 1986).

7. Michael Moravcsik and John Ziman, in 'Problems of Science Development', to be published by *World Scientific*, Singapore.

8. Noam Chomsky, *Language and Problems of Knowledge – The Managua Lectures*, (Cambridge, Mass., MIT Press, 1988).

3. The War Between Science and Medieval Christianity

The wife of the Bishop of Worcester, when informed about Darwin's theory, commented, 'Descended from the apes! My dear, let us hope that it is not true, but if it is, let us pray that it may not become generally known.'

The rigidly orthodox of every faith — including the fundamentalist Muslim of today — has never been comfortable with the method and discoveries of science. But historically, it is the Christian orthodoxy which fought the longest and most bitter battle against science. For a thousand years before the Renaissance, the Christian Church had ruled Europe with an iron hand. Intolerance, prejudice, suspicion and superstition had made scholarly learning an impossibility. Suspicious of every attempt at independent thinking, the Church violently suppressed all teaching that was not in direct conformity with its preachings. Religious tribunals sentenced tens of thousands of suspected witches and heretics to death by torture. Convicts were tied between horses and torn apart, disembowelled, hung or burnt at the stake. Even the dead were not forgiven. The famous Archbishop Ussher had concluded from his study of the Bible that the world began at 9 a.m., Sunday 23 October 4004 B.C. — this despite the fact that a long dead scientist, Wycliffe, had provided evidence based on fossils and geology that the earth was at least some hundred thousand years old. Unable to tolerate this insolence, the Church ordered that Wycliffe's bones be dug up, broken in pieces, and thrown into the sea so that the germs of dissent and doubt might no longer contaminate the earth.

Why was the Church so adamant in its position and so bitterly opposed to men with new ideas, such as Bacon, Wycliffe, Bruno, Galileo, and tens of thousands of lesser thinkers? I think that the cause of this rigidity can be understood from the following chain of arguments:

(1) The entire social order was predicated on a literal observance of specific rules laid down by the Church. There was a rule for everything from worshipping rites, to eating and drinking, to marriage and sex. Medieval Christianity was a complete code of life.

(2) These rules — and the ability of the Church to enforce them — depended on the total and unquestioning acceptance of Church dogmas.

(3) Rejection of even one of these rules — whether by science or otherwise — could, given the rigidity of dogma, bring about collapse and a disintegration of the entire social order.

(4) Hence science and free-thinking were a threat and had to be proscribed.

It is in this context that the condemnation of Galileo ought to be viewed. Galileo's punishment by the Church — though by no means the most severe example on record — has special significance because it was the first effective prohibition of a scientific thesis which, subsequently, became established truth. Bernard Shaw has made the following astute observations:

> Galileo is a favoured subject with our scientists; but they miss the point because they think that the question at issue was whether the earth went around the sun or was the stationary centre round which the sun circled. Now, that was not the issue. Taken by itself, it was a physical fact without any moral significance, and therefore of no consequence to the Church. But what the authorities had to consider was whether the Christian religion, on which to the best of their belief not only the civilization of the world but its own civilization depended, and which had accepted the Hebrew scriptures and the Greek testament as inspired revelations, could stand the shock of the discovery that many of its tales, from the tactics of Joshua in the battle of Gideon to the Ascension, must have been written by somebody who did not know what the physical universe was really like.[1]

Because the suppression of scientific thought by the medieval Church represents one of blackest periods of human history, many scholars have studied this period with great care. Worth special mention is a remarkable two-volume treatise entitled *A History Of The Warfare Of Science With Theology*, published in 1896 by Andrew Dickson White. White later became the first president of Cornell University. From the many fascinating accounts in this compendium, here are but a handful:

● The doctrine of the spherical shape of the earth, and therefore the existence of the antipodes, was bitterly attacked by theologians who asked: 'Is there any one so senseless as to believe that crops and trees grow downwards? . . . that the rains and snow fall upwards?' The great authority of St Augustine held the Church firmly against the idea of the antipodes and for a thousand years it was believed that there could not be human beings on the opposite side of the earth — even if the earth had opposite sides. In the sixth century, Procopius of Gaza brought powerful theological guns to bear on the issue: there could not be an opposite side, he declared, because for that Christ would have had to go there and suffer a second time. Also, there would have had to exist a duplicate Eden, Adam, Serpent, and Deluge. But that being clearly wrong, there could not be any antipodes. QED!

● Diseases, Saint Paul had declared, were the malignant work of devils. Said the church authority, Origen: 'It is demons which produce famine, unfruitfulness, corruptions of the air, pestilences; they hover concealed in clouds of the lower atmosphere, and are attracted by the blood and incense which the heathen offer to them as gods.' And Augustine, the most influential of the early Church authorities, wrote that: 'All diseases of the Christians are to be ascribed to these demons; chiefly do they torment fresh baptized Christians, yea, even the guiltless new-born infants.' By the orders of Pope Pius V, all physicians were required to call in a 'physician of the soul' on the ground that 'bodily infirmity frequently arises from sin'. The cause of disease being established as devils and evil spirits, the cure was naturally their exorcism through means such as holy relics. Enormous revenues flowed into various churches and monasteries noted for the possession of healing relics. The Church was not only the guardian of the Christian's soul, but also of his physical well-being.

• Because plagues, such as those of smallpox and cholera, were also considered Divine retribution by the Church, inoculation against them was bitterly denounced by the orthodox. The argument used was that smallpox is a 'judgement of God on the sins of the people', and that 'to avert it is but to provoke him more.' A lighted grenade was thrown into the house of a man who gave shelter to the pioneer of smallpox vaccine, Dr Boylston. From the pulpits a steady stream of abuse was heaped upon the advocates of vaccination. But the facts were too strong — with inoculation people lived, and without it they died. And so inoculation was eventually accepted by the Church, although the resistance has never totally died out.

• A serious obstacle in the development of scientific medicine was the opposition to the dissection of dead bodies. St Augustine referred to anatomists as 'butchers' and denounced this practice in unequivocal terms. A general dread existed that mutilating a dead body might result in some unimaginable horror on the day when all bodies would be resurrected. To this argument, the Church added one more: 'the Church abhors the shedding of blood.' This was indeed a remarkable argument — the obvious delight with which the Church burnt thousands of suspected heretics and witches suggested little abhorrence to shedding blood when that was in the Holy interest.

• Around 1770, a remarkable phenomenon was observed in various parts of Europe. Detailed statements were sent to the Royal Academy of Science that water had turned to blood. Ecclesiastics immediately saw in this an indication of the wrath of God. When a miracle of this sort was observed in Sweden, an eminent naturalist, Linnaeus, looked into the phenomenon carefully and found that the reddening of the water was caused by dense masses of minute insects. When news of this discovery reached the bishop, he roundly denounced the scientific discovery as a 'Satanic abyss' and declared that 'the reddening of water is not natural.' Now, Linnaeus was not a bold man and he knew too well what had happened to Galileo. In the face of this, he retreated and ultimately declared that the truth of the matter was beyond his understanding.

- Ecclesiastics and theologians of the medieval Church vigorously promoted the view that comets are fireballs flung by an angry God against a wicked world. Churchmen illustrated the moral value of comets by comparing the Almighty sending down a comet to the judge laying down the sword of execution on the table between himself and the criminal in a court of justice. Others denounced people who heedlessly stared at such warnings from God and compared them to 'calves gaping at a barn door'. Even up to the end of the 17th century, the oath taken by professors of astronomy prevented them from teaching that comets were heavenly bodies obedient to physical laws. But ultimately, science could not be suppressed. Halley, using the theory of Newton and Kepler, observed the path of one particularly 'dangerous' comet and predicted that it would return in precisely 76 years. He calculated to the minute when it would be seen again at a well-defined point in the sky. This was incredible. But 76 years later, when Halley and Newton were both long dead, Halley's comet returned exactly as predicted.

- Christian orthodoxy also held geology to be a highly subversive tool in the service of the devil. Not only did geological evidence refute Archbishop Ussher's assertion of the earth's age, but it also showed that creation in six days was impossible. The orthodox declared geology 'not a subject of lawful inquiry', denounced it as 'a dark art', called it 'infernal artillery', and pronounced its practitioners 'infidels' and 'impugners of the sacred record'. Pope Pius IX was doubtless in sympathy with this feeling when he forbade the scientific congress of Italy to meet in Bologna in 1850.

- During the Middle Ages, the doctrine of the diabolical origin of storms was generally accepted, receiving support from such unassailable authorities as St Augustine. Storms, it was held, were the work of demons. Against this supernatural 'power of the air' various rites of exorcism were used, the most widely employed being that of Pope Gregory XIII. Whereas in earlier times the means of exorcism amounted simply to various chantings and ringing of church bells during storms, in the 15th century there evolved a tragic belief that certain women may secure infernal aid to produce whirlwinds, hail, frosts, floods, and like. On the 7th of December 1484, Pope Innocent VIII issued a papal bull, inspired by the scriptural command 'Thou shalt not suffer a witch to live'. He exhorted the clergy of Germany to detect sorcerers and witches who cause evil weather and so destroy vineyards, gardens, meadows, and growing crops. Thereupon thousands of women found themselves writhing on the torture racks, held in horror by their nearest and dearest, anxious only for death to relieve them of their suffering.

- The thunderbolt, said Church dogma, was a consequence of five sins: impenitence, incredulity, neglect of repair of churches, fraud in payment of tithes to the clergy, and oppression of subordinates. Pope after pope expounded on this instrument of divine retribution, calling it the 'finger of God'. And then in 1752 Benjamin Franklin flew his famous kite during an electrical storm, discovering in this dangerous experiment that lightning was but electricity. Immediately there followed the lightning rod, a sure protection from even the most furious storm. At first the Church refused to concede its existence. Then, as the efficacy of these lightning conductors became widely recognized and more and more were installed, the orthodox took up cudgels against them. The earthquake of 1755 in Massachussetts was ascribed by them to the widespread use of Franklin's rods in Boston, and preachers fulminated against those who attempted to control the artillery of the heavens. The opposition would undoubtedly have lasted longer but for the fact that churches without lightning rods were frequently devastated by lightning. In Germany, in the period between 1750 and 1783 alone, about 400 church towers had been damaged and 120 bell ringers killed by lightning. On the other hand, the town brothel, with its protruding lightning rod, stood smug and safe even in the worst of storms. The few churches which had installed rods were also never touched. And so, grudgingly to be sure, lightning rods received the Holy Sanction and were used to protect most churches by the end of the century.

- When Immanuel Kant presented the theory that there exist nebula as well as stars, throughout the theological world there was an outcry against such 'atheism'. The rigidly orthodox saw no reference to it in the Scriptures. Hence nebula should not exist. These opponents of nebular theory were overjoyed when improved telescopes showed that some patches of nebular matter could indeed be resolved into stars. But with time came the discovery of the spectroscope and spectrum analysis; the light from nebula was clearly from gaseous matter. And so the orthodox were ultimately forced to retreat.

The list of means by which medieval Christianity brutalized the human spirit and crushed scientific inquiry is much longer than the few selections given above. Also, I have made no attempt to discuss that great battle between science and Christian theology which followed the publication of Darwin's *Origin of Species* in 1859. This battle overshadowed all earlier ones — even that of Galileo. Indeed, humanity has found it much more difficult to be scientific about life itself than about falling rocks or heavenly bodies. The power of growth and spontaneous movement of living bodies were, and still are, infected by deep superstitions.

The conflict on this particular issue between science and orthodox Christianity is still manifest today in the Creationist movement in the United States. This movement was born during the period of Ronald Reagan's presidency in the 1980s, and continues to remain a significant force in many states. Creationism has as a cardinal belief that all life in the universe was created out of nothing about 6,000 years ago, in exactly seven days, and exactly as described in the first chapters of Genesis. So, for example, the Great Flood is taken as a historical fact, not as merely allegorical. Creationism attacks all areas of astronomy and geology which do not put a limit of 10,000 years on the age of the earth. Radioactive carbon dating is rejected. Above all, it is Darwin's theory of evolution which draws the greatest vituperation. Recently, Judge Braswell Deen, a creationist and judge of the Georgia State Court of Appeals, has written that the 'monkey mythology of Darwin' causes 'permissiveness, promiscuity, pills, prophylactics, perversions, pregnancies, abortions, pornotherapy, pollution, poisoning, and proliferation of crimes.'[3]

In spite of this resurgence of religious irrationalism in Western countries, the battle for sanity has by no means been lost. It is heartening to observe the numerous reversals suffered by Christian fundamentalists and particularly their inability to make any significant inroads into the scientific establishment in the West. They have not succeeded in their efforts to force schools to give equal time to scientific and biblical versions of creation. Indeed, with the departure of Reagan, Creationism suffered a significant reversal of fortunes.

Moreover, the modern world has not allowed the Roman Catholic Church to forget its past cruelties, the most symbolic of these being the persecution of Galileo and the forced renunciation of his scientific views. It was undoubtedly a significant event when, on 9 May 1983, at a special ceremony in the Vatican, Pope John Paul II issued what must be considered the first official apology:

> The Church's experience, during the Galileo affair and after it, has led to a more mature attitude. . . . It is only through humble and assiduous study that [the Church] learns to dissociate the essential of the faith from the scientific systems of a given age.

The apology comes 350 years too late. It also omits far more than it admits. Nevertheless to the Holy Pontiff's declaration of intent we can all say, with deep feeling, 'Amen'!

References

1. *The Complete Prefaces of Bernard Shaw*, (London, Paul Hamlyn, 1965), p. 369.

2. Andrew Dickson White, *A History of the Warfare of Science with Theology*, 1896. (Reprinted by Peter Smith, Gloucester, Mass., 1978).

3. *Creationism, Science, and the Law — The Arkansas Case*, edited by M. C. La Follette, (Cambridge, Mass., MIT Press, 1983).

4.   The State of Science in Islamic Countries Today

There is no question, but today, of all civilizations on this planet, science is weakest in the lands of Islam. The dangers of this weakness cannot be over-emphasized since honourable survival of a society depends directly on its strength in science and technology in the condition of the present age.

Professor Abdus Salam

To someone travelling by aeroplane, the view of cities from Karachi to Tehran, and Dubai to Riyadh, differs but little. This uniformity comes not from the common faith shared by their inhabitants, but from Western technology in the form of skyscrapers made of steel and glass, modern airports with sleek looking airliners on the tarmac, highways crammed with cars, and television antennae sprouting from every dwelling. Also imported from abroad are the technologies from which these societies derive their basic sustenance. Oil exploration, drilling, extraction, refining, and transportation are particularly important examples. They permit nations like Saudi Arabia and Iran to exchange natural wealth for manufactured goods ranging from AWACS early warning aircraft to rifle bullets, and from oil refineries to can openers. For some decades to come, a slippery, subterranean hydrocarbon will continue to provide the basic sustenance of these countries, finance their wars, allow experimentation with new social structures, and temporarily — but only temporarily — grant exemption from that inexorable law of history which relegates unproductive societies to destruction or marginalization. It is now perfectly routine to lament this critical dependence on oil and Western technology and ritualistically to call for a transfer of technology from developed to developing countries. Often, diabolical theories of international conspiracy, with varying degrees of credibility, are invoked as explanations for Muslim scientific backwardness. But these are not very fulfilling. Indeed, the damage to the collective self-esteem cannot be undone by such means, and thoughtful Muslims must seek sounder reasons.

In seeking an explanation for scientific underdevelopment, one must recognize at the outset that the environment for science in Islamic countries today is replete with paradoxes. On the one hand, all these countries are in the full grip of Western technology and market-based consumerism, which are the products of the Scientific Revolution. This has legitimized science as essential knowledge, and mastery over it as necessary for economic development and national power. Hence no group which seeks to win public support can afford to condemn science totally. But, on the other hand, technology and the market bring about homogenization and threaten old collective identities. Perceived as even more threatening to traditional norms and thinking is the attitude prescribed by science — an attitude which demands persistent query and examination of ideas. Muslim modernists and pragmatists have persistently sought to amalgamate the new with the old. But their attitude towards science is oftentimes a schizophrenic one, particularly in those Muslim countries where orthodoxy wields state power.

This point is exemplified by the views expressed by Saudi delegates to a high level conference held in Kuwait in 1983. The ostensible aim of the conference, attended by rectors from 17 Arab universities, was to identify and remove bottlenecks in the development of science and technology in the Arab world. But a single topic dominated the proceedings: is science Islamic? The Saudis held that pure science tends to produce 'Mu'tazilite tendencies' potentially subversive of belief. Science is profane because it is secular; as such — in their opinion — it goes against Islamic beliefs. Hence, recommended the Saudis, although technology should be promoted for its obvious benefits, pure science ought to be softpedalled.

To return to the issue of where Muslim countries stand today in the area of science and technology, we must ask what criteria ought to be used to gauge this status. This makes necessary the specification of a theoretical framework which should be both broad and precise enough to facilitate useful judgements.

Measuring Science

How one measures science, or scientific progress, naturally depends on what one means by science.[1] But contrary to expectations, this is not an easy task because science permeates our lives in such a large variety of ways, and has changed its form so greatly in the course of history. Nevertheless, it is useful to identify four key ways in which science manifests itself in the contemporary world:

(1) As a major factor in the maintenance and development of the productive processes needed to sustain society;

(2) As a collective and organized body of practitioners (scientists) who are professionally engaged in its full-time pursuit;

(3) As a major element of the educational system within a society;

(4) As one of the most powerful influences moulding people's beliefs and attitudes towards the universe — the scientific world view, which employs a methodological procedure wherein observation, experiment, classification and measurement are used to derive knowledge about the physical world.

I would regard this description of science as broad enough within which to discuss the state of science in Muslim countries, although there are presumably alternative criteria that one could employ.

Science in Production

There is a view that science exists in the modern world principally because there is an economic need for it. Marxists, in particular, emphasize that science has developed in response to economic forces, and not because of some inner compulsion which drives the individual into investigating his environment. In 1894, Friedrich Engels wrote a letter to Starkenburg forcefully emphasizing this point:

> If society has a technical need, that helps science forward more than ten universities. The whole of hydrostatics (Toricelli etc.) was called forth by the necessity for regulating the mountain streams of Italy in the sixteenth and seventeenth centuries. . . . But unfortunately it has become the custom in Germany to write the history of the sciences as if they have fallen from the skies.[2]

One also recalls Marx's argument about the Greeks having discovered steam power, but never building locomotives because these were simply not an economic need in a society which had slaves available to it. The case of the 17th century chemist Leblanc is yet another example: this French scientist invented a means for making soda from common salt, sulphuric acid, lime and coal. As such, it was a landmark in the history of industrial technology. But Leblanc suffered years of poverty and finally in frustration blew his brains out; the chemical industry had simply not developed to the point where it could usefully use what he had invented.

While the above are persuasive examples, and there are many others of a similar kind, where science has progressed in response to the demands of a society's economy, one need not subscribe to this view in its entirety. It does not, for example, explain satisfactorily what led Newton to discover the laws of motion, or Einstein the theory of relativity. And how could any economic need have led to the discovery of imaginary numbers? The fact that a negative number like minus one could have a square root was the last thing one could imagine being relevant to society even though, eventually, it turned out to be so important that, without it, the development of the radio would have been impossible. So, it is clear that science does possess its own internal dynamics which push it to proceed from discovery to discovery without any obvious external reasons. Otherwise there is simply no explanation about what motivated men of genius towards those various fundamental discoveries which appeared at the time to be completely innocent of any consequence for human society.

It is therefore clear that there exist both internal and external forces propelling scientific development. Especially in modern times, scientific growth is obviously stimulated when there exists a tangible need for society to develop its productive forces and when it leads to obvious economic benefits. IBM and Bell Labs certainly do not maintain huge laboratories for altruistic reasons. One must, therefore, ask the question: to what extent does there exist a technical need for science in Muslim countries today? The answer must be sought in the light of the following facts:

- One important indicator of the scientific–technological development of a country is the extent to which industry and manufacturing are part of its economy. This is, in turn, estimated by the 'value added' in manufacturing. As an example, iron ore and coke could be imported and turned into steel domestically, leading to a product of value greater than the ingredients. In economics manufacturing is taken to include machinery and transport equipment, chemicals, textiles, etc. The list below, derived from data published by the World Bank,[3] gives an indication of the role of manufacturing in the more populous Muslim countries compared to the highly industrialized countries.

Table 1
Value Added in Manufacturing, 1986 ($ per capita)

Country	Value Added
Bangladesh	11
Sudan	23
Pakistan	49
Indonesia	61
Egypt	87
Turkey	253
Algeria	320
United States	3,428
Japan	4,697

- The structure of merchandise exports provides another indicator of industrialization. The table below gives the percentage share of machinery and transport equipment of the total exports from selected countries.[3]

Table 2
Exports of Machinery and Transport Equipment as a %age of Total Exports

Country	% of Total Export
Bangladesh	0%
Sudan	3%
Pakistan	3%
Indonesia	3%
Egypt	17%
Turkey	7%
Malaysia	27%
India	32%
United States	47%
Japan	65%

- Of 46 Muslim states, only 24 produce cement, 11 produce sugar, 5 have heavy engineering industries, 6 produce textiles, and 5 produce light armaments.[4]

- By and large, Muslim countries are producers of raw materials, oil being the most important among these. These countries produce about 56% of the world's oil exports, 37% of natural gas, 80% of jute, 70% of rubber, 75% of palm oil, 25% of food grain, 13% of cotton, and 10% of sugar cane.[4]

- Trade with non-Muslim countries accounts for 94% of all foreign trade; trade between Muslim countries accounts for a mere 6%.

- The table below shows that, relative to other Third World countries, Muslim countries are considerably wealthier. The richest Muslim country is the United Arab Emirates, with a per capita GNP of $15,830, which exceeds even that for Japan ($15,760). Crude birth rates in 1986 were considerably live in cities,[3] and that urbanization generally leads to a reduction in the birth rate.

Table 3
Muslim Countries and the Third World: Selected Indicators

Indicator	Third World	Muslim Countries
Per Capita GNP	$300	$856
Urbanization	34%	40%
Crude Birth Rate	3.1%	4.1%

The message which these statistics send is rather clear: the nature of the economy in key Muslim countries — particularly the oil-producing ones — is basically extractive or agricultural. Even in the relatively advanced non-oil exporting countries, of which Egypt and Pakistan are examples, value added in manufacturing is a minor part of the total economy. To be sure, scientific methods are needed for oil extraction, mining and agriculture, and these do create some demand for learning and developing new techniques. But the technology for extraction is basically imported, as is some of the agricultural research on new crops and varieties. Hence the overall importance of science to production in the Muslim countries is peripheral, and present incentives for its indigenous growth are not large.

Science as an Institution

Until it was invented by Whewell in 1840, the term scientist did not exist. Indeed, the practitioners of science were not numerous enough at that time to warrant the introduction of a new word into the English language. But in the 20th century, science has become an institution in which hundreds of thousands of men and women find their profession. Throughout the world, and in the developing countries as well, a new universal community of scientists is rapidly emerging.

But in Muslim countries, the speed of this growth is quite a bit slower. The size of the scientific community in Muslim countries, and the productivity of scientists, is considerably below that for the rest of the world. This is so even in comparison to the average for Third World countries. Some figures, mostly following Moravcsik, are given below:[5]

Table 4
The Number of Scientific Authors, 1976

World Wide	352,000	
Third World	19,000	
Muslim Countries	3,300	
Israel	6,100	(approx.)

Among Muslim countries, the largest producers of scientific literature were Egypt, Iran, Pakistan, Nigeria, Turkey, Malaysia, and Lebanon.[5] Another listing, which gives the contribution to scientific authorship for selected countries, follows below.

Table 5
Scientific Authorship for Selected Muslim Countries as %age of world output, 1976

Country	%
Egypt	0.21
Iran	0.043
Iraq	0.022
Libya	0.002
Pakistan	0.055
Saudi Arabia	0.008
Syria	0.001
India	2.260

Another measure of the scientific output of Muslim scientists is simply to count the number of authors with Muslim sounding names in key scientific research journals. To this end, this author carried out a small-scale survey of the 1989 international scientific literature and obtained the results set out in Table 6. Allowing for the fact that some Muslims may not have Arabic/Persian/Turkish sounding names, at a rough estimate one should increase the numbers in the right-hand column by some 30–40 per cent. This does not, however, alter the conclusion that these numbers are woefully small. It is also significant that about half of the Muslim authors had institutional addresses in the West.

Table 6
Scientific Authorship in Physics, Mathematics and Chemistry, 1989

	Total number of authors surveyed	*Number of Muslim authors found*
Physics	4,168	46
Mathematics	5,050	53
Chemistry	5,375	128

A similar picture emerges upon inspecting the Science Citation Index, which contains a fairly comprehensive guide to recent scientific literature.

Table 7
Publications Quoted in Science Citation Index, 1988

Country	*Population (in millions) (1987)*	*Relative number of publications (1988)*
Argentina	31	25
Bangladesh	104	1.8
Brazil	141	33
Egypt	49	17
India	700	90
Indonesia	150	2.5
Iran	50	2
Iraq	17	4
Israel	4.5	72
Malaysia	16.5	4
Pakistan	102	4
Turkey	51	10.5

Source: A. Sadiq and N.A. Khattak.

The above results are not inconsistent with other estimates. Comparing Arab and Israeli scientific outputs on a per capita basis, A. B. Zahlan finds the Arab output to be a mere 1% of that of Israel.[6] Material resources are clearly not the problem. Arab GNP increased from $25 billion in 1967 to more than $140 billion in 1976, yet scientific output rose only modestly. It is interesting to note that at the time of the 1967 war, the Arab defeat was widely ascribed to a technology gap between Israel and the Arabs. There was some speculation, therefore, at the time that this would spur an Arab quest for modern science and technology. The available data indicate that this expectation was not fulfilled.[7]

I shall now briefly remark on the institutional aspect of science in the context of Pakistan, the Muslim country I am most intimately acquainted with. There are, on paper, 133 science and technology institutions in Pakistan. In size they range from large research and development organizations such as the PAEC (atomic energy), PCSIR (industrial research), and SUPARCO (space research) to small units occupying only a few rooms of office space. Equipment is generally plentiful, salaries are 30–50% higher than in neighbouring India, and perks such as foreign travel are common. The organizations maintain public relations offices, have good access to the state media, send employees for overseas training, and organize conferences all year round. On the face of it these are signs of busy, productive, and effective activity. But, with some exceptions, their scientific research output is minuscule by any reasonable standard, and the impact on the technology that exists or the national economy imperceptible. Pakistan's nuclear programme, which is by far the most advanced among Muslim countries, is often held up as the symbol of the nation's technical prowess. But the only declared achievement of significance is the reasonably successful operation of, and fuel fabrication for, the single Canadian supplied reactor located in Karachi, KANUPP. Unlike India, Pakistan cannot hope to design and construct its own reactors in the foreseeable future, which is why it entered into a deal in 1990 for purchasing a turn-key French supplied reactor.

Many causes are commonly attributed to the ineffectiveness of Pakistani R. & D. organizations. The principal among these is an open door import policy enforced by foreign aid agencies which discourages the indigenization of technology and forestalls any increase in the tiny numbers of highly skilled scientists and engineers. The validity of this last point can be gauged from seeing that the total number of Ph.D.'s throughout the country in natural sciences and engineering is only about 1,000. The corresponding number in India is estimated to lie between 70,000 and 80,000.

Given that per capita incomes in Pakistan ($350) and India ($300) are not so very different, the huge discrepancy in levels of scientific attainment must be sought elsewhere. The explanation lies in education.

Science in Education

Scientific research and development — and hence the growth or decay of science as an institution in society — are inescapably connected with education. In fact, the ultimate expression of the philosophy to which a society subscribes is to be found in the manner by which it educates its young. It is here where one faces squarely the question of whether education should be a means of transforming and modernizing society, or whether it should principally seek to conserve tradition. Leaving for later discussion all other dimensions — such as objectives, quality, and method — let us first look at the present scale of education in Muslim countries. Some relevant statistics are given in Table 8.[3]

Table 8
Educational Enrolments for Selected Countries, 1986 (%)

	Primary		Secondary		Tertiary
	male	*female*	*male*	*female*	*total*
Bangladesh	69	50	24	11	5
Sudan	59	41	23	17	2
Pakistan	55	32	25	10	5
Indonesia	121	116	45	34	7
Egypt	96	77	77	54	21
Morocco	96	62	39	27	9
Turkey	121	113	56	33	10
Third World	113	92	42	27	3

Note: Percentages of relevant age group enrolled may exceed 100% because pupil age standards vary. (For methodology, consult Ref. 3)

The above enrolment figures do not reveal any very dramatic differences between Muslim and other Third World countries, although one would expect the former to be substantially ahead in view of their greater average per capita GNP. More importantly, the figures say nothing about the quality and objectives of the educational systems.

Lacking detailed knowledge of the real situation of education in other Muslim countries, I shall confine myself in the remainder of this section entirely to the case of Pakistan. A recent report of the World Bank gives an accurate, but gloomy, picture:

> The unusually low educational attainments of Pakistan's rapidly growing population, particularly the female population, will become a serious impediment to the country's long-term development. . . . The weak human resources base on which Pakistan's economic development is being built endangers its long-term growth prospects and negatively affects the distributional benefits to be derived from such growth.[8]

Seventy-five million Pakistanis can neither read nor write. Pakistan government figures put the average (both sexes) literacy rate at 26 per cent, and the female literacy rate at only 15 per cent. While these figures are low even by Third World standards, the actual situation is probably considerably worse. Independent sources estimate that the true figures may be 30–40 per cent lower than stated. Pakistan's Asian neighbours have enrolment levels averaging

70–90 per cent, whereas Pakistan's at the primary level is only 55 per cent. Pakistan devotes about 2.0 per cent of its GNP to education compared to 2.4 per cent in Nepal, 2.6 per cent in India, and 6.7 per cent in Malaysia. As a percentage of the budget the educational expenditure is 6 per cent in Pakistan as against 9 per cent in Nepal, 11.2 per cent in India, and 26 per cent in Malaysia. A Pakistan government sponsored study of book reading habits and book publishing found that Pakistan ranked the lowest in South Asia.

No government in Pakistan, whether democratic or military, has ever given education any reasonable status in the list of national priorities. But the military regime of General Zia stands out particularly. A damning indictment of this regime's achievements in the field of education is to be found in a report by a US research concern, which was given a contract in 1986 by the government to analyse the state of education in Pakistan. The report concludes that:

> Most dramatic was the difference between the projections of the 5th five year plan and actual performance during this period (1978–83) which fell over 50% below the planned level and represented the lowest level of national effort in support of education in the independent nation's history.[9]

In earlier periods of Pakistan's history, such low levels of attainment in education had been admitted with quiet shame, but the objectives of education were tacitly taken to be essentially universal, modernistic ones. However, following the coup of 1977 which brought General Zia-ul-Haq to power, the military government, in alliance with political parties of fundamentalist orientation, declared its intention of creating an Islamized society and a new national identity based exclusively on religion. Education immediately became a key instrument to be used towards this end. Consequently, a number of important changes were officially decreed. These included the following:

- Imposition of the chadar for female students in educational institutions;
- Organization of *zuhr* (afternoon) prayers during school hours;
- Compulsory teaching of Arabic as a second language from the 6th class onwards;
- Introduction of *nazra* Qur'an (reading of Qur'an) as a matriculation requirement;
- An alteration of the definition of literacy to mean religious knowledge;
- Elevation of *maktab* schools to the status of regular schools;
- The recognition of *madrasah* certificates as equivalent to master's degrees
- The grant of 20 extra marks for those applicants to engineering universiti who have memorized the Qur'an;
- Creation of the International Islamic University in Islamabad;
- Organization of numerous national and international conferences on various aspects of Islamization;
- Introduction of religious knowledge as a criterion for selecting teachers o science and non-science subjects;
- Revision of conventional subjects to emphasize Islamic values.

General Zia and his followers pursued their concept of Islamized education with great seriousness, and most of the above decrees were implemented at least to some degree. But zealotry was tempered with pragmatism when powerful interests were at stake. For example, the government left almost untouched that exclusive set of expensive, private, English medium schools to which military officers, bureaucrats, and wealthy citizens send their children. Elite institutions such as the Karachi Grammar School, Aitchison College, Burn Hall, and many others, boast of a content and quality of education which is comparable to the better ranking schools in the West. In contrast to Urdu medium schools — which are intended for the masses — these provide instruction of a modern and basically secular character to roughly one per cent of the population. Apart from relatively minor changes, they continued to function during the Zia era as in the years before.

The overall impact of General Zia's Islamization policies on Pakistani education, setting aside the special case of elite schools, has been tremendous. The successor civilian government of Benazir Bhutto, which was not known for seeking bold initiatives, did not dare to make any meaningful changes during its tenure in office. With the demise of her government, and the accession to power of the Islamic Democratic Alliance, it is almost certain that the Islamization of education will be accelerated. The conscious effort to substitute traditional religious education in favour of modern secular education produced changes within the system which will be felt by the generations to come. From colonial times onwards, the assumption had been that modern education was necessary for social progress — and that social progress was desirable. This was explicitly renounced in 1977. Instead, the restoration of past Islamic glories was declared as the goal. Achievement of this required that all modern disciplines — the humanities, social sciences, and natural sciences — be Islamized. Of this, more will be said later on in the book.

But let us now turn to the issue of the quality and kind of science education in Pakistan. By and large, this education is alienated from the spirit of scientific inquiry. The well known Indian-born chemist, J. B. S. Haldane, recounts an instance which particularly impressed upon him the manner in which science is generally taught and learned in Pakistan:

> I was walking near my house one Sunday afternoon when I heard a male voice raised in a monotonous chant. I supposed that I was listening to some mantras, and asked my companion if he could identify them. The practice of repeating religious formulae is, of course, about as common in Europe as in Pakistan.
>
> But my companion stated that the language of the chant was English and the subject organic chemistry. We returned, and I found that he was right. The subject of the chant was the preparation of aliphatic amines, with special reference to various precautions.[10]

Rote learning dominates science teaching in Pakistan to an extent which appears to be even greater than 25 years ago when Haldane made the above observation. In part this can be ascribed to a defective system of examination, incompetent and underpaid teachers, and widespread corruption in the educational apparatus. One should not underestimate the effects of these. But, to a significant degree, the rote nature of contemporary education can be traced to attitudes inherited from traditional education, wherein knowledge is something to be acquired rather than discovered, and in which the attitude of mind is passive and receptive rather than creative and inquisitive. The social conditioning of an authoritarian traditional environment means, as an inescapable consequence, that all knowledge comes to be viewed as unchangeable and all books tend to be memorized or venerated to some degree. The concept of secular knowledge as a problem-solving tool which evolves over time is alien to traditional thought.

To assess the quality of science teaching in Pakistan in quantitative terms is problematic because few quantitative measurements have been made. To examine changes in standards over time is still harder. But to talk about education in Pakistan without reference to its quality misses a great deal. So, while recognizing that true quantitative measures are still lacking, I have attempted to piece together various fragmentary measurements of the quality of science education which are available.

- Lost and buried in the dusty archives of Harvard's Widener Library is a Ph.D. dissertation, submitted in 1964 to that university by a Pakistani student, Wali Muhammad Zaki, entitled 'The Attitudes of Pakistani Science Teachers Towards Religion And Science'. Although it is probably the only serious work done in this important area, this thesis has not, to my knowledge, ever been quoted or its results published in the intervening 25 years.

In his thesis, Zaki sought to discover the extent to which secondary school teachers in West Pakistan understood and appreciated the nature of the scientific enterprise. He then attempted to determine if there existed any relationship between their understanding of science and their attitude towards religion. The methodology consisted of randomly selecting a sample of teachers who were requested to complete a questionnaire designed to measure their attitude towards religion, their attitude towards science, and their understanding of science.

The results of Zaki's research are as follows:

(1) High school *students* in the US understood the nature of the scientific enterprise, and the methods and aims of science, significantly better than did the high school *teachers* of West Pakistan.

(2) The understanding of science, as well as the attitudes towards science, were found to have significant negative correlation with attitudes towards religion. Science teachers who had received their education in post-independence Pakistan were found to be more favourably inclined towards religion and less towards science, relative to those who had been trained in pre-partition days.

(3) The denominational sects of Ahmadis and Protestants indicated a significantly more favourable attitude towards science relative to Sunnis.

(4) Similar differences were found between regional cultures with teachers belonging to Sind showing a significantly more favourable attitude towards science.

(5) Science teachers with backgrounds in the biological sciences understood the nature of the scientific enterprise better than those in the physical sciences.

There are several counts on which one can fault the above study. Lack of ease of the respondents with English, the possible inappropriateness and cultural bias of some of the questions asked, and the flaws of carrying out a survey by mail, are among the important criticisms that can be made. But is this the reason why Zaki's dissertation met the fate of obscurity and oblivion?

• In 1983 the National Institute of Psychology (NIP) administered a science and mathematics test to compare the skills of schoolchildren in various foreign countries against those of their Pakistani counterparts.[11] Some 420 children in the Rawalpindi area were given this multiple choice test after NIP workers had adapted it for local conditions. The results for 6th class children providing an unsatisfactory comparison, the test was also administered to the 7th, 8th, 9th 10th, and 11th (first year F.Sc — i.e. Intermediate) classes. Some results are shown in the following charts.

Major conclusions drawn by the NIP researchers were:

(1) The lowest score of 6th class overseas children exceeded that of 6th, 7th, 8th, and 9th class Pakistani children in all cases. In fact, the highest score in mathematics of 6th class Japanese students (50.2) exceeded that of 11th class Pakistani students (38.80). The report concludes that 'ultimately, many of our students of grade 11 remain less proficient in science and mathematics than grade 6 students of other countries.'
(2) The growth of scientific reasoning rises very slowly in successive classes. According to the report, 'what is probably most significant is the extremely slow pace of learning. During the three years of middle school (from grade 6 to 8) there is no significant increase in science and mathematics learning.'
(3) Contrary to the belief that the standard of education is much higher in English medium schools as compared to Urdu medium schools, the NIP report found no major difference between the two in the learning of science and mathematics. In fact a small, and statistically insignificant, bias was found towards the Urdu schools.

• Since 1985, Pakistan's Ministry of Science and Technology has been sending several hundred students every year to the US and Britain for Ph.D. work in

Figure 1: Comparison of Sixth Class Pakistani and Overseas Children in Mathematics and Science (exam results in %)

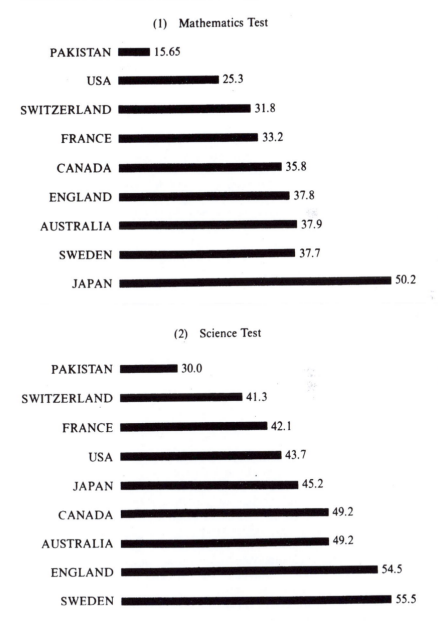

(1)   Mathematics Test

PAKISTAN 15.65
USA 25.3
SWITZERLAND 31.8
FRANCE 33.2
CANADA 35.8
ENGLAND 37.8
AUSTRALIA 37.9
SWEDEN 37.7
JAPAN 50.2

(2)   Science Test

PAKISTAN 30.0
SWITZERLAND 41.3
FRANCE 42.1
USA 43.7
JAPAN 45.2
CANADA 49.2
AUSTRALIA 49.2
ENGLAND 54.5
SWEDEN 55.5

scientific and technical fields. Those selected are supposedly the cream of the nation's talent, and each student sent to the US costs the Pakistani government between US$30,000 and US$35,000 a year. But this programme is failing badly because of the poor quality of the students selected. For example, in 1985–86, 187 students were sent to the US for Ph.D. work. As of 1991, only 9 had received Ph.Ds, and 39 had been given M.Scs. In the same year, 191 students were sent to the UK. Of these, 65 received Ph.Ds. This relatively larger number indicates the less rigorous nature of the British system.

- On 29 January 1986, the Centre of Basic Sciences in Islamabad administered a test designed by the Nobel prize winning physicist, Samuel Ting. About 120 students from all over Pakistan, and with qualifications ranging from M.Sc. to M.Phil. to Ph.D., took the test. Students were allowed to bring any notes and books they wanted. This 5-hour long test consisted of 200 multiple choice questions on various aspects of physics. Since each question had three alternative answers, random guessing would give an average score of 67 marks. Students who scored more than 160 would be granted admission to MIT.

Not a single student passed. Not one came anywhere close to the pass mark. The highest recorded score was 113, and the average score was 70 — a scant 3 points above that which a group of illiterates would have attained, had they been allowed to randomly tick off the answers. The authorities which had allowed the test to take place now sought to suppress its results, but the cat was out of the bag.

- An important estimate of the quality of science education can also be inferred from the kind of questions that students are expected to answer in examinations, as well as their results. On looking at examination papers set for the Intermediate and B.Sc. levels by the Federal Board of Education over the last three years, the following salient features can be discerned:

(1) A very high degree of repetition was present in all science subjects. Between 40 and 70 per cent of exactly the same questions had been set in the past three years. Instances exist where the entire exam paper of a previous year has been repeated unchanged in a subsequent year.
(2) Between 60 and 80 per cent of marks are reserved, even in science subjects, for questions of the type 'write a short note on . . .', or 'discuss . . .' These test memorization, not understanding.
(3) Even where a calculation was required in the question, this was either identical or a simple variant of an example in the prescribed textbook.
(4) In many examinations, students are only required to attempt half the number of questions in the paper. This enables students to ignore a large portion of the actual syllabus.

- A batch of physics teachers, all of whom had master's degrees and had been teaching for several years in Pakistani colleges and universities, and who were due for a refresher course at Quaid-e-Azam University in 1984, were administered a surprise test comprising entirely basic questions at the Matriculate and Intermediate (F.Sc.) level. Although these teachers had been teaching at a much higher level to B.Sc. and M.Sc. classes, *less than 10 per cent of them were able to answer any of the questions.* A closely similar test was administered in 1988 to fresh students, all of whom had obtained firsts in their Master's degree and were applicants for technical posts in the Pakistan Atomic Energy Commission. Almost simultaneously, students entering Pakistan's premier science institutions — Quaid-e-Azam University — were also given the test. The results were slightly, but not substantially, better. This is unmistakable evidence that the vast majority of Pakistani teachers and students do not internalize and make part of their mental machinery even very elementary material.

The well established pattern of examination questions has encouraged the mushrooming of 'coaching centres' which boldly enter into a contractual agreement with an individual student, wherein a certain level of marks is assured for a certain period of attendance at the coaching centre in return for an agreed sum of money. Pakistani newspapers periodically expose the sale of degrees, certificates and mark sheets, as well as widespread cheating during examinations. Definitive statistics on the extent of such activities are not available. However, because they are common knowledge, students feel deeply discouraged in making efforts towards meaningful accomplishment of learning.

The de-emphasis of secular subjects, and reduced levels of performance in these, is in considerable measure a result of the fundamental changes in educational priorities. The emphasis on religious and nationalistic indoctrination has caused most literary works to be replaced by moralizing essays, classical poetry by religious poetry, and the teaching of history and geography to be confined to that of Muslim periods and areas. The vision of a universalistic world civilization remains hidden from the pupil's view. Most importantly, the role of reason and creativity in the learning process has been denigrated.

Protests and opposition have not challenged the policy of indoctrination through education. Instead, most parents who can afford the extra expense choose to send their children to private English medium schools. These schools have a higher content of secular learning, and mostly use textbooks published overseas. Whether unwittingly, or by design, the government's policy of Islamizing education was an important reason for the vast expansion of the private education sector. In Zia's Pakistan, these alone offered some measure of escape from doctrines imposed by the state apparatus. The subsequent civilian government proved too weak to make any significant changes.

The years of General Zia's rule also saw the virtual extinction of intellectual activity in Pakistani universities. Public lectures, debates, drama, musical events, and even *mushairas* (poetry recitals) were virtually banished from the campuses. In part this was due to the efforts of university authorities obsessed with the desire to maintain law and order, and in part to active threats by religious student groups who consider drama and music as un-Islamic. The latter force has not disappeared with Zia's death.

Producing little new research or ideas of consequence, Pakistani universities are among the poorest in quality in South Asia. Compare Indian universities with Pakistani ones. This is especially relevant because of obvious historical and cultural similarities. India has more than a dozen well established institutes in the physical sciences and engineering. These include the five Indian Institutes of Technology (IIT's), the Bhabha Atomic Research Centre (BARC), the Tata Institute Of Fundamental Research (TIFR), the Saha Institute, the Indian Institute Of Science, etc. Just one of these — the IIT at Kanpur — has an educational and research output which exceeds by far the entire output of all Pakistani institutions put together. Between 1982 and 1985, a total of 37 Ph.D. degrees, most of these being in the biological sciences, were awarded by Pakistani universities. No Ph.D. in engineering has yet been awarded. But, during the same period, the IIT at Kanpur alone awarded 202 Ph.D. degrees in science and engineering. The total number of science Ph.D. degrees awarded in India in 1980 exceeded 2,000.

Given the state of intellectual impoverishment, bright young people — some of whom have established enviable reputations overseas in their fields — tend to avoid a university career in Pakistan. Occasionally, however, a rare young man or woman can be persuaded to take a daring risk and enter the world of Pakistani academia. But the chances are high that he or she will run foul of some university selection board.

With the intention of preserving the universities from unwanted change, there has evolved an elaborate system whereby the university faculty is selected so that contamination by the germs of intellectual and professional competence is avoided as much as possible. This task of sanitization is one which the university selection boards are entrusted with. The means by which this task is accomplished includes, among others, forcing candidates to answer questions wholly unrelated to their subject of specialization, and which bear no relevance to any possible professional activity of the candidate.

This point is well illustrated by successive meetings in 1987 and 1988 of the selection board of Quaid-e-Azam University, which is considered to be Pakistan's premier university. The candidates who appeared before the interviewing panel, including some superbly qualified specialists with Ph.D. degrees in scientific subjects, were confronted with questions like this:

- What are the names of the Holy Prophet's wives?
- Recite the prayer Dua-e-Qunoot.
- When was the Pakistan Resolution adopted?
- What is the difference between different azan's?
- What does your [the candidate's] name mean?
- Give the various names of God.

Questioning candidates on Islam and Pakistan during selection interviews became established official policy during the Zia era. Candidates who refused to submit themselves to such questioning were generally turned away. The government of Benazir Bhutto did not repudiate the policy, and the successor IJI government has reaffirmed it.

The issue of what should be expected of university faculty is indivisibly linked with the desired role of the university in the society at large. In dynamic and progressive societies, universities are the magnets which attract the best and most creative minds. Not only do they transmit knowledge between generations, but they also extend the boundaries of knowledge and give to society the intellectual impetus needed for its growth. Modern society relies crucially on the vigour and vitality of its universities, and would become static and dormant without them.

In contrast to this, Pakistani society appears to have cultivated nothing but docility in its universities. This docility does not mean renunciation of physical violence — the use of Kalashnikovs and automatic weapons has become increasingly common on the campuses. Rather, the docility is intellectual, reflecting a chronic inability to think independently, analytically and creatively. Consequently, the Pakistani university has become a centre towards which the least able members of society — meaning students and teachers who have failed in all else — tend to gravitate. Where all means of expression are denied, and only crudities of absolute right and wrong exist, violence becomes a natural, even inevitable act.

Science as a World View

The distinction between science and technology becomes increasingly murky as one proceeds to the very frontiers of technology. Genetic engineering, robots and artificially intelligent systems, computers, nuclear fusion, and space travel were all brought into existence by sophisticated theoretical science and depend heavily upon these for further progress. But it would be a mistake to think that science and technology are synonymous or interchangeable terms. They are directed towards different goals, and the demands which they make at the philosophical and conceptual level are quite different. Whereas, for example, designing and constructing an oil refinery or motor manufacturing plant places little strain on values and beliefs, the appreciation and mastery of science possibly does. The fact that science cannot do away with questioning means that conflict with traditional modes of thought is almost inevitable.

We have already encountered the uneasiness of important Saudi administrators. They are not the only ones who see this clash between the world view of science and the demands of faith; such fears have long been articulated by orthodox practitioners of all religions. As I shall endeavour to demonstrate in the remainder of this chapter, the intellectual climate in several Muslim countries is, at the present time, not particularly propitious for free thinking and science as the following cases will illustrate.

- Nowhere is the conflict between scientific and traditional modes of thinking more visible than in the dispute over miracles. Precisely to underscore the belief in the efficacy and existence of miracles, a large-scale international conference entitled Scientific Miracles Of Quran And Sunnah was held in October 1987 in the capital city of Islamabad. Inaugurated by the late President of Pakistan, General Zia-ul-Haq, and organized jointly by the International Islamic University and the Organization Of Scientific Miracles based in Mecca, this much heralded conference was attended by several hundred pious participants from Muslim countries. The Scientific Miracles Conference was a significant event because it was one of the many of its kind supported by the Pakistani state in the recent past, and because it clearly portrayed the mind-set of those who wielded state power in Pakistan. The thrust of the conference was towards the following:

(1) Affirmation of the existence of 'scientific' miracles;
(2) Proving that all known scientific facts can be traced to either the Qur'an or Sunnah;
(3) New conjectures related to physical phenomena, ostensibly based on the holy texts;
(4) A condemnation of secular 'Western' science.

The appendix, 'They Call It Islamic Science', at the end of this book looks at some of the papers presented at this conference.

- The new moon of the month of Ramazan is the subject of bitter argument between the scientifically inclined and the ulema, and amongst the ulema themselves. Often the dispute among the ulema over whether or not the new moon had appeared has led to Muslims starting the Ramazan fast at different times, or celebrating the Eid festivals on different days, depending on which community follows which ulema's authority. In order to eliminate the confusion and disputes, the scientifically inclined insist that modern astronomy can predict the position and time of the new moon to excellent accuracy. Hence, in their opinion, disagreements between different observers can be eliminated and the date of Eid announced beforehand. Most of the ulema vehemently disagree and insist that there can be no substitute for visual sighting. The Pakistan government, anxious to avoid divisive decisions on a sensitive issue, has created the *Ruet-i-Hilal* (moon-sighting) committee which is taken aloft in an aeroplane at the opportune time. Agreement on even this procedure, however, is not unanimous among the ulema.

- Weather prediction is another issue where modern and orthodox views continue to clash. Muslim modernists take the position that physical laws determine weather in general, and rainfall in particular. However, they are careful to reconcile this with Islamic beliefs on the subject, derived from a *sura* in the Holy Qur'an which prescribes special prayers (*namaz-i-istisqa*) for rain. According to the modernist interpretation, prayers for rain express only an ardent wish for rain and one cannot expect that God will suspend the laws of nature on account of them. However, if there is an element of chance either way, then the believer implores Allah to send rain. Under modernist influence, it has come about that most Muslim countries maintain modern meteorological departments which, on the basis of satellite supplied data and the equations of fluid physics, provide anticipated weather patterns including predictions for rainfall. These are regularly broadcast by the media, according to the normal practice in the rest of the world.

The orthodox hold a view on this issue which is almost diametrically opposite to the modernist. Many, if not most, orthodox ulema contend that prediction of rain lies outside of what can be lawfully known to man, and infringes on the supernatural domain. Consequently, between 1983 and 1984, weather forecasts were quietly suspended by the Pakistani media, although they were later reinstated. Belief in direct supernatural intervention in influencing weather exists at the official level. Hence, when drought appears imminent, special prayers for rain are organized by the government of Saudi Arabia. General Zia's government in Pakistan also revived the practice in 1981. The special prayers are generally attended by tens of thousands of believers.

- Perceiving Darwinism as a threat to Faith, the reaction in the Muslim world to the evolutionary theory of biology has been, for the most part, a highly negative one. Introduced by Shibli Shumayyil into the Arab world in 1910, it became the subject of intense denunciation and emotional polemics by traditionalists who proclaimed 'jihad against the poison of Darwinism'. Jamaluddin Afghani, who was generally an advocate of Western science, also reacted strongly and was, in fact, the first major Islamic figure to speak out against Darwinism. Afghani, like many of those who opposed it, had a rather strange notion of the theory and argued against it saying that, if it was correct, then 'it would be possible that after the passage of centuries a mosquito could become an elephant and an elephant, by degrees, a mosquito'.[12] The response of the Arab world to Darwinism has been examined in a recent book by Adel Ziadet.[13]

To hold views supporting evolutionary biology, even today, is dangerous in many Islamic countries and there are specific laws against its being taught. Most recently, an eminent biologist in Sudan, Farouk Mohammed Ibrahim of the University of Khartoum, was jailed in 1990 for teaching his students Darwin's theory. In a letter smuggled out of jail, he details how he was whipped, kicked, and beaten in the presence of a member of the regime's revolutionary council. This treatment has, however, elicited strong outrage from a section of the Muslim community in Britain. Zaki Badawi, principal of the Muslim College in London and chairman of the Imams and Mosques Association, said: 'I don't believe it. They [the Sudanese authorities] must have gone mad . . . They might justifiably arrest people for their political, but not for their scientific, views.'[14]

- Even in the present day, the traditional curriculum of Muslim universities teaches Ptolemaic astronomy, embedded in a frame of geocentric cosmology and philosophy. A modern system is available as an option but presented as a 'hypothesis'.[15]

- The Ptolemaic system continues to inspire Sheikh Abdul Aziz Ibn Baz of Saudi Arabia, the well-known president of Medina University and recipient of the 1982 Service to Islam King Faisal international award. The Sheikh authored in the same year a book in Arabic entitled *Jiryan Al-Shams Wa Al-Qamar Wa-Sukoon Al-Arz*. This translates into 'Motion of the Sun and Moon, and Stationarity of the Earth'. The earth is the centre of the universe and the sun moves around it, says the venerable Sheikh. In an earlier book, he had threatened dissenters with the dire *fatwa* of *takfir* (disbelief), but did not repeat the threat in the newer version. Now, Sheikh Baz is an important personage in Saudi Arabia, and his views are taken with great seriousness in that country. This might suggest to some readers that progress is not considered a virtue there. But Saudi Arabia is also the first — and so far only — Muslim country to have sent an astronaut into space. Carried aloft in NASA's space shuttle, the first Muslim astronaut could certainly have commented on the Sheikh's thesis if he had not been preoccupied with the urgent task of determining the direction of Qibla for his prayers.

Although the victory of science over superstition is said to be assured, the battle is far from being won today. The tragic consequences rarely, if ever, make it into the news. There is, however, an occasional exception. The famous Hawkes Bay incident of February 1983 is one such exception. One wintry morning, hundreds of villagers from northern Pakistan, inspired by a village maiden's dream, jumped into the stormy waters of the Arabian sea on a Karachi beach. They were hoping to make the pilgrimage to the Holy Karbala in Iraq, and had been assured that the sea would give safe passage. Over thirty corpses were recovered. The police, uncertain about how to deal with the issue, acted in classic bureaucratic fashion: the survivors were put under arrest for attempting to leave the country without passports. But they were soon released, and this attempted pilgrimage was lauded by some influential ulema. After a fund-raising drive the survivors were sent off for pilgrimage by air. What is significant is the amount of social support, and even praise, which this ill-fated venture garnered from the population at large.

References

1. What follows is similar to the criteria devised by J. D. Bernal in his classic work, *Science in History*, Vol. 1, (Cambridge, MIT Press, 1971), pp. 27–53.

2. F. Engels in *The Origins of the Scientific Revolution*, ed. H. Kearny, (London. Longmans Green, 1964), pp. 64–6.

3. *World Development Report*, (Oxford, Oxford University Press, 1989).

4. Data on trade and technology in Muslim countries has been collected in useful form in the *International Conference on Science in Islamic Polity, Vol. 1*, (Islamabad, Ministry of Science and Technology, 1983).

5. Michael Moravcsik, in Reference 4 above, pp. 340–54.

6. A. B. Zahlan in *Science and Science Policy in the Arab World*, (London, Croom Helm, 1980), Chapter 2.

7. A. B. Zahlan, *Journal of Palestine Studies*, I(1972), pp. 17–36.

8. *World Bank Report*, 1986.

9. Development Associates' Report on Primary Education in Pakistan, prepared for USAID and the Government of Pakistan, p. 5.

10. J. B. S. Haldane, 'Is Science a Misnomer?', *The Hindu Weekly Review*, August 31, 1959.

11. National Institute of Psychology, Quaid-e-Azam University, Islamabad, unpublished report, 1983.

12. Nikkie Keddie, *An Islamic Response to Imperialism*, (University of California Press, 1983), p. 15.

13. Adel A. Ziadat, *Western Science in the Arab World — The Impact of Darwinism, 1860–1930*, (London, Macmillan Press, 1986).

14. *New Scientist*, 17 March 1990, p. 21.

15. G. Santillana in the preface to *Science and Civilization in Islam*, by S. H. Hossein, (Cambridge, Mass., Harvard University Press, 1968), p. xi.

5. Three Muslim Responses to Underdevelopment

The fact that science and technology in its present form did not develop in Islam is not a sign of decadence, as is claimed, but the refusal of Islam to consider any form of knowledge as purely secular.

Syed Hossein Nasr

The slow growth of science and modern ideas in most Muslim countries — even relative to other similar non-Muslim countries — is impossible to hide. Although Muslims form one-fifth of the world's population, they are barely noticeable in the world of scientific research, and Muslim countries are the most abjectly dependent among developing countries upon Western technology and know-how. The Gulf war was a recent and powerful illustration of this glaring, but more than two-hundred-year-old, fact. Now, whether this reality ought to be lauded as a demonstration of tenacity against corrupting Western influences — as the above quote from the scholar, Syed Hossein Nasr, suggests — or whether it should be lamented is immaterial to its veracity. Rather than engage in a futile attempt to refute an unpleasant reality, it would be infinitely more productive for us to try and understand why science and modernism have developed at a relatively slower pace in Muslim countries.

The simplest thing to do, of course, is to hold the Islamic Faith responsible. The common Western view of Islam, wherein it is viewed as a monolithic set of beliefs, takes this almost for granted. The scientific backwardness of Muslim states is proffered as proof that Islam is fundamentally retrogressive and incapable of sustaining a modern scientific culture. Indeed, many Orientalist scholars have long asserted that Islam produces fatalism, is oriented to the past rather than the future, and discourages new experiences and innovation. They go on to say that Islam and modernity are essentially at odds because the line between this-worldly and other-worldly spheres is confused, and because true Islam rejects a rational and scientific culture.[1] 'Islam is absolutely defenceless against modernization,' claims Daniel Lerner, a leading Western sociologist.[2] Another Orientalist, Manfred Halpern, writes that the Islamic system that once upon a time 'connected man, God, and society together is falling apart in the teeth of modernization which is tearing off its repetitive pattern of balanced tensions'.[3] A particularly influential intellectual – but one who barely concealed his ethnic and racial prejudice – was the German sociologist, Max Weber. One of his principal contentions was that Islam, as a religion of warriors, produced an ethic fundamentally incompatible with a rational capitalist society. Yet without this rational ethic, a society is doomed to a medieval existence. More will be said about Weber's views later.

The Orientalist's analysis does, at times, contain elements of truth. But it is often simplistic and needs to be viewed with suspicion. In an area of human concern where the strict criteria of scientific objectivity do not apply, there is ample scope for malevolence and manipulation. For example, at the behest of some well-known Orientalists, the University of Manitoba recently sponsored a conference with the provocative title 'Islamic Terrorism in the Nineties'. Such outrages indicate that many Orientalists bear a psychological hostility against the object of their study. Indeed, the well-known Islamist, Montgomery Watt, advises Western scholars of Islam to be cognizant of existing prejudices lest they intrude on the quality of their professional work:

> The difficulty is that we are heirs of a deep seated prejudice which goes back to the 'war propaganda' of the medieval times . . . . From about the eighth century A.D. Christian Europe began to be conscious of Islam as her great enemy, threatening her in both military and the spiritual spheres . . . . The image created in the twelfth and thirteenth centuries continued to dominate European thinking about Islam and even in the second half of the twentieth century had some vestigial influence. According to this image, Islam was a perversion of Christian truth, even an idolatrous religion; it was a religion of violence, spread by the sword; it was a religion without asceticism, gaining adherents by pandering to their sexual appetites both in this world and in the world to come.[4]

I shall not attempt here to debate in detail the phenomenon of Orientalism in its full generality. Others, such as Edward Said,[5] have done this far more competently, and have forcefully emphasized the heartless nature of a scholarship which lacks empathy with the object of its study. The basic problem with the Orientalist viewpoint is that it takes a strictly formal and textual view of Islam, and generally sets aside as irrelevant the diverse intellectual currents which have historically coexisted within Muslim civilization. Instead, it has long dwelt upon the stereotype of the backward Muslim without adequate recognition of the long and honourable intellectual tradition within Islam. A predictable consequence of this bias and hostility has been the triggering of a defensive reaction and hardening of attitudes among Muslims so that *all* critical scholarship tends to get confused with malevolent scholarship. This has led to a certain closing of minds, and has decreased the ability of many Muslims to appreciate the enormity of the crisis which envelopes the Muslim world today.

What do *Muslims* consider their situation in the world to be, and what causes do they assign to it? Faced with a fundamental crisis and only too manifest decline, three distinct responses have emerged from within Islamic civilization in the colonial and post-colonial periods. To borrow the characterizations of Eqbal Ahmed, they are: restorationist, reconstructionist, and pragmatist. These categories provide a useful analytical framework within which one can examine the problems and possibilities of developing a rational and science-oriented society in the Islamic world.

The Restorationist Line

Among Muslims the Restorationist response is the most visible one today. It seeks to restore some idealized version of the past, and assigns all failures and defeats to a deviation from the True Path. The mushrooming of fundamentalist Islamic movements in the 1970s and 1980s is its most concrete manifestation. From nominally secular Egypt to the Wahabi Islamic Kingdom of Saudi Arabia, from the revolutionary Shi'ite state of Ayatollah Khomenei to the Islamic Republic of Pakistan, the trumpets call incessantly for Holy War. Holy War against the secular, rationalist and universalist ideal. Holy War against capitalism, socialism, and communism alike. Holy War to establish one or other vision of an ideal Islamic state. Holy War to fight against the principle – first enunciated by the Arab (and Muslim) philosopher Ibn Rushd some 800 years ago – that human reason is the only instrument which should be allowed to guide human society. And Holy War against the foundations of modern, secular, scientific thought and method.

In what follows, I take the case of Pakistan as a particularly interesting reaction against science and modernity.

The Jamaat-e-Islami of Pakistan

The vanguard of the restorationist reaction in Pakistan has been the Jamaat-e-Islami, a politico-religious party which derives its support from the urban middle class and students, and which is by far the most well organized among such parties. It is a sister organization of the 'Ikhwan-ul-Muslimeen', a fundamentalist organization which operates in numerous Arab countries, and which recently won a large representation in Jordan's first parliamentary elections. Although the Jamaat has never achieved a significant share of the popular vote in any Pakistani national election, its influence on urban middle class politics is considerable. By penetrating the educational establishment, it significantly altered the content of education during the Zia era – a change which subsequent, more liberal governments have found difficult to negate. The disputes that other religious political parties have with the Jamaat are essentially fights over turf, and not over fundamental matters such as what the role of science ought to be in Islamic society.

The Jamaat's most articulate spokesperson on matters of science and modernity has been Maryam Jameelah. A Jewish American convert to Islam, Jameelah compares the pursuit of science and modernism with idolatry:

> All modernist ideologies are characterized by man worship. Man worship most often appears under the guise of science. Modernists are convinced that progress in scientific knowledge will eventually confer upon them the powers of Divinity.[6]

Science, in her view, is intrinsically evil because of its godless nature:

> Modern science is guided by no moral value, but naked materialism and arrogance. The whole branch of knowledge and its applications is contaminated

by the same evil. Science and technology are totally dependent upon the set of ideals and values cherished by its members. If the roots of the tree are rotten, then the tree is rotten; therefore all its fruits are rotten.[7]

Tradition, says Maryam Jameelah, is where all goodness and the solution to all problems can be found. She decries the emphasis that modern science puts on constant progress and change:

> [In Islamic society] originality, innovation and change were never upheld as intrinsic values. The ideal of Islamic culture was not mechanical, evolutionary progress but the permanent, immutable, transcendental, divinely revealed moral, theological, and spiritual values of the Qur'an and Sunnah.[8]

Therefore, in Maryam Jameelah's view, it is neither necessary nor desirable for Muslim science to 'catch up with the West', given the evil and godless nature of Western science. The old times were so much better; modernity brings nothing but corruption of the soul. She justifies her position ideologically from Ahadith such as the following, displayed on the front page of one of her books:

> Ayesha reported that the Messenger of Allah said: 'Whoever introduces a new innovation into this thing of ours (Islam) which is not of it, he is cursed.' (Muslim, Bukhari)

Maulana Abul Ala Maudoodi, founder of the Jamaat-e-Islami and one of the most influential Islamic thinkers of our times, also bitterly criticizes Western science. In a lecture on Islamic education, he stated that geography, physics, chemistry, biology, zoology, geology and economics are taught without reference to Allah and his Messenger and are hence a source of *gumrahi* (straying from the truth):

> Reflection on the nature of modern education and customs immediately reveals their contradiction with the nature of Islamic education and customs. You teach young minds philosophy, which seeks to explain the universe without Allah. You teach them science which is devoid of reason and slave of the senses. You teach them economics, law and sociology which, in spirit and in substance, differ from the teachings of Islam. And you still expect them to have an Islamic point of view?[9]

To avoid this evil the Maulana presents a solution wherein all education should be converted into Islamic education. He writes:

> The entire blame for this sorry state of affairs rests on the separation of *dini* (spiritual) from *dunyawi* (worldly) education. As I have just pleaded, this separation is totally unIslamic. In the new system of education a new course on *dinyat* is not needed. Instead, all courses should be changed into courses of *dinyat*.[10]

With the passage in May 1991 of the Shariat Bill by Pakistan's National

Assembly and Senate, the ulema's dream of a completely Islamized education, free from contamination by modern science, has presumably been brought a step closer to reality.

Inspired by the Maulana's wisdom, the Institute for Policy Studies in Islamabad, which serves as an intellectual centre for the Jamaat-e-Islami, has set about the task of redefining science and drawing up guidelines for writing suitably Islamized science textbooks. A sample of the IPS's recommendations is summarized below:

(1) No phenomenon or fact should be mentioned without referring to the benevolence of Allah. For example, in writing a science book for Class 3 children one should *not* ask 'What will happen if an animal does not take any food?'. Instead, the following question should be asked: 'What will happen if Allah does not give the animal food?'[11]

(2) A science textbook should be written only by a man who believes strongly in Islam as the only code of life, and who is thoroughly familiar with the Qur'an and Sunnah. All possible care must be taken in this regard.[12]

(3) Effect must not be related to physical cause. To do so leads towards atheism. For example, says the IPS recommendation, 'there is latent poison present in the subheading *Energy Causes Changes* because it gives the impression that energy is the true cause rather than Allah. Similarly, it is unIslamic to teach that mixing hydrogen with oxygen automatically produces water. The Islamic way is this: when atoms of hydrogen approach atoms of oxygen, then by the will of God water is produced.'[13]

(4) The first chapter of, say, a chemistry book should necessarily be entitled: 'The Holy Qur'an and Chemistry'. Every chapter should begin with an appropriate Qur'anic verse or Hadith.[14]

(5) No laws or principles should be named after scientists. For example, it is unIslamic to speak of Newton's Laws, Boyle's Law, and so on because this is tantamount to *shirk* (idolatry). Naming laws in this manner gives the impression that such laws were created rather than discovered by scientists.[15]

(6) God should be introduced into science classrooms. 'Our science textbooks should present the arguments for Divine existence and the Hereafter. Such a study of these subjects should be taken as a study of science and not Islamiat.'[16]

(7) Maulana Maudoodi's *Tafhim-ul-Quran* (Interpretation of Qur'an) should be used at the outset of a zoology course as guidance.[17]

(8) The birth of all sciences should be traced to the Muslim period. Nuclear

physics owed its origins to Ibn Sina, chemistry to Jabir Ibn Hayyan, etc. The Greeks do not deserve credit because they knew nothing about experimental science.[18]

These recommendations of the Institute of Policy Studies merit two brief comments. First, we should note that the basic assumption of science – that each physical effect has a corresponding physical cause – is being specifically refuted. Instead of physical forces, it is continuous divine intervention which moves matter. Secondly, nowhere in the recommendations does one find a call to excite the curiosity of children, to develop in them an attitude of questioning, or to place the idea in the child's mind that authority can sometimes be wrong. Truly, in the fundamentalist doctrine there is no mandate for real science. In a closed, static and pre-ordained universe, what use is it anyway?

The Jamaat-e-Islami position on science and modernity is characteristic of the fundamentalist viewpoint generally. Sayyid Qutb of the Ikhwan-ul-Muslimeen, who was hanged together with other fundamentalists by Gamal Abdul Nasser in Egypt, expressed his views on science in the book *Fi-Zalal-ul-Quran*. These are virtually identical to those of the Jamaat and a separate discussion appears unwarranted.

The Reconstructionist Line

The reconstructionist position – in sharp contrast to the virulent anti-science and anti-modernism of the orthodox – is essentially to reinterpret the faith in order to reconcile the demands of modern civilization with the teachings and traditions of Islam. This school of thought holds that Islam during the lifetime of the Prophet and Khilafa-i-Rashida (the four righteous Caliphs) was revolutionary, progressive, liberal and rational. The subsequent slide towards stultifying rigidity and reactionary dogmatism is ascribed to the triumph of *taqlid* (tradition) over *ijtihad* (innovation).

On the Indian sub-continent, two individuals – Syed Ahmed Khan and Syed Ameer Ali – were its most influential early exponents.

Sir Syed Ahmed Khan (1817–1898)

The attempt to make a transition from medieval to modern Islam in the 19th century was spearheaded by the Indian Muslim, Syed Ahmed Khan. The failure of the 1857 uprising against the British, and the subsequent trauma of Indians and particularly Indian Muslims, spurred him into seeking a new interpretation of Islam. He was the most radical among major Islamic thinkers in modern times and remains a controversial figure almost a century later.

Born into an aristocratic family of Mughal ancestry, Syed Ahmed Khan was convinced that desperate remedies were needed if the Muslims of India were ever to become anything other than 'stableboys, cooks, servants, hewers of wood, and drawers of water'. As he saw it, backwardness was a direct result of superstitious beliefs and rejection of *maaqulat* (reason) in favour of blind obedience to *manqulat* (tradition). So he set about the task of reinterpreting Muslim theology, making it compatible with post-Renaissance Western humanistic and scientific ideas, and extracting the 'pure' Islam from fossilized and irrelevant dogma:

> My enquiring mind never left me . . . . This made me arrive at the truth which I believe to be *thet* Islam (pure Islam) although conventional Muslims may hold it to be *thet kufr* (pure unbelief).[19]

It was a difficult enterprise to take on. For Muslims of the Indian sub-continent, the period after the end of Akbar's reign had been one of unbroken anti-science and anti-rationalist conservatism. Some 200 years before Syed Ahmed Khan, Sheikh Ahmed Sirhindi and other influential religious figures had issued *fatwa*s against mathematics and the secular sciences, demanding that the education of Muslims be exclusively along religious lines. Rebelling against this view, Syed Ahmed Khan wrote:

> Now with great humbleness I ask: of the different religious books which exist today and are used for teaching, which of them discusses Western philosophy or modern scientific matters using principles of religion? From where should I seek confirmation or rejection of the motion of the Earth, or about its nearness to the sun? Thus it is a thousand times better not to read these books than to read them. Yes, if the Mussulman be a true warrior and thinks his religion right, then let him come fearlessly to the battleground and do unto Western knowledge and modern research what his forefathers did to Greek philosophy. Then only shall the religious books be of any real use. Mere parroting will not do.[20]

For Syed Ahmed Khan as a religious scholar, the task of scientific exegesis was of paramount importance. In a startling break with tradition, he proposed that the Qur'an be reinterpreted so as to remove all apparent contradictions with physical reality. Since the Qur'an was the word of God, he argued, and since scientific truths were manifestly correct, any contradiction could only be apparent and not real. So, he suggested a mode of interpretation of the Qur'an according to the following methodology:[21]

(1) A close enquiry be made into the use, meaning and etymology of Qur'anic language so as to yield the true meaning of the word and passage in question.

(2) The criterion employed to decide whether a given passage needed metaphorical interpretation, and which of several interpretations ought to be selected, is the truth established by science. Such truth is arrived at by *aqli dalil* (rational proof) and demands firm belief.

(3) If the apparent meaning of the Scripture conflicts with demonstrable conclusions, it must be interpreted metaphorically. In this, Syed Ahmed Khan follows Ibn Rushd in his problem of reconciling *maaqul*

(demonstrative truth) with *manqul* (scripture truth). Yet, he makes clear that such metaphorical and allegorical interpretation is precisely what the Author of Scripture intended.

This methodology often led Syed Ahmed Khan into a radical reinterpretation of theology and some highly unconventional positions on major issues. For example, he accepted the Darwinian theory, arguing that the fall of Adam and Eve was actually a symbol for man to distinguish between good and evil and to become *mukallaf* (under obligation) in distinction from other living beings. He also proposed allegorical interpretations for the Great Flood, the miracles of Jesus, the Ascension, and other phenomena which he felt conflicted with nature. For Syed Ahmed Khan the Qur'an was a book meant for moral guidance, not a book in which to seek scientific knowledge.

For the religious of his time, the most objectionable element of Syed Ahmed Khan's theology was his dismissal of the Shari'at, the code by which all Muslims are expected to live, as irrelevant to the Muslims of modern India. This, expectedly, drew wide condemnation. Significantly, Syed Ahmed Khan did not attempt to create a new Shari'at. In the view of William Cantwell Smith, a well-known Orientalist, this frontal attack on traditional authority was an inescapable element in the transition from a pre-bourgeois to a bourgeois society:

> Not only was the authority in question now outdated and irrelevant – it answered questions which in capitalist society do not arise – but all moral codes now in principle are superseded . . . . The individual himself became morally responsible and had to decide questions on his own . . . . Thus it is that Sir Sayyid Ahmed Khan, on rejecting the old Shar'iat, did not replace it with a new one, nor has any of his successors done so but only emphasized the general moral 'principles' of the Qur'an.[22]

Although Syed Ahmed Khan is revered in Pakistan as the first exponent of Muslim nationalism, his views on religion and science have found few takers. In truth, he is a controversial figure. His cringing tributes to the imperial British, and his anti-woman attitudes, do not endear him to many present-day nationalists and progressives. Nevertheless, he is certainly the most important among those who have tried to build a bridge between Islam and modernity.

Syed Ameer Ali (1849–1924)
Educated in England and a firm disciple of Syed Ahmed Khan, Syed Ameer Ali wrote his magnum opus *The Spirit Of Islam* with a definite goal in mind – to prove that true Islam is revolutionary, rational, and progress oriented. First published in 1891, and repeatedly enlarged upon until 1922, the book underwent innumerable reprints and was read throughout the Muslim world. For Western educated Muslim modernists of the early 20th century, it was a definitive and comprehensive work which challenged the hostile representations of Islamic history, values, and theology put forward by most Orientalists. But it was also a work for which its author was repeatedly dubbed an apologist who

pandered to modern Western ideals at the expense of true Islamic ideas.

Syed Ameer Ali's concern with the issue of scientific progress and Islam permeates much of his book. His views on this can be summarized as follows:

- The Holy Qur'an and sayings of the Prophet (PBUH) give supreme value to knowledge. Knowledge is to be understood as including science. This is what motivated the early Muslims to study science.

- Aristotelian philosophy and rationalist thinking were entirely in accordance with Islam, and the Mu'tazilite movement is to be sympathized with even if it went a bit too far sometimes. The Muslim philosophers and scholars – Al Kindi, Al Farabi, Ibn Sina, Ibn al-Haytham, Ibn Rushd – are true heroes of Islam.

- It was the fanatics and rigid dogmatists who caused Islamic science and culture to collapse. Syed Ameer Ali identifies those most responsible as Al Ashari, Ibn Hanbal, Al Ghazzali, and Ibn Taymiyya.

- Science needs to be brought back from the West into Islam; it is not something foreign to Islam and not by any means unIslamic.

Syed Ameer Ali rhetorically asked the question: why have science and philosophy died out among Muslims and an 'anti-rationalistic patristicism' taken possession instead? In his opinion, Islam needed to be rescued from the mujaddids and imams, and the mind of the Mussulman freed from the bondage of literal interpretations. The present situation, he argues, is much the same as in European medieval times when the Church consigned myriads of people to the flames on charges of heresy, and proved itself to be the mortal enemy of science until the revolt of Luther. So, said Ameer Ali, Islam needs a reformation just as Christianity did. In a passage which outraged some of his co-religionists, he compared the 'Sunni Church' with the Church of Rome, and termed Mu'tazilism a form of 'Islamic Protestantism':

> For five centuries Islam assisted in the free intellectual development of humanity, but a reactionary movement then set in, and all at once the whole stream of human thought was altered. The cultivators of science and philosophy were pronounced to be beyond the pale of Islam. Is it possible for the *Sunni Church* to take a lesson from the Church of Rome? Is it impossible for her to expand similarly – to become many-sided? There is nothing in Mohammed's teachings which prevents this. *Islamic Protestantism*, in one of its phases – Mu'tazilism – has already paved the way. Why should not the great *Sunni Church* shake off the old trammels and rise to a new life?[23] (emphasis added)

Syed Ahmed Khan and Syed Ameer Ali's passionate defence of science and philosophy was coupled with a general liberalism on issues of social importance. They rejected polygamy and purdah as unsuited to the modern age, interpreted jihad as actually meaning intellectual war, asserted that the Holy Prophet battled with his foes purely in self-defence, stated that amputation of the hand for theft or stoning to death for adultery were suitable only for tribal societies lacking prisons, and believed that the Qur'an was written in a language suitable for the common folk of the desert. So, for example, the hooris of Heaven are creatures of Zoroastrian origin, while Hell in the severity of its punishments is Talmudic.

In their determination to go back to the 'pure' Islam of the Prophet and prove the 'modernity' of Islam, Muslim modernist–reconstructionists have walked a tight-rope. It will never be resolved satisfactorily whether their attempts to reinterpret Islam were motivated by deeply held inner beliefs, or by more pragmatic concerns for the fate of the Muslim peoples. Several forces appear to have acted simultaneously: true conviction, fear of the orthodoxy, the belief that Muslims are doomed should they persist in rejecting modern civilization and progress, and the urge to 'look good' in the eyes of the West. Syed Ahmed Khan's efforts epitomize this struggle. He took on the full fury of the orthodoxy. Aligarh Muslim University, which was his creation, was boycotted. Numerous *fatwa*s of *ilhad* (apostasy) and *kufr* (unbelief) were issued by the ulema. The *mutawalli* (keeper) of the Holy Kaaba declared him to be an enemy of Islam and *wajib-i-qatl* (deserver of death). However, his defence of Muslim interests has preserved his name for posterity.

The Pragmatist Line

There is overwhelming evidence that it is the Muslim pragmatist who constitutes the silent majority of Muslims today. Preferring to treat requirements of religion and faith as essentially unrelated to the direct concerns of political and economic life, or to science and secular knowledge, the pragmatist is satisfied with a vague belief that Islam and modernity are not in conflict, but is disinclined to examine such issues too closely. The preoccupation of reconstructionists in searching for Qur'anic interpretations strikes him as being somewhat redundant and arcane. Nevertheless, on substantive issues, including opposition to fundamentalist thinking, there is essential agreement.

A fascinating example of the early pro-modernity and pro-science pragmatist is Syed Jamaluddin Afghani (1838–1897). By studying this prototype of pragmatic thought, I believe that a great deal can be understood about Muslim responses to modernizing Western influences today.

Afghani is important because his ideas deeply influenced Muslims in their struggle against Western colonialism, and his stress on Islam as a force for militant anti-imperialism continues to inspire liberals as well as fundamentalists. He is occasionally identified as the pioneer of the Islamic Resurgence in the contemporary world and, in Arabic literature, is referred to as the Sage of the East. It is specially interesting to study Afghani's views on science and modernity because, in contrast to reconstructionists such as Syed Ahmed Khan (who was also his contemporary and rival), Afghani did not make a serious attempt to reinterpret Muslim theology. Instead, he stressed Islam as a unifying force against the colonial West. His real contribution lies in having inspired the Muslim masses to resist the yoke of foreign domination, and infusing in them a sense of purpose and pride.

According to his biographer, Nikki Keddie, Afghani was born not in Afghanistan, as he claimed, but in Asadabad, Iran.[24] He was deeply influenced during his early schooling by the works of the Islamic rationalist philosophers such as Ibn Sina. Although such works had been proscribed as heresy in much of the Sunni world, Shia Iran had a long philosophical tradition. Steeped as he was in a rationalist tradition, it was not surprising that Afghani's religious views were frequently a cause of great uneasiness to the orthodox. In 1870 Afghani was expelled from Istanbul under pressure from the clergy. His crime was the advocacy of a Darul-Funun, a new university devoted to the teaching of modern science.

There is no question that Jamaluddin Afghani was deeply enamoured with the power of modern science and was eager to learn the secret of the West's strength. In his 1882 lecture in Calcutta he said:

> Thus I say: If someone looks deeply into the question, he will see that science rules the world. There was, is, and will be no ruler in the world but science . . . . The benefits of science are immeasurable; and these finite thoughts cannot encompass what is infinite.[25]

Islam, he said, brought with it a spirit of inquiry:

> The first Muslims had no science, but, thanks to the Islamic religion, a philosophic spirit arose among them . . . . This was why they acquired in a short time all the sciences with particular subjects that they translated from the Syriac, Persian, and Greek into the Arabic language at the time of Mansur Davanaqi.[26]

In the same speech, Afghani went on to lament the existing state of Muslims who spurned philosophy, literature, logic, and the sciences. Whereas the early Muslims had eagerly sought science and knowledge, the later ones had become totally stagnant. He delivered a blistering attack on the Indian ulema, saying:

> It is strange that our ulema read Sadra and Shams al-Baria and vaingloriously call themselves sages, and despite this they cannot distinguish their left hand from their right hand, and they do not ask: Who are we and what is right and proper for us? They never ask the causes of electricity, the steamboat, and railroads . . . . our ulema at this time are like a very narrow wick on top of which is a very small flame that neither lights its surroundings nor gives light to others . . . . The strangest thing of all is that our ulema these days have divided science into two parts. One they call Muslim science, and one European science. Because of this they forbid others to teach some of the useful sciences.[27]

The pragmatist element in Jamaluddin Afghani is revealed nowhere more clearly than in his exchange with Ernest Renan, the renowned 19th century French Islamist. This exchange is undoubtedly a landmark, since it was a debate between an ardent champion of Muslim causes and a Westerner who was an acknowledged atheist and enemy of all religions. But, as Keddie points out, this debate has been distorted in the Muslim world. It is assumed that since Renan had called Islam hostile to science, Afghani must have retorted that Islam was friendly to the scientific spirit. This is false, and the newly translated papers of Afghani show that he put forward one face before the Muslim masses but rather a different one before the West.

Here is how the famed debate began. In March 1883, Ernest Renan delivered a lecture, subsequently published in the *Journal des Debats*, on Islam and Science. In this, he lashed out against all religions but concentrated on Islam because, in his opinion, it did not separate the spiritual and temporal realms. This made its dogma 'the heaviest chain that humanity has ever borne'.[28] In a later article, he expressed another strong view:

> The human mind must be freed of all supernatural belief if it wishes to work on its essential work, which is the construction of positive science. This does not imply violent destruction nor brusque rupture. The Christian does not have to abandon Christianity nor the Muslim Islam. The enlightened parties of Christianity and Islam should arrive at that state of benevolent indifference where religious beliefs become inoffensive. This has happened in about half the Christian countries, let us hope that it will happen in Islam.[29]

Did Afghani respond in a spirit of outrage to such a direct assault? One certainly would have expected that. But the answer is no! In fact, quite to the contrary, he agreed with Renan on this aspect of his argument, saying:

> All religions are intolerant, each one in its way . . . . I cannot keep from hoping that Muhammadan society will succeed someday in breaking its bonds and march resolutely in the path of civilization after the manner of Western society . . . . I plead with M. Renan not the cause of the Muslim religion, but that of several hundreds of millions of men, who would thus be condemned to live in barbarism and ignorance. In truth, the Muslim religion has tried to stifle science and stop its progress.[30]

Afghani has no fundamental dispute with Renan on the issue that blind dogma kills science and enquiry. In fact, he echoes much the same ideas:

> A true believer must, in fact, turn from the path of studies that have for their object scientific truth . . . . Yoked, like an ox to the plow, to the dogma whose slave he is, he must walk eternally in the furrow that has been traced for him in advance by the interpreters of the law. Convinced, besides, that his religion contains in itself all morality and all sciences, he attaches himself resolutely to it and makes no effort to go beyond . . . . What would be the benefit of seeking truth when he believes he possesses it all? . . . Whereupon he despises science.[31]

There have been claims that the letter to Renan was not written by Jamaluddin

Afghani but, instead, by some other Afghani. It has also been suggested that some anonymous person may have tried to disgrace him. But this appears unlikely because Afghani's letter to Renan precipitated vigorous hostility and controversy among the Muslim youth in Paris. Afghani was certainly aware of this, but never refuted the letter. He is also known to have refused permission to his disciple Mohammed Abduh to reprint it in Egypt.

One might perhaps have expected that, insofar as they were both modernists and rationalists, Syed Jamaluddin Afghani and Syed Ahmed Khan would have been allies, at least to some degree. But far from it – Afghani was a declared enemy of Syed Ahmed and accused him repeatedly of heresy and deviating from Islam. In one of Afghani's articles, he launches a frontal assault:

> It so happened that a man named Ahmed Khan Bahadur was hovering around the English in order to obtain some advantage from them. He presented himself to them and took some steps to throw off his religion and adopt the English religion. He began his course by writing a book demonstrating that the Torah and Gospel were not corrupted or falsified . . . . His doctrine pleased the English rulers and they saw in it the best means to corrupt the hearts of the Muslims. They began to support him, to honor him, and to help him build a college in Aligarh, called the Muhammadan College, to be a trap in which to catch the sons of the believers . . . . Ahmed Khan wrote a commentary on the Koran and distorted the sense of words and tampered with what God revealed . . . . He called openly for the abandonment of all religions.[32]

It should now be clear to the reader why one ought to consider Syed Jamaluddin Afghani a pragmatist *par excellence*. It is not for us to pass judgement on whether he was true to his belief as a Muslim, but abundant evidence has been presented showing that he was far from orthodox in his beliefs. He was conscious of the power of modern science and recognized that its development was suffocated by the orthodoxy of his times. But, as a pragmatist, he did not turn his guns primarily on the ulema. On the contrary, where it suited his political ambitions, he made full use of religious symbolism. For example, as we saw in the above quote, he chose to attack Syed Ahmed Khan using the idiom of the orthodox. The reason is evident: in his mind any collaborator of the imperial British was a despicable traitor to be attacked by whatever means were available. To attack Syed Ahmed Khan for heresy was a particularly effective way of doing so, and guaranteed to get support from the anti-British orthodox Indian ulema.

Afghani was perhaps the first major modern pragmatist, a man who was conscious of the enormous power of religious sentiment in mobilizing the masses. Others have not exploited religion as a political force, emphasizing instead its separation from economic and political life. The example of pragmatists in Ataturk's Turkey is foremost. An official slogan, invented by Zia Gokalp in the days of the revolution, was 'Belong to the Turkish nation, the Muslim religion, and European civilization.'

Conclusion

The post-colonial era saw the emergence of numerous pragmatists as popular leaders of the Islamic world. Mohammed Ali Jinnah, Gamal Abdul Nasser, Ahmed Sukarno, Habib Bourguiba, Zulfiqar Ali Bhutto and even Saddam Hussein were among those who called their peoples to action rather than an admiration of Islam. Although the ascendancy of the restorationist-fundamentalist trend is the most visible in contemporary Islam, pragmatist Muslims still form the majority. The electoral defeats of the fundamentalist parties in several Muslim countries strongly suggest that most Muslims will not accept fundamentalist versions of the Faith when there is an alternative.

It is impossible, however, to hide the fact that both the capacity and will of Muslim societies to accept the challenges of modernity have been significantly eroded in the last decade. The future of science and civilization in Islam depends critically on whether the silent majority reasserts itself and snatches back control of civil society, or whether it buckles before the ferocious onslaught of nascent revivalism.

References

1. An interesting and detailed discussion of Islam and modernity from an Islamic modernist point of view is given by Ghulam Nabi Saqib in *Modernization of Muslim Education*, (Lahore, Islamic Book Service, 1983).

2. Daniel Lerner, *The Passing of Traditional Society: Modernizing the Middle East*, (Illinois, Free Press of Glencoe, 1958), p. 199.

3. Manfred Halpern, *The Politics of Social Change in the Middle East and North Africa*, (New Jersey, Princeton University Press), p. 25.

4. William Montgomery Watt, quoted in Ref. 1 above.

5. Edward W. Said, *Orientalism*, (New York, Vintage Books, 1979).

6. Maryam Jameelah, *Islam and Modernism*, (Lahore, Muhammad Yousuf Khan Publisher, 1977), pp. 16–17.

7. Maryam Jameelah, *Modern Technology and the Dehumanization of Man*, (Lahore, El-Matbaat-ul-Arabia, 1983), p. 8.

8. Ibid.

9. Abul Ala Maudoodi, *Taalimat*, (Lahore, Islamic Publishers, n.d.) p. 20.

10. Ibid.

11. *Planning Curricula for Natural Sciences: The Islamic Perspective*, (Islamabad, Institute of Policy Studies, 1983), p. 8.

12. Ibid., p. 10.

13. *Kimiya Ki Tadrees Ka Nazriati Pehloo*, (Islamabad, Institute of Policy Studies, 1982), p. 27.

14. Ibid., p. 10.

15. Ibid., p. 27.

16. 'Knowledge For What?', Proceedings of the Seminar on the Islamization of Knowledge, Islamic University, Islamabad, 1982, p. 73.

17. See Ref. 13, p. 65.

18. See Ref. 11, p. 31.

19. Syed Ahmed Khan, *Tasanif-e-Ahmadia, Vol. 1*, (Aligarh, 1983), p. 2.

20. Syed Ahmed Khan, *Maaqulat-e-Sir Syed, Vol. 1*, (Lahore, Majlis-e-Tarraqi-e-Adab, 1962), pp. 97–8.

21. C. W. Troll, *Sayyid Ahmad Khan – A Reinterpretation of Muslim Theology*, (Karachi, Oxford University Press, 1978), pp. 168–70.

22. William Cantwell Smith, *Modern Islam in India*, (Lahore, Shaikh Muhammad Ashraf, 1963), p. 70.

23. Syed Ameer Ali, *The Spirit of Islam*, (Karachi, Pakistan Publishing House, 1976), p. 454.

24. The authoritative work on Syed Jamaluddin's political and religious views is by Nikki R. Keddie, *An Islamic Response to Imperialism*, (Berkeley, University of California Press, 1983). Most of the comments on Afghani in this section are derived from Keddie, and from Afghani's original writings which are contained in its Appendix.

25. Ibid., p. 102.

26. Ibid., p. 103.

27. Ibid., pp. 106–7.

28. Ernest Renan, *l'Islamisme et la science*, (Paris, 1883), p. 17, quoted in Keddie, op. cit., p. 85.

29. Ernest Renan, *Ouevres complètes, I*, (Paris, 1947), pp. 960–5, quoted in Keddie, op. cit., p. 93.

30. Syed Jamaluddin Afghani in 'Réponse de Jamal ad-Din al-Afghani à Renan', quoted in Keddie, op. cit., p. 86.

31. Ibid., p. 87.

32. Syed Jamaluddin Ahmed, 'The Materialists in India', published in *al-Urwa al-Wuthqa*, August 28, 1884, quoted in Keddie, op. cit., pp. 176–7.

6. Bucaille, Nasr and Sardar – Three Exponents of Islamic Science

Whether Hindu, Christian, Jewish, or Islamic, fundamentalism is essentially about once and for all revelation. Knowledge is inevitably finite; it consists in whatever has been revealed. For fundamentalists, therefore, any increase in knowledge consists only of finding new interpretations of holy writ. Fundamentalists often claim that every major discovery of modern science was long anticipated in the holy scriptures of their faith. Read the text carefully, they say, and you will find that it is there. But if you don't find it, either you have not done a good job at reading or the so-called scientific fact is false. This type of reasoning must be contrasted with that of ordinary believers, who generally hold that no new knowledge contradicts the scriptures and some new knowledge may even strengthen old beliefs.

The type of claims and arguments used by fundamentalists is quite irrespective of the particular religion. As an example, let me quote from a recently published book on the sciences of ancient India.[1] The author, who appears to be an ardent believer in the Hindu faith as well as Hindu supremacy, asks his readers to ponder on Bhagavad Gita 2–16 which says:

नासतो विद्यते भावो ना भावे विद्यते सत: ।

'what does not exist cannot come into existence, and what exists cannot be destroyed'. This line, proclaims the author triumphantly, is definitive proof that a pillar of modern physics – the law of conservation of matter and energy – was also known to the Ancients thousands of years ago. It establishes the divine nature of the Gita, and proves that there is nothing new which has been added to the stock of human wisdom since the time the scriptures were set down.

There is no lack of other Indian examples. Certain Hindu fundamentalists have described with great seriousness the Vedic vision of the creation of the universe from *Prakriti* (primeval matter) over a period of several *kalpas*, and have arrived at the happy conclusion that all this is just what modern physics and the Big Bang theory of creation say. Other orthodox Hindus consider the laws of Manu to be statements of physical fact, and argue that the differences between various substances arise from varying amounts of *gunas* (qualities) and *tanmatras* (subtle states) in each. Still others are greatly satisfied that human rebirth is now a scientifically established fact, choosing to believe certain parapsychologists who claim evidence that the moment a man dies his mass suddenly decreases by 50 grams. This is clear indication, they say, that the *atman* (spirit) has left the body in preparation for making a new being somewhere else. None of these observations, however has ever been shown to be repeatable or to have survived careful investigation. They are therefore rejected by scientists.

One can find any number of dubious examples. But, because it typifies the fundamentalist argument, let me come back to the first example given here and examine it more closely. There are two questions to be asked. First, is the scriptural statement 'what does not exist cannot come into existence, and what exists cannot be destroyed' a correct one? Secondly, does it imply the law of conservation of matter and energy of modern physics as alleged?

The answer to the first question is 'maybe'. It all depends on how the word 'exist' is to be interpreted. Take a piece of paper and burn it in the fire. Clearly, it no longer exists as a piece of paper. But, one could argue, the essence of the paper's existence was the atoms which comprised it. The act of burning merely transformed the paper into gases, keeping the original atoms intact. Thus, provided it is suitably interpreted, there is no contradiction of Gita 2–16 with experience. Or, put differently, the verse is vague on the definition of existence, and its refutation is impossible.

The answer to the second question is 'most definitely not' – no physicist of any worth will accept Gita 2–16 as a valid statement of physical law, even though a few physicists may well hold that that text embodies some superior metaphysical doctrine. Does Gita 2–16 refer to the spirits? To thoughts? To what? Nobody has ever managed to use this statement for anything relevant to physics. The point is that modern physics is a very precise subject. It does not tolerate inexact or vague statements; every statement of value to physics must be verifiable and lend itself to quantification. The statement that 'matter and energy cannot be created or destroyed' is by itself not useful. There must also be a clear procedure available for measuring the mass of a body, together with an operational definition of what energy is and a procedure for measuring the rate at which it is radiated or generated. If we do not have a precise and mathematical way of ascertaining these quantities, any statement relating them could mean so many different things that it is useless for physicists. Put in another way, vague statements such as 'what does not exist cannot come into existence' are not predictive. We cannot, using such statements, make any definite prediction of physical phenomena or build new machines or suggest new experiments. Of course, once something is known to be true, one or the other scriptural passage can always be massaged to give the right meaning.

At times the desire to relate all science to various holy texts leads to very interesting intellectual gymnastics. The respected Indian astrophysicist, J. V. Narlikar, points out that during the time that the Steady State theory of creation of the universe was in vogue, abundant scriptural evidence was gathered by religious Hindus to show how this was in perfect accord with the Vedas. Alas, this theory was eventually discredited and replaced by the Big Bang theory of creation. Not the least discomfited, Hindu fundamentalists quickly found other Vedic passages which were in perfect accord with the newer theory and again proudly acclaimed it as a triumph of ancient wisdom.

Certain exegetes of the Holy Qur'an have also attempted to derive scientific facts from the Holy Book in a manner much like that described above. Among these, Maurice Bucaille is by far the most prominent and widely read.

Maurice Bucaille

A French surgeon who turned spiritualist, Monsieur Bucaille shot into prominence throughout the Islamic world with the publication of his exegesis, *The Bible, The Qur'an, and Science*. Translated into numerous languages, hundreds of thousands of copies of the book have been printed and distributed free of cost by Muslim religious organizations throughout the world. At international airports and American university campuses, it is the spearhead with which evangelical students seek to win conversion to Islam. Most Muslim intellectuals that I know of have either read the book, or at least have heard about it. As for the author, his popularity is unquestionable. One wonders how much of this arises from the fact that he is a white man; for it cannot be denied that even with the demise of colonialism the white skin still commands much authority. In any case, Monsieur Bucaille is in great demand at conferences, such as the First International Conference of Scientific Miracles of the Qu'ran and Sunnah, of which he was a chairman.

Bucaille's method is simple. He asks his readers to ponder on some Qur'anic verse and then, from a variety of meanings that could be assigned to the verse, he pulls out one which is consistent with some scientific fact. He thereupon concludes that, whereas the Bible is often wrong in the description of natural phenomena, the Qur'an is invariably correct and that it correctly anticipated all major discoveries of modern science. To this end, he marshals an impressive number of Qur'anic references to bees, spiders, birds, plants and vegetables of different kinds, animal milk, embryos, and human reproduction. His discussion of inanimate matter ranges from the planets of the solar system, to galaxies and interstellar matter, and then to the expansion of the universe and the conquest of space. He ends the discussion of each topic with the ritual conclusion that the marvellous agreement of Qur'anic revelations with scientific facts is proof of its miraculous nature.

Whereas Monsieur Bucaille appears eminently satisfied with his methodology, Muslims who wish to combine reason with faith will readily detect at least two fundamental flaws in it even though they accept the divine nature of the Qur'an.

First, it will be recognized that the proof of a proposition is meaningful only if the possibility of disproof is also to be entertained. What sense does it make to assume that the sum of the angles of a triangle equals 180 degrees, and then 'prove' the same? Since believers know that it is impossible for the Qur'an to be wrong in any manner, all attempts at 'proving' its divine nature are entirely specious right from the start.

Second, hanging an eternal truth on to the changeable theories of science is a dangerous business. Our understanding of the universe may change drastically with time, and science is quite shameless in its abandonment of old theories and espousal of new ones. Will this not wreak havoc if one attempts to anchor a theological idea on to these shifting sands?

Consider the following. Monsieur Bucaille has 'discovered' that the Qur'an speaks of a universe which is continually expanding. Now, let us overlook the fact that it was only after astronomical observations established the truth of this phenomenon that the expansion of the universe was suddenly 'discovered' as a long-known religious fact. Consider, instead, what would happen if some new astronomical observations were to indicate that the universe was contracting rather than expanding. Indeed, cosmologists suspect that a few billion years hence, the universe will cease expanding and then start contracting. Under the extreme assumption that life will continue to exist in the present form, we can ask what options a Bucaillist living a few billion years hence will have when faced with the contracting universe. Possibly, he may refute the astronomical evidence in favour of what he believes to be a religious truth. But, more likely, he will discover hitherto undiscovered subtleties of the Arabic language which persuade him that earlier interpretations were incorrect, and he will then find a suitable passage which fits the new facts.

Observe that in Bucaille's book there is not a single *prediction* of any physical fact which is unknown up to now, but which could be tested against observation and experiment in the future.

Pseudo-scientific attempts, of which the above are examples, to derive the physical sciences from the Qur'an have been courageously criticized by some of the great Muslims of modern times. One finds, for example, a point of view diametrically opposed to fundamentalist thinking of the Bucaillist variety in the works of Sir Syed Ahmed Khan, the founder of Aligarh University in India. Syed Ahmed Khan believed that it was futile to regard the Qur'an as a work on science. A good portion of his own labours as a religious scholar were, in fact, aimed at disentangling what he considered to be the essential message of the Qur'an from certain confusing and wrong beliefs of Greek astronomy. Although he believed the Qur'an to be divinely revealed, he also held the view that attempts to derive scientific truths from the Book were entirely misplaced. Syed Ahmed Khan wrote that:

> The Qur'an does not prove that the earth is stationary, nor does it prove that the earth is in motion. Similarly, it cannot be proved from the Qur'an that the sun is stationary. The Holy Qur'an was not concerned with these problems of astronomy; because the progress in human knowledge was to decide such matters itself . . . . the real purpose of a religion is to improve morality . . . . I am fully convinced that the Work of God and the Word of God can never be antagonistic to each other; we may, through the fault of our knowledge, sometimes make mistakes in understanding the meaning of the Word.[2]

Here is the crux of Syed Ahmed Khan's belief: 'the real purpose of religion is to improve morality'. Let scientific truths be established by observation and experiment, he says, and not by attempting to interpret a religious text as a book of science. By having explicated these beliefs in such clear terms, and by virtue of his well recognized role as the protector of Muslim interests in British India, Syed Ahmed Khan's philosophy provides in principle a credible antidote against the various strains of Bucaillism which have gained such enormous currency in the Muslim world today.

Seyyed Hossein Nasr

In arguing for the compatibility between Islam and modern science, the Muslim modernist line of argument is that science did once blossom in the lands of Islam and maintained its radiance for almost five centuries. It is concluded, therefore, that Islam is indubitably supportive of modern science. This modernist line has been challenged by some orthodox Muslim scholars. From among these the most influential, and also the most sophisticated and articulate, is Seyyed Hossein Nasr.

A Shiite Iranian by birth and early education, Seyyed Hossein Nasr went to the US for an undergraduate degree in physics at MIT and then for a Ph.D. in history at Harvard. His reputation as a scholar and historian of Islamic Science derives from the large number of impressive books he has authored, and appears well deserved. It is the brilliance and clarity of his expositions, rather than the originality of his research, which is the more striking. This ability to communicate has made Nasr by far the most influential of Muslim historians who write on Islam and science. His prestige would have been still greater were it not for the fact that, because of his former position as president of an officially sponsored Iranian writers organization and his declared support for the Shah in pre-revolutionary Iran, he has now to live outside of Iran. Nasr is currently a professor at an American university.

Seyyed Nasr will have no truck with liberals and modernists who claim consistency between Islam and modern science. In his opinion, they deliberately distort Islam to suit their own ends. He fiercely excoriates those:

> modernistic Muslim apologetic writings which would go to any extreme to placate modernism and would pay any price to show that Islam is 'modern' after all and that in contrast to Christianity it is not at all in conflict with 'science'.[3]

According to Nasr, those modernistic writings which claim that Islam is compatible with modern science – meaning the science which Galileo and Newton are usually credited with having initiated – are irredeemably flawed. The pitfall in all these writings, says Nasr, is that the Arabic word *ilm*, whose pursuit is a religious duty, is wilfully distorted into meaning science and secular learning. This is false because *ilm* refers to knowledge of God, not to knowledge of the profane. Modernists must recognize this, Nasr insists, because modern science is a cancer which is today steadily eating away the marrow of the Islamic faith:

No amount of denying that the problem exists and of proclaiming in loud slogans the 'scientific' nature of Islam will prevent the spreading of this kind of science – based on the forgetting of God – from corroding the foundations of the citadel of Islamic faith.[4]

A scientist, says Nasr, who consistently uses the tools and techniques of modern science will, even if he is a devout Muslim, inevitably damage the fabric of Islam because:

Whatever devout Muslim scientists may believe as individuals, they cannot prevent their activity as modern scientists from emptying the Islamic intellectual universe of its content unless this science is shorn away from its secular and humanistic matrix where it has been placed since the Renaissance.[5]

The problem with modern science is that it relies solely on reason and observation as the arbiters of truth. For Nasr's brand of Islamic orthodoxy, this is entirely unacceptable.

But what of the ancient sciences? About these, Nasr has kind words because they:

were never a challenge to Islam in the same way as modern science has been. Young Muslim students in traditional madrassahs did not cease to perform their prayers upon reading the algebra of Khayyam or the al-chemical treatises of Jabbir ibn Hayyan as so many present-day students lose their religious moorings upon studying modern mathematics and chemistry.[6]

Is this alleged difference between medieval science and modern science in fact correct? So important is this question that we must understand it in some depth.

In truth, two vastly different conceptual frameworks underlie medieval science and modern science. Medieval scientists, whether Muslim or Christian, worked within the boundaries of a paradigm which was a complex web of supernatural beliefs, beliefs held by custom, and logical hypotheses. The stated function of natural science was teleological; it had to find the divine order of the universe whose main features had been provided by revelation. In other words, science was seen principally as a means of illustrating theological truths and for emphasizing the need to go beyond material existence. The answers were known in advance; science, as the handmaiden of theology, had to prove that faith was supported by reason and physical facts.

Even mathematics — which we today view as abstract and completely detached from theology — was thoroughly enmeshed in religious beliefs. Most early numerical systems ascribed a supernatural origin to numbers. Arithmetic was a priestly privilege, the domain of the temple and the palace. Under the Greeks, geometry was exalted and regular figures were associated with the gods. Indeed, the secularization of mathematics and freedom from dogmatic conflict took humanity thousands of years.

It is true that general principles – such as that of falling bodies – were sometimes sought, but their importance and universality were impossible to understand or appreciate on the basis of extant knowledge. Speculations were occasionally hazarded, but the body of tested knowledge was too small to conclude the existence of physical laws that could explain, and even predict, much that was of significance. It was beyond the power of medieval science to explain why earthquakes and volcanic eruptions take place; how the sun shines and the earth moves around it; what causes winds to blow and rain to fall; how plagues are caused and how they may be combated; and so on. The colossal state of ignorance is evident from the fact that, in medieval Europe, Jews were regularly massacred in large numbers by Christians during every outbreak of plague because they were considered responsible for bringing the wrath of God on to whichever community they lived in.

On reflection, one can see that it could scarcely have been otherwise. In those days, the art of observation, let alone experimentation, was so undeveloped, that science simply could not be what it is today: an instrument for prediction and control. As Sarton remarks:

> Whatever positive knowledge [our ancestors] had was not very reliable; any one of their scientific statements could easily be challenged. Compared with that, the theological constructions seemed unshakeable; they were not based on observation, hence no amount of observation could destroy them; they were not based on deduction, hence no amount of logic could impugn them.[7]

Because the scientific facts needed for resolving various issues were simply unavailable in those days, theological reasoning was used as a substitute. So, for example, one finds Al-Biruni engaged in fierce battle against the arguments of Aristotle for the eternity of the world, and advocating instead a creation *ex-nihilo*. (Today we are almost at the point where this question can be answered on scientific grounds.) Among Christians, the question of whether the earth had antipodes was debated and rejected on grounds that there would have to be a second Christ on the other side of the world who would have to suffer a second crucifixion. Even for Roger Bacon, who was a radical and put in prison by the Church for carrying out scientific research, the main end of science was the buttressing of revelation.

The medieval world picture was complete and hierarchical, built around an elaborate ethereal, cosmological scheme of a rigid theological–physical universe of spheres and orbs. First in this majestic picture came the spheres of the moon and sun, then the spheres of the planets, and then the great spheres of the fixed stars beyond which lay Heaven. Religious cosmology was intimately connected with angelology because angels played a basic role as movers of the heavens. Ibn Sina's cosmology, for example, is permeated by these concepts. The cosmic order, which the angels maintained, also implied the existence of a social order, and even an order inside the human body. For example, the Ikhwan-ul-Safa (The Brethren of Purity), who formed a secret society of rationalistic Ismaili thinkers in the 10th and 11th centuries, made the following correspondence between the motion of the planets and the ailment of various parts of the human body:[8]

Eyes	–	Jupiter
Ears	–	Mercury
Nostrils and nipples of breast	–	Venus
Channels of excretion	–	Saturn
Mouth	–	Sun
Navel	–	Moon

Physical sicknesses were described as analogous to the eclipse of a heavenly body; the cosmic correspondence indeed extended to everything.

Another major difference of outlook between medieval and modern science lies in the concept of progress. In modern times we have almost unconsciously accepted as natural and inevitable that succeeding generations become more knowledgeable and advanced. But, in medieval times, it was hard to believe that life had been very different in the remote past or that the people of those times knew less. For example, Al-Biruni believed that the peoples of the ancient world (Byzantines, Egyptians, Greeks) possessed *more* knowledge than the peoples of his own time, and wrote that 'what we have of our own sciences is nothing but the scanty remains of bygone times'.[9] Instead of a belief in unilinear progress, medieval scholars subscribed to a cyclical vision of history. The history of humankind was a rhythmic rise and fall — any time a people became too clever or powerful, divine retribution would descend in the form of earthquakes, plagues and floods which would periodically devastate the earth. Such cataclysmic events served the twofold purpose of punishing people for their sins, and reminding them that God never stops intervening in this world.

One cannot, therefore, disagree with Nasr that the conceptual framework of medieval science was formally defined by theology. On the other hand, he appears not to appreciate the fact that the only lasting achievements of this science — whether practised by Greeks, Muslims, or Christians — were of universal and secular character. These are precisely the elements which it has in common with modern science. For example, motivated by frankly utilitarian concerns, alchemists sought to convert base metals into gold. In this they failed, but many interesting chemical principles were discovered. The mechanics of falling bodies, levers and simple machines, the properties of lenses, the life of plants and insects, the geography and topography of the earth, etc. were also studied with the aim of deducing general principles. The motivation evidently came from natural human curiosity and cannot be specifically connected with divine edicts.

To conclude the discussion on the differences between the epistemological and philosophical presumptions of modern science and those of medieval Islamic science, I believe that Nasr has indeed raised an important point by questioning an assumption which lies at the heart of the Islamic modernist thesis and is rarely explicated. But his strident rejection of modern science as anti-Islamic can only be accepted by the rigidly orthodox.

Nasr is not only a historian of science. He is also an advocate and propagandist for a new 'Islamic' science which, according to him, should not be constrained by the tyranny of logic:

> A truly Islamic science cannot but derive ultimately from the intellect which is Divine and not human reason . . . . The seat of intellect is the heart rather than the head, and reason is no more than its reflection upon the mental plane.[10]

These words ring beautifully, and conjure up before us a magnificent vista of unblemished knowledge. Unfortunately, what they mean in real terms is as clear as mud. Any science which claims to derive 'from the intellect which is Divine and not human reason' is certainly excellent if practitioners of that science have direct access to the Divine intellect, but otherwise could be very contentious and problematic indeed. The success of Dr Nasr's new 'Islamic' science is obviously contingent upon finding interpreters of the Divine intellect, who are presumably to be chosen from among the holy and the pious.

Engrossed in passionately advocating his ethereal vision of a new Islamic science, which is 'shorn away from the secular and humanistic matrix [of modern science]', and in which 'the seat of the intellect is the heart rather than the head', Dr Nasr appears to have had little time for sorting out issues of a practical, mundane nature. Alas, as the following not-so-unlikely example shows, there could be problems:

- **Example 1**: Scientist A and Scientist B subscribe to Dr Nasr's vision of science. Both are investigating the origin of the continents, taking their respective seats of the intellect to be their hearts rather than their heads. Scientist A is inspired by a certain scriptural passage, which he takes to be supportive of the belief that the continents were all joined together at some remote time in the past. But Scientist B is convinced that the continents arose spontaneously from the sea, and quotes another scriptural passage which he says supports his belief. The evidence for either position is not compelling enough, and so the matter is referred to the Supreme Religious Council. The pious and knowledgeable men in the Council deliberate on this weighty matter, and after much study and prayer and incantations they give their final verdict that the continents were formed by . . . . Meanwhile, in the faraway land of communist Russia, a team of geologists announces a major breakthrough in plate tectonics which finally resolves the issue scientifically. The Council denounces their results as the work of atheists.

Dr Nasr berates what he called Western science for being destructive of man and nature. One can scarcely disagree with him here. But, he goes on to construct an ethereal vision of a perfectly harmonious and peaceful Islamic science utterly free both of fault and of a meaningful set of rules by which it would be governed. Again, a not-so-unlikely example illustrates the emptiness of Nasr's vision:

- **Example 2:** Scientist C is a chemist and lives in a country called Irna. Scientist D is also a chemist but lives in a country called Irqa. Both have read Dr Nasr's book on the plight of modern man and agree on the decadence of Western culture and the destructiveness of modern science. They have been convinced by Dr Nasr's arguments that the ethics of a science based upon religion will not permit science to be destructive of human life. But then begins a dreadful war between Irna and Irqa, and nerve gas becomes the need of both countries. Scientist C is requested by the government of Irna, and Scientist D by the government of Irqa, to begin research on synthesizing the compound diphenylchlorotetrasine which is known to cause involuntary defecation and convulsions before the victim finally succumbs. This is considered to be militarily desirable because severe loss of morale in the enemy population accompanies the casualties. Both scientists are initially reluctant, especially since the two countries share the same religion. But, from the Supreme Religious Council in the city of Muq there comes a proclamation declaring the adversary as infidels. Simultaneously, the Council of the Most Righteous and Pious in the city of Dadbagh announces that the doors of Heaven are open to those who exterminate the incarnation of evil in this world . . . . The next morning, after a hearty breakfast and with a clear conscience, Scientist C and Scientist D whistle as they work in their respective laboratories on synthesizing diphenylchlorotetrasine.

Ziauddin Sardar

The self-perception of a fundamentalist today is that of a David locked in battle against the Goliath of modern science.

One cannot deny that it takes courage to demand that the enormous edifice of modern science be torn down and another, whose blueprints are not yet made, be erected in its stead. But this boldness is not, however, altogether admirable. Armed with the sword of faith, but lacking the armour of disciplined reason, very few of the modern Davids are scientists. Nor can they appreciate the magnitude of the task they have set for themselves. As for those exceptional ones who do lay claim to a scientific education, it so happens that none of them is particularly distinguished for their work as scientists. But this small matter is no source of discouragement for those who are never troubled by doubt.

A less admirable trait is that of intellectual plagiarism. Those who argue for a science based on religion begin their case with a critique of modern science which questions the value-free nature of science, emphasizes the destructive nature of certain of its products, and points out that its application has led to the dehumanization and robotization of society. Now, these are all serious and valid criticisms. But they do not necessarily derive from profound insights emanating from a particular faith. The fact that the practice of modern science has created serious problems for human society was not a discovery of born-again fundamentalists. As a matter of fact, the most devastating critiques of science in industrial civilization have been made by Marxists and anarchists. Marcuse, Kuhn, Ellul and Feyerabend are among the most noteworthy.

Having put the evil colossus of modern science to the sword, the doughty Davids press on. Each has a pet version of a science which is supposed correctly to embody divine instruction. We have already seen Professor Nasr's version of Islamic science. Yet another set of views is that of Ziauddin Sardar, a Pakistani born emigré living in Britain and the author of half a dozen books on Islam and science.

In an article published in the prestigious journal *New Scientist* entitled 'Why Islam Needs Islamic Science',[11] Sardar declares that the quest for Islamic science is the most urgent task facing Muslims today. Presumably the abysmally poor educational level of Muslims, their widespread unfamiliarity with basic science, and total dependence upon Western technology, are the least pressing of concerns for Mr Sardar. What he calls Western science is obviously unsuitable, he says, not only because its applications have been harmful but also because its epistemology is basically in conflict with the Islamic view.

Setting aside for the moment what Ziauddin Sardar means by Islamic Science, it is worth pointing out that he is not particularly happy with the suggestions of other exponents of Islamic science. He chides the late Al-Faruqi, a highly conservative Muslim who was the most influential exponent of Islamizing science, and who had suggested that the Islamization of knowledge required one to establish the specific relevance of Islam to each area of modern knowledge. Says Sardar, this is like putting the cart before the horse because 'it is not Islam which needs to be made relevant to modern knowledge, it is modern knowledge which needs to be made relevant to Islam'.[12] Criticizing Al-Faruqi's methodology as being merely a pious statement of belief, he says that: 'Unfortunately, Al-Faruqi's methodology amounts to very little'.[13] As for Hossein Nasr, his views on Islamic science are to be generally admired. However, 'he errs by overemphasizing the metaphysical aspects of Islamic science at the expense of its quantitative aspects'.[14]

For all his voluminous writings in favour of Islamic science, Sardar adds little which would make clear the meaning of this nebulous term. Science and technology, he says, are related to a set of ten basic Islamic values, which include *tawheed* (unity of God), *ibadah* (worship), and *khilafah* (trusteeship). Further, Islam is opposed to the concept of science for science's sake, and to *zalim* (tyrannical) science and technology. If the reader wants more than platitudes, he will be disappointed.

Borrowing the vocabulary and outward trappings of modern science (but, alas, none of its logic), Sardar embarks on grandiose flights of fancy. For example, complete with a computer style flowchart with seven boxes and numerous charts and diagrams,[15] he has designed what he calls project UMRAN to regenerate the entire Muslim system and prepare for its entry into the 21st century. The flowchart of the Project begins from a box titled Model of Medina State, and ends in a box with the rather intriguing title Muslim PAYOFF, where PAYOFF = Plans and Assessment to Yield Options for the Future. If cuteness of acronyms were all that was needed to make projects fly,

UMRAN would be up in the sky. But the sad fact is that ideas of substance are necessary, and UMRAN being innocent of content, its future is rather bleak.

Whatever the particular merits, or otherwise, of proposals by individuals such as Nasr and Sardar, there is a broader issue to which we must turn. Can there be an Islamic science of the physical world? Since one is treading here on the terrain lying between ideology and science, it is also interesting to ask several related questions. Can there exist a specifically Marxist science different from ordinary Western or capitalist science? And what of a unique Third World science?

References

1. Nem Kumar Jain, *Science and Scientists in India*, (Delhi, Indian Book Gallery, 1985), p. 1.

2. W. T. Bary, *Sources of Indian Traditions*, (New York, Columbia University Press, 1958), p. 743.

3. S. H. Nasr in *Islam and Contemporary Society*, (London, Longman Group, 1982), p. 176.

4. Ibid., p. 179.

5. Ibid., p. 180.

6. Ibid., p. 179.

7. G. Sarton, *Introduction to the History of Science, Vol. 1.*, (New York, Krieger Publishing, 1975), p. 5.

8. S. H. Nasr, *An Introduction to Islamic Cosmological Doctrines*, (Bath, Thames and Hudson, 1978), p. 101.

9. Al-Biruni, quoted in Nasr, op. cit., p. 121.

10. Nasr in Ref. 3., p. 179.

11. Ziauddin Sardar, 'Why Islam Needs Islamic Science', *New Scientist*, April 1982.

12. Ziauddin Sardar, *Islamic Futures – The Shape of Ideas to Come*, (New York, Mansell Publishing), p. 101.

13. Ibid., p. 95.

14. Ibid., p. 174.

15. Ziauddin Sardar, *The Future of Muslim Civilization*, (New York, Mansell Publishing), pp. 122–36.

7. Can There Be An Islamic Science?

The answer to this question, in my opinion, is simple. No, there cannot be an Islamic science of the physical world, and attempts to create one represent wasted effort. This is in no way a discredit to Islam — as Sir Syed Ahmed Khan has argued, the purpose of religion is to improve morality rather than specify scientific facts.

Islamic Science?

I shall now try to show why it is futile to try and create a new physical science based on religious principles.

- **First, Islamic science does not exist. All efforts to make an Islamic science have failed.**

Modern science, on the other hand, has a definite and palpable existence. Without it factories could not produce, armies could not fight, and disease could not be combated. It enables a person's picture to be received instantaneously thousands of miles away, jet aircraft to traverse continents, defective hearts to be remedied mechanically, and new genetic varieties of plants and animals to be created in the laboratory. In industrial society, science dictates the lives of individuals, forms their world view and habits of thought, and enters even into human relationships. Some of this is to be deplored, and some to be welcomed. But none can deny that the power of modern science is real and enormous.

As for Islamic science, although impassioned arguments for why it should exist have been around for some decades now, and although numerous international conferences have been devoted to the subject, the efforts to create a science endowed with a new epistemology have uniformly failed. This strongly suggests that there was little substantive content in these discussions. To my knowledge, Islamic science has not led to the building of a single machine or instrument, the synthesis of any new chemical compound or drug, the design of a new experiment, or the discovery of some hitherto unknown, testable physical fact. Instead, the practitioners of Islamic science have directed their enquiry towards issues which lie outside the domain of ordinary science.

These include such untestable matters as the speed of Heaven, the temperature of Hell, the chemical composition of jinns, formulae for the calculation of *munafiqat* (hypocrisy), explanations of the Holy Prophet's Ascension based on the theory of Relativity, and the numerous other instances described in the article 'They Call It Islamic Science' at the end of this book. Whether these so-called discoveries of Islamic science are consistent with the Islamic Faith is highly questionable. As for meeting the criteria of scientific theories, they most certainly do not fulfil these.

- **Second, specifying a set of moral and theological principles – no matter how elevated – does not permit one to build a new science from scratch.**

Suppose that Scientist A believes in the unity of God, Scientist B is a polytheist, and Scientist C an atheist. Let's say that their field of research is the physics of elementary particles — a highly sophisticated and mathematical field in which there are a large number of theoretical constructs. In spite of their varied beliefs, their professional work will be judged by only one standard: does it, or does it not, meet the challenge of experiment? I have already quoted the example of Abdus Salam and Steven Weinberg, two physicists who shared the 1979 Nobel Prize in Physics for having unified the weak and electromagnetic forces existing in nature. Salam, who declares himself to be a believer, and Weinberg who is an avowed atheist, were both geographically and ideologically remote from each other when they conceived the same theory of physics.

The impossibility of decreeing that such and such science should exist arises from the fact that science has its own internal logic which cannot be tampered with from outside. Even the scientist himself has sometimes no choice. For example, both Galileo and Newton were devout Christians and had little desire to change the beliefs of their times. Newton was, at times, deeply troubled by the conflict with Christian dogma but he opted ultimately for objectivity. Ultimately, their discoveries set into motion a tidal wave of scientific growth which swept away much of the power of the Church. Had Newton known that this was to happen, he might well not have published his *Principia*.

In spite of being provided with ideological principles and clear political motivations, and in spite of numerous attempts, it has proved impossible to define what Islamic science ought to be in practical terms. Consider, for example, the fact that Islamization of science education was, in General Zia's regime, a goal which was repeatedly stated and emphasized. Numerous learned bodies were constituted, and countless meetings held. But, eleven years of trying led to pitifully little progress. What constitutes an Islamized science syllabus? To this day there is no available answer, and advocates of Islamization avoid discussion on the matter. How badly the exercise failed can be gauged from the fact that, aside from a concerted assault against the theory of evolution — which has led to its being altogether dropped from the Intermediate and B.Sc. biology courses in Pakistan — the essential content of science courses has not changed since 1977. But the damage it has caused to the structure and quality of science education is so enormous that years of patient reconstruction will be needed to achieve previous levels — which in themselves were not very high.

It is interesting to recount some of the attempts made to Islamize science during the years of General Zia's rule. The first serious indication was a public declaration that all knowledge — including science — would shortly be made Islamic. This was in early 1982, when an important seminar on the Islamization of knowledge was held jointly by the International Islamic University in Islamabad and the U.S. based International Institute of Islamic Thought. It was inaugurated by General Zia.

The keynote address was given by the Islamic University rector, the late Mr A. K. Brohi. Of Mr Brohi it must be said that he was a highly articulate lawyer of the old English school who became a national figure following the coup of 1977. Much of his fame derived from the creation of an ingenious Doctrine of Necessity which declared legitimate and necessary the new military regime because it had moved in to save the country from anarchy and chaos. In recognition of his services to the military government, he was buried with full state honours in 1987. In his speech, Mr Brohi expressed little sympathy for the 'dubious contribution of contemporary thought that is reflected in sciences like Physics and Chemistry'.[1] The textbooks used in universities today were the particular objects of his ire because they: 'bear on the face of their pages indelible imprint of the findings that have been recorded by some, at least, of the outstanding irreligious thinkers like Darwin, Freud, Karl Marx.'[2]

Mr Brohi found Einstein's theory of relativity to be objectionable and incompatible with Islam: 'In my considered opinion, the Einsteinian view of the behaviour of moving particles — or the ultimate constituents of matter — regarded from the Islamic perspective, is false'.[3]

Mr Brohi was not a physicist — let alone that special kind of physicist who spends a part of his life simply acquiring the mathematical tools without which Einstein's theory of relativity cannot be comprehended, much less challenged. Lesser men, or those who admit to a small amount of doubt or ignorance in some matters, would have probably refrained from commenting on matters outside their ken lest they appear a little foolish. But, like the venerable Archbishop Ussher who had concluded from his study of the Bible that the world began at 9 a.m. on Sunday 23 October 4004 BC, Mr Brohi, too, was a man of conviction who gave priority to his interpretation of faith over the exigencies of scientific reasoning.

Another affirmation of the view that science should be subordinated to religion was provided by Dr M. A. Kazi, adviser to the President on Science and Technology. This high position in the Pakistani scientific establishment did not prevent him from expressing distaste for the methodology of modern science. In a speech entitled Islamization of Modern Scientific Knowledge, Dr Kazi announced the imperative need to write new science textbooks for all levels such that 'whenever we have to prove a scientific theory or principle on the basis of available information and arguments, we must provide an additional proof by quoting a relevant reference from Qur'an and Sunna if the same is available.'[4]

Of course, the fact that past efforts to define Islamic science have failed is unlikely to deter the really determined. For them, the moral is simply that they will have to look harder. The adoption in 1991 of the fundamentalist-inspired Shariat Bill in Pakistan, which calls for the complete Islamization of education, is certain to lead to a renewed quest.

- **Third, there has never existed, and still does not exist, a definition of Islamic science which is acceptable to all Muslims.**

Long before the advent of modern science, there had been severe disagreement among Muslims over what constitutes legitimate science. Rationalists such as Ibn Sina, Ibn al-Haytham, and Ibn Rushd were locked in conflict with members of the Asharite school. It is fortunate for Muslim science that the orthodox did not hold political power for several centuries and thus could not prevail over rationalism. Had it been otherwise, there would have been no Golden Age of Islamic scientific achievement.

In the present age, sectarian problems are at least as serious as they were in the past. Add to this the complication of national disputes between different Muslim states. Iran, for example, has boycotted all meetings on Islamic science in recent years. In these circumstances, a consensus on the nature of Islamic science is close to impossible.

Issues of a hypothetical Islamic technology are no less difficult than those of Islamic science. Utopians like Seyyed Hossein Nasr would have us believe that Muslims in past centuries, although they were quite capable of it, never made complicated machines or guns because this would have upset the delicate balance between man and nature, and have reduced the spiritual quality of his existence. Even if this were true — and I think it more than just doubtful — such an ascetic view of science is unlikely to be acceptable to the majority of Muslims today who want complicated machines of every sort and weapons of the most sophisticated kind. It is also not *a priori* obvious that advanced technology would be used by Muslim states in a manner very different from that by non-Muslim states. Indeed, it must be considered extremely fortunate for Muslims as a whole that neither Iran nor Iraq possessed nuclear weapons during the course of their conflict.

Can There Be a Marxist Science?

Although our interest centres around the issue of Islamic science, it is of great relevance to explore the encounter of science with ideology in another context.

During the years 1930–1960, the philosophy of Marxism inspired large numbers of Soviet, as well as some Western, scientists to seek a science of the physical world whose epistemology would be based on dialectical materialism. Armed with Engel's *Dialectics of Nature* and Lenin's thesis on *Materialism And Empirio-Criticism*, they sought to bring into existence a Marxist science which would be distinct from, and superior to, the bourgeois science practised in capitalist society. Dutifully looking for thesis, antithesis, and synthesis they applied the filter of ideological conformity to areas of the physical sciences as diverse as quantum mechanics, relativity, and genetics.

This attempt to create a socialist science was not just a failure, it was an unmitigated disaster. The classic example of this is Lysenko's socialist biology in Stalin's Russia. So important is this phenomenon in the history of socialist thought that numerous books, both by Marxists and anti-Marxists, are devoted to its examination.[5] Only the briefest summary can be attempted here.

Lysenko, a plant breeder of peasant origin, appeared on the scene of Soviet biology in the earlier 1930s and set about challenging the work of the academic geneticists, who almost uniformly belonged to the privileged classes. Because Lysenko's scientific claims were couched in the language of class struggle and dialectics, they were adopted as official doctrine by the Russian state under Stalin. His supporters were soon able to gain access to the apparatus of state terror, and thereafter began the elimination of scientific opponents from all positions of authority. The most infamous case is that of Nikolai Vavilov, a pioneer of plant genetics and himself a man with socialist leanings. Vavilov was sentenced to death by a military court for allegedly committing agricultural sabotage and various other crimes. Although the sentence was later commuted to ten years imprisonment, he died in prison after serving three years.

Based on highly dubious arguments and falsified data, Lysenkoism was an attempt to refute Mendelian genetics. It claimed that heredity is not determined by genetic structure but, instead, is a result of the interaction between the organism and the environment. The experiences of the organism over its lifetime are transmitted on to its progeny. The natural corollary of this is that man determines himself — a highly attractive ideological proposition from a socialist angle. But, as biologists can prove with massive amounts of evidence, acquired characteristics are not transmitted and the proposition is simply false. Another of Lysenko's false claims was that plants of the same species showed 'socialist solidarity' and would not compete against each other for survival. He also insisted that trees of the same species planted close together would help each other survive. Forestry in Russia suffered considerably on account of this false belief.

Lysenkoism set Soviet biology back by about 20 years, caused much human suffering through the persecution of opponents, and did considerable damage to Soviet agriculture. Not until the Khrushchev era did it fall into open discredit. As could be expected, opponents of socialism were quick to seize upon this debacle as demonstrating the illogic and tyranny of Marxism.

The reactions of socialists to Lysenkoism were varied. On the one hand, long after it was discredited in Russia, ultra Maoists parroted it as the supreme realization of Engels' dialectics and criticized the Soviet renunciation of Lysenkoism as revisionist. Others searched for the material conditions, such as the poor state of Russian agriculture and Stalin's failure at farm collectivization, which gave rise to a desperate search for magical and irrational solutions such as Lysenkoism. Still others dismissed it as the case of an ambitious and opportunistic individual operating in an authoritarian environment. Because it was but an individual case, they said, little of abiding interest could be read into it.

But the Lysenko experience should not be dismissed so lightly. While it was the most dishonourable example of a Marxist science, there were other instances too. The probabilistic nature of quantum mechanics, and the philosophical implications of Einstein's theory of relativity, made both of them ideologically suspect in Stalin's Russia. It was feared by party ideologues that the quantum mechanical indeterminacy of the physical world would spill over into the world of politics, and perhaps go against the deterministic evolution of societies advocated by Marx. Similarly, Einsteinian relativity was considered as a prologue to moral relativism. One sees how, in the books and monographs written during that era, even very respectable physicists (such as V. Fock) went to absurd lengths in attempting to explain how their work was derived from Marxist–Leninist principles.

These experiences have been instrumental in liberating progressive scientists from the misplaced notion that nature can be forced into obeying an ideology. As for the uses that science is put to, that is altogether a different issue.

And What of a Third World Science?

It's an unjust world that we live in. Third World nations, with over three-quarters of the world's population, earn less than 20% of the Gross Global Product and consume only 22% of the world's natural resources. An American, on the average, consumes 1,000 times more energy than an African. Developing nations produce four times more non-renewable raw materials than they consume, thus exhausting their own soil for the benefit of foreign clients. Their dependence upon the industrialized countries pervades every aspect of their existence. In the economic sphere, this is highlighted by the fact that Third World countries paid the staggering sum of $150 billion in 1989 for debt servicing to banks in the industrialized countries.

This dependence is not accidental by any means — the self-interest of the industrialized countries, in spite of rhetoric to the contrary, is for maintenance of the *status quo*. This becomes clear upon examining policies made by the industrialized countries through international agencies, banks and lending organizations. Many of these are of devastating consequence for the Third World. For example, elites in these countries are being deliberately inspired with a policy of unbridled greed for imported consumer goods. Their military adventurism is being nourished by sophisticated arms supplies from military-industrial complexes in the developed countries. However, only very rarely, such as when Iraq used these weapons against the West and its clients, does this become an issue worthy of attention. National resources are plundered by transnational corporations which chop down forests and pollute rivers for profits. Numerous countries are subject to the dumping of chemicals and pesticides which threaten to destroy the local ecology, and they are easy victims to Bhopal-like disasters.

These matters of fact are upsetting to all those who believe in a just world. Perhaps understandably — although not justifiably — it has led to a reaction against all things Western, including science. Hence we find today a variety of arguments that the Third World must abandon modern science. It is pointed out that science, as practised today in the Third World, is not very creative or original, and for the most part functions in isolation from society at large. In form however — although not in quality — it is no different from the science practised in the West, and as such is indeed divorced in spirit and substance from the knowledge and philosophies which existed in pre-colonial times. And so, it is argued, because science is a colonial implant, it cannot be expected to take deep root in non-Western countries.

Does this mean that the Third World needs a new Third World science?

According to some, it does. One of the most vocal advocates of Third World science is Susantha Goonatilake, a Sri Lankan intellectual. In common with his Islamic contemporaries like Nasr and Sardar, Goonatilake is in love with the romantic idea that the most profound sources of wisdom are to be found in the distant past.[6] The difference is that he searches for these sources in the civilizations of pre-colonial South Asia rather than the Islamic period. Again, like Nasr and Sardar, Goonatilake believes that modern science is fast approaching a state of terminal collapse and only the ancient civilizations contain wisdom deep enough to rescue it. So, in the field of medicine, the 'Ayurvedic past could be screened for new growth-points which could be married to contemporary scientific knowledge', and new directions in atomic physics and cosmology can be found by going back to the 'rich historical scientific and conceptual traditions such as those of South Asia or China'.[7] Otherwise, says Goonatilake, we in the Third World are doomed to mere imitative science whose centre is the West.

Similar sentiments are generally echoed by other advocates of Third World science, some of whom gathered in 1986 in Penang for an international conference entitled Crisis in Modern Science. The conference declared that modern science and technology are based on Western experience and epistemology, and therefore ill-suited to the needs of the Third World. It was stressed that the most difficult aspect of the fight was to 'debrainwash' the people of the Third World from the First World's penetration, and to fight 'foreign-trained scientists' who are 'the greatest germ-carriers of the Western virus against which our societies are seeking immunity.'[8]

Although the motivations for a politically based science are different in detail from the motivations for a religiously based science, in my opinion they are equally unsound. Every objection to the latter concept applies *in toto* to the former. To repeat: no such science exists; every proposal for such a science made so far is excessively vague and often self-contradictory; it does not enjoy any consensus as to its appropriate form outside small groups of individuals who often have nothing to do with science; and it negates the spirit of universalism. Since these arguments have been elaborated upon at length earlier in this chapter, they will not be repeated here.

For all these reasons, I believe that Third World science, regarded as a quest for a new epistemology for science, is an illegitimate concept which is nothing but a waste of time, and whose pursuit can only serve to accelerate the backwardness, poverty, and ecological destruction of the Third World. But it is an altogether different issue when one looks at the role of modern science as the major factor in producing inequality between different cultures. Indeed, this disparity did not exist in earlier times; no single culture was powerful enough to dominate and devalue the others until the point when modern science was born in Europe. It is now perfectly visible that science, regarded as a factor of production, is excellent at producing, but terrible at distributing — justice is a concept which lies outside science. Indeed, the cumulative nature of science is such that the haves continue to have more, and the have-nots less and less. This makes it imperative to bring about a conscious intervention in terms of which that part of humanity which does possess science helps those parts which do not. For the developing countries, it is necessary that the tools of science be mastered, not abandoned. Only by doing so can they possibly ensure their own survival and the continued existence of a global civilization.

References

1. A. K. Brohi in 'Knowledge For What?', proceedings of the Seminar on the Islamization of Knowledge, Islamic University, Islamabad, 1982, p. xv.

2. Ibid.

3. Ibid.

4. M. A. Kazi in 'Knowledge For What?', op. cit., pp. 67–8.

5. Z. Medvedev, *The Rise and Fall of T. D. Lysenko*, (New York, Columbia University Press, 1969). Also R. Lewontin and Richard Levins, 'The Problem Of Lysenkoism', in *The Radicalisation of Science*, eds. Hilary Rose and Steven Rose, (London, Macmillan Press, 1976), pp. 32–64.

6. Susantha Goonatilake, *Aborted Discovery – Science and Creativity in the Third World*, (London, Zed Books, 1984).

7. Ibid.

8. *Modern Science in Crisis – A Third World Response*, (Penang, Third World Network and Consumers Association of Penang, 1988).

8. The Rise of Muslim Science

Most historians portray the Middle Ages as being an exceptionally dark period in human existence. But this notion is a rather parochial one; it arises from concentrating exclusively on Western cultural history. The Dark Ages were the dark ages of Europe, not all humankind. In fact, at the time when Europeans were preoccupied with burning witches and disembowelling heretics, Islamic civilization was at its brilliant best. The remarkable achievements of this period are acknowledged by all historians of repute. For example, George Sarton's encyclopedic treatise on the history of science — which is considered as the definitive work on the subject — forcefully emphasizes this fact.

> From the second half of the eighth to the end of the eleventh century, Arabic was *the* scientific, *the* progressive language of mankind . . . . It will suffice here to evoke a few glorious names without contemporary equivalents in the West: Jabir ibn Hayyan, al-Kindi, al-Khwarizmi, al-Farghani, al-Razi, Thabit ibn Qurra, al-Battani, Hunain ibn Ishaq, al-Farabi, Ibrahim ibn Sinan, al-Masudi, al-Tabari, Abul-Wafa, Ali ibn Abbas, Abul-Qasim, Ibn al-Jazzar, al-Biruni, Ibn Sina, Ibn Yunus, al-Karkhi, Ibn al-Haytham, Ali ibn Isa, al-Ghazzali, al-Zarqali, Omar Khayyam! . . . . If anyone tells you that the Middle Ages were scientifically sterile, just quote these men to him, all of whom flourished within a relatively short period, between 750 and 1100.[1]

A similar point of view is expressed in a recent issue of the prestigious scientific journal, *Nature*:

> At its peak about one thousand years ago, the Muslim world made a remarkable contribution to science, notably mathematics and medicine. Baghdad in its heyday and southern Spain built universities to which thousands flocked. Rulers surrounded themselves with scientists and artists. A spirit of freedom allowed Jews, Christians, and Muslims to work side by side. Today all this is but a memory.[2]

It is worthy of note that paying such lavish — and well deserved — tributes to Islamic scientific achievement is entirely a 20th century phenomenon. One does not find anything resembling this in the Orientalist literature of the 18th and 19th century. The reason is rather clear. Until the period of decisive European supremacy, Islam had represented the principal military and moral threat to Christianity because it was a powerful and vigorous alternative faith. So, in order to explain the spread of Islam, Christian theology had developed a defensive theory which demonstrated that Islamic success was the product of Muslim violence, lasciviousness and deceit. This was indeed very convenient to assume at a time when European mercantile imperialism was on the rise. By doing so, the 'white man's burden' not only became easier to bear, but also military conquest assumed the form of a moral imperative when the conquered peoples could be portrayed as barbarians ignorant of scientific and artistic refinement. Hence the existence of a strong disincentive towards any impartial scholarship which might lay such assumptions open to doubt.

The perception that, by and large, Western scholarship is rigged against them has generated among Muslims an intense search for an alternate perspective on intellectual and cultural history. Rescued from dry history books, medieval history becomes the tale of past Muslim glories, and a part of the living imagination today of Muslims throughout the world. Scientific achievements of earlier periods, in particular, take on extraordinary significance. Although a millennium has passed, the key which will unlock the doors to another Golden Age is seriously thought by some to be lying somewhere along the unlit road leading back into the past. If we find out what went wrong, the argument goes, then we will know what to do in the future.

For this reason, over the last 200 years — and continuing to this day with undimmed vigour — identifying the causes of civilizational decline has been a major preoccupation for Muslims right across the ideological spectrum. But, as is generally the case in disputations based on historical reasoning, lessons are drawn to authenticate or reinforce already held positions.

From the orthodox–restorationist angle, the Golden Age is seen as divine reward for the pious behaviour of Muslims. As long as they prayed punctiliously, performed Haj, fasted in the month of Ramazan, gave Zakat, and rigorously observed the rituals of faith, they prospered. Conversely, the decline is ascribed to the practice in the courts of the caliphates of vices such as drinking, singing, dancing and sexual laxity. In this view, a restoration of former glories today demands a return to the enforcement of the Sharia (divine law) and strict adherence to the ritualistic aspects of religion. The sceptic, however, points to the fact that the most significant periods of intellectual progress are associated with rulers, such as Harun-al-Rashid and Al-Mamun, whose liberalism was a source of great displeasure to the orthodoxy of their times.

The modernist–reconstructionist Muslim, by contrast, looks for a different moral. He is quick to find in the record of past Islamic scientific achievement solid proof of the harmony between Islam and science. The Golden Age becomes triumphant vindication of the numerous exhortations of the Qur'an and the Prophet to seek knowledge, and these exhortations are specifically understood as instructions to acquire *scientific* knowledge in the modern sense. It has become fairly commonplace to find assertions that 750 verses of the Qur'an — nearly one-eighth of the book — exhort believers to study nature and pursue modern science. Thus, the argument goes, Golden Age scientific success proves that Islam is completely supportive of science and that the pursuit of science is both a religious duty as well as a pragmatic necessity.

The history of science in the Muslim world of old is important to the future of science in Islamic civilization now. For this reason, it is necessary to enter into disputation on a number of contentious issues. Among these, there are three of particular importance:

- Was the science developed by Muslims specifically of Islamic character, hence deserving to be called Islamic science? Or was it universalistic and therefore more appropriately called Muslim science?

- Is the thesis that Golden Age science was developed primarily by the Arabs correct? How important was the role of non-Muslim and non-Arab scholars?

- Did the major institutions of medieval Muslim society truly accept, assimilate, and internalize the rational sciences?

Consideration of these questions will occupy the remainder of this chapter.

Was it Islamic Science or Muslim Science?

This is by no means a quibble over semantics. The question is whether the science developed by Muslims in medieval times was uniquely connected with Islamic theology and beliefs, or whether its presumptions and techniques were essentially those of other human civilizations as well. This attempt to demarcate the particularistic from the universalistic is equivalent to asking whether the science of the Golden Age should be called Islamic science or Muslim science.

The reason that this issue has been the source of so much confusion is that science in medieval times did not at all mean that what it means today. For example, the study of Shari'at is referred to as a science by Al-Ghazzali, but this would be quite contrary to the modern use of the word. Indeed, there were different sciences, and different medieval scholars who classified them according to very different schemes. According to the Ihsa al-ulum of Al-Farabi, jurisprudence, *ilm-ul-kalam* and metaphysics are considered as much part of science as geometry and optics. So also with Shams al-Muli who divided science into two categories *ulum-al-awa'il* (sciences of the earlier peoples such as Greeks and Indians, and comprising ethics, logic, music, philosophy, mathematics, astronomy, etc) and *ulum-al-awa'khir* (sciences of the later people, and comprising of shari'at, sufism, history, etc). As for Al-Ghazzali, he also had his own typology of knowledge, and so on. None of these categorizations correspond with what is generally understood by science today.

So, to sharpen the debate, we must agree to let science take its present

meaning in the following discussion. One can then meaningfully ask whether
the achievements of Muslims in mathematics, optics, mechanics, astronomy,
chemistry and medicine are to be considered as advances in Islamic science or
Muslim science.

Consider mathematics. The kind of mathematical problems that the major
Muslim mathematicians considered worthy of attention were no different from
those which Egyptian, Babylonian, Indian, and Greek mathematicians had
attempted thousands of years earlier, or which were the subject of investigation
several centuries later. The nature of the achievements in this field bear witness
to this fact. For example, Muslims used their knowledge of Indian numerals to
invent the modern decimal representation of numbers; Jamshid al-Kashani
worked out the binomial theorem and by doing so anticipated this work of
Newton by 700 years; Abdul Wafa established the law of sines in trigonometry;
Al-Khwarizmi systematized the study of equations through his study of
algebra, *al-jabr*; Omar Khayyam developed a geometric solution of cubic
equations; and so on.[3] While it has been argued that this love for mathematics is
directly connected with the doctrine of Unity (*Tawhid*), it is obvious that other
cultures have also developed an identical mathematics. Pythagoras and
Diaophantine were certainly not monotheists! Of course, a part of the work of
medieval mathematicians was related to matters originating from the
particularities of religious belief. For example, al-Khwarizmi devoted half of
his text on algebra to problems of inheritance law. However, none of this work
had any enduring value as it was too specific.

To conclude, there is nothing in Muslim mathematics which could be called
Islamic mathematics. If there is a difference, then that difference is simply that
Muslim civilization did better than any of the others for the 500 years of its
Golden Age.

Much the same can be said about optics. The work of Ibn al-Haytham on
lenses or the refraction of light was directed towards issues in optics that had
engaged the minds of scientists both before him and after him. His place in
history is secure because he was the first to discover certain optical phenomena.
The fact that such men could be produced redounds entirely to the credit of the
Islamic civilization, but it has no link with any theological doctrine. This fact is
unpalatable for certain amongst the orthodoxy even in present times. For
example, a Saudi financed journal published from London openly alleges that
Ibn al-Haytham's achievement, as well as those of other great Muslim
rationalists, was but a 'natural and logical extension of Greek thought', and so
it is 'no wonder that he [Haytham] was generally regarded as a heretic, and has
been almost totally forgotten in the Muslim world.'[4]

It is absurd to think that the scientific views of a Muslim scientist are
necessarily connected with his religious belief, or that he necessarily derives
inspiration for his scientific work from faith. This was as true a thousand years
ago as it is now. Alchemy provides an excellent example. Developed extensively
by Jabir Ibn Hayyan and Al-Razi, and based on certain myths going back to
Arius and Pythagoras, it was one of the most important Muslim contributions.
Of course, today everyone knows that alchemy was scientific nonsense: there

cannot be anything like the Philosopher's Stone, and the transformation of base metals like copper or tin into silver or gold by chemical means is an impossibility. However, alchemy, regarded as embryonic chemistry, did turn out to be exceedingly important. Alchemists learned the art of mixing in precise proportions, the properties of acids and alkalis, the affinities of certain elements for others, and so on. But these are the fortunate by-products of a programme which was fundamentally misdirected. Surely, it would be false to say that inspiration for Muslim alchemy came from Islam!

Was Science in the Golden Age Arab Science?

In the famous dispute between the 19th century French Islamist Ernest Renan and the Muslim modernist–pragmatist Syed Jamaluddin Afghani, Renan had argued that not only had science and philosophy been introduced into the Islamic world by non-Arabs, but they were also responsible for sustaining and nurturing these disciplines. He pointed out that only one of the great Islamic philosophers, Al-Kindi, was Arab by birth. Hence, asserted Renan, Arab science is a misnomer and science and philosophy should be considered more accurately to be of Greek or Persian origin.[5]

Similar arguments have been repeated by others. It therefore requires us to explore in some detail the manner in which the sciences were introduced into Islam's society and their subsequent evolution. We shall also see what arguments Afghani used in his reply to Renan.

To set the stage for discussion, it is useful to demarcate medieval Islamic history into four more or less distinct periods: before 750 (the period of genesis), 750–1000 (the classical Abbasid period), 1000–1250 (the high Middle Ages), and 1250–1500 (the late Middle Ages).

There was no science or philosophy in the period of genesis — these only entered the world of Islam during the classical Abbasid period. (Some alchemical, astrological, and medical works were, however, translated on the initiative of the Umayyad prince Khalid bin Yazid (d. 704), who had turned to the study of alchemy when his claims to the caliphate were thwarted). This latter period was an era in which Islam was in a state of vigorous territorial and commercial expansion, and Islamic society was vibrant and dynamic. Prosperity from trade and conquest had created a leisure class at home free from the mundane tasks of simple survival, and hence able to pursue tasks demanding a higher level of intellectual sophistication. Cultivation of the arts and sciences began in these times.

The monumental task of translating and systematizing the works of Greek science, philosophy, and medicine was the first step. Starting at Jundishapur, and then moving on to Baghdad, this work was carried out by scholars who were, for the most part, non-Muslims. Sabra[6] points out that, in fact, the majority of translators were Christians belonging to the Nestorian sect who had carried on a tradition of learning in schools and monasteries dispersed over the Near East and Central Asia. The greatest among them, Hunayn Ibn Ishaq, trained and led a number of translators, including his son Ishaq, who were responsible for translating a sizeable body of Greek works in medicine, philosophy and mathematics into Arabic. Thabit Ibn Qurrah, another master of translation, came from the community of Sabians in Harran, who comprised a pagan cult deeply influenced by astrology and Pythagorean mysticism. Other major translators, such as Abu Bishr Matta and Yahya bin Adi, were Jacobites. Baramika, of Indian Buddhist ancestry, was the guiding spirit behind the Bait-ul-Hikma and helped in the introduction of Indian medicine, mathematics and astronomy before the translations from Greek were made. This first stage of Islamic scientific development was essentially an assimilation of imported knowledge and Muslim scholars had only a secondary role to play as translators.

The contributions of Muslim scholars in this beginning stage were not of great importance, and Renan's argument is basically correct if limited to this period. However, it should also be recognized that the translation effort would have been impossible without the full support and encouragement of the Muslim ruling elites. Indeed, the court of the Caliph and the homes of the nobility received sages and scholars of all creeds as dignitaries. They were venerated and respected, not simply tolerated. Nurtured by this environment of liberalism and religious open-mindedness, science quickly took root in the lands of Islam.

By the high Middle Ages, the translation effort had been completed. Science in the Islamic civilization now entered into its second phase of development. Arabic, not Greek, now became the vehicle of intellectual thought. In contrast to the earlier period, most scholars in the lands of Islam were now Muslims. At this high point, Islamic civilization produced *Muslim* scientists such as Ibn al-Haytham (965–1039), Al-Biruni (973–1051), Omar Khayyam (1038–1123) and Nasir-ud-din Tusi (1201–1274). To recount here the major contributions of Muslim scientists is impractical. Many of these were subsequently assimilated by Renaissance science in Europe. Roger Bacon — much to the displeasure of the Christian Church — began his experiments based on Ibn-al-Haytham's treatise on optics; the Latin translation of Ibn Sina's *Canon of Medicine* was taught for centuries in Western universities; and Ibn Rushd was destined to become the first philosopher of the Reformation.

And now for Jamaluddin Afghani's reply to Renan's argument.

Afghani began his reply by pointing out that the Arabs, though ignorant and barbaric in origin, had nevertheless taken up what had been abandoned by the civilized nations, and rekindled the extinguished sciences. The Europeans welcomed Aristotle when he had in a sense emigrated and become Arab; but they did not think of him at all when he was Greek and their neighbour. It is true, said Afghani, that after the fall of the Arab kingdom in the Orient the great centres of science, like Iraq and Andalusia, fell again into ignorance and became the centres of religious fanaticism. However, one cannot conclude from this that scientific and philosophic progress of the Middle Ages was not due to the Arab people who ruled at that time.

Afghani then challenged Renan's assertion that very few of the great Islamic scholars had been of Arab origin:

> M. Renan has said that the philosophers of the first century of Islam as well as the statesmen who became famous in this period were mostly from Harran, from Andalusia, and from Iran. There were also among them Transoxanian and Syrian priests. I do not wish to deny the great qualities of the Persian scholars nor the role that they played in the Arab world; but permit me to say that the Harranians were Arabs and that the Arabs in occupying Spain and Andalusia did not lose their nationality; they remained Arabs. Several centuries before Islam the Arabic language was that of the Harranians. The fact that they preserved their former religion, Sabaeanism, does not mean that they should be considered foreign to the Arab nationality. The Syrian priests were also for the most part Ghassanian Arabs converted to Christianity.
>
> As for Ibn-Bajja, Ibn-Rushd, and Ibn-Tufail, one cannot say that they are not just as Arab as al-Kindi because they were not born in Arabia . . . . And if all Europeans belong to the same stock, one can with justice claim that the Harranians and the Syrians, who are Semites, belong equally to the great Arab family.[7]

One might add here — although Afghani omits this rather important point — that the language of science was Arabic, regardless of where the scholar hailed from. Texts in Persian, for example, were usually of an introductory nature; all serious work was in Arabic.

Renan's reply, published the next day in the same journal, and reproduced by Keddie in her book on Afghani, acknowledges the justice of the reply for the most part. Afghani's argument is balanced and reasoned. Without denying the seminal contributions of non-Arabs and non-Muslims, he effectively refutes Renan and emerges as the winner in this part of the debate. But on a different issue — the alleged role of religions in impeding free thought and science — we have already encountered the astonishing concurrence of Afghani's and Renan's views.

Was Science Accepted by Medieval Muslim Society?

It would be of great interest to discover the extent to which the institutions of medieval Muslim society accepted, assimilated, internalized and transmitted the rational sciences. Knowledge of this would enable us to guess the extent to which science became part of that society.

Before asking such a question, one must recognize that science played a very different role in all traditional societies, including medieval Christian society. In modern times, we have become thoroughly accustomed to science as a large body of full-time practitioners engaged in performing very specialized tasks, and usually communicating in a language quite incomprehensible to those outside particular fields. This body creates, and in turn is created by, the major institutions of modern society. Economic, social, educational and political institutions have evolved around major technological advances. Civilization, as we know it today, is defined in large measure by science.

This was not so in earlier periods of history. In all traditional civilizations, including Islamic civilization, both the reasons for practising science and the way in which it was practised were very different from the present. Of course, there does exist certain common ground. Both pre-modern and modern science derive from a certain species characteristic — human curiosity. The strange properties of numbers, eclipses and tidal phenomena, the vast expanses of the cosmos, the intricacies of the human body — such phenomena have fascinated human beings from time immemorial. The urge to know, and the ability of the human mind to construct abstractions, lies behind all of science. This force has been present throughout the ages, and been nurtured to a greater or lesser degree by every society. So it is certainly correct to say that science has been around almost as long as humanity itself.

The point, however, is that the symbiosis between science and technology had not occurred in any traditional civilization, including the Islamic civilization. Ancient science did not lead to notable improvements in agriculture, housing, clothes and, with some exceptions, even in the weapons of war. The extant technology was basically empirical, *ad hoc*, and without deep theoretical underpinnings. A great deal of the science of those times dealt with book learning and disputation, and the searching test of practical use arose only seldom. This meant, among other things, that the full possibilities of Islamic science could not be realized in the framework of the civilization which had nurtured it. The systematization of algebra by Al-Khwarizmi was indeed beautiful and a milestone in the history of abstract thought. But, in this embryonic stage of intellectual development, it was by no means obvious that science and mathematics had anything of use to offer. Not until the birth of modern civilization in Europe did mathematics make essential contact with technology. Indeed, even there, modern technology owed more initially to experimental genius; technology as an application of science did not emerge until as late as the 19th century. In the 17th and 18th centuries most inventions and experimental discoveries preceded theoretical developments. For example, the steam engine came first and the development of thermodynamics followed.

So, as I have argued above, science and mathematics did not have very much immediate application to the concerns of medieval Islamic society. Exceptions existed, but they were of marginal significance. One can point to the fact that practical problems arising in commerce, land surveying, and cartography led to the introduction of basic mathematics in the madrassa curriculum. Another use of mathematics was to determine the direction of the Qibla (Mecca) at different points on the globe, and to compile tables for prayer timings. The mosque time keeper (*muwaqqit*) sometimes used trigonometry and algebra for his work. It is also possible to find occasional examples in engineering and civil works. For instance, Ibn al-Haytham was engaged by the Fatimid Caliph al-Hakim to work on an ambitious project to regulate the flow of the Nile. Unfortunately this was doomed to failure because the earth-moving technology of the time was much too primitive.

In ruling out the possibility of technology as a major motivation for developing science in medieval Islamic society, we are left with the basic question: to what causes may one, then, ascribe the flowering of science in Islam?

A basic element appears to be the patronage of enlightened caliphs and princes, for whom science and learning provided an intense fascination. Even the French aristocracy of the Enlightenment cannot match the extent and seriousness of this patronage. Rulers vied with each other in attracting the best scholars to their courts. Al-Kindi in the court of Caliph Mamun, Fakr-ad-din Razi in the court of Sultan Mohammed Ibn Tukush, Ibn Sina as a physician to various princes, Ibn al-Haytham as a consultant to al-Hakim, Ibn Rushd under Al-Mansur, and so on. Practically all great scholars of medieval times were associated with the royal courts which conferred upon them professional fame, social prestige, access to libraries and observatories, and, perhaps most importantly, generous stipends. The Caliph's patronage was also crucial in keeping at bay those fanatics who believed that the scholar's works amounted to heresy. Without this protection there would have been no Golden Age of Islam.

But dependence on royal patronage was also a dangerous structural weakness for Muslim science. The personal proclivities of the patron, the prevailing fortunes of the ruling dynasty, and the intrigues of court life; it was these which determined both the type of learning to be promoted and the fate of individual scholars. A change of rulers often meant disaster for courtiers and scholars of the old court. For example, rationalist scholars who had been cultivated in the court of Mamun, such as Al-Kindi, fled for their lives when the conservative Al-Mutawwakil took over the Caliphate. All colleges and universities were closed. Literature, science and philosophy were indicted, and the rationalists were hunted from Baghdad. But the reasons for a scholar's hasty departure were not always ideological. Ibn Sina's history shows that the life of a physician often dangled from a very slender thread — particularly when someone in the royal family was incurably sick. Sometimes, fleeing at midnight on horseback, and sometimes disguised as a dervish, his adventures as he fled from court to court read like an action packed novel. Some of his contemporaries were not so lucky, and were forced to exit this world somewhat sooner than they wanted.

In conclusion, it appears that science — and for that matter all secular learning — remained a highly esoteric subject confined to the enlightened upper strata of Muslim society. This seems a reasonable deduction in view of the following.

(1) The possible applications of science — meaning here systematized methods based on theoretical principles — were much too few to have a major impact on the technology of the times. Science did not create institutions of economic importance, or generate major economic activity, or create concentrations of expertise. Hence there was no real need to take it to the people.

(2) Courtly patronage, though entirely laudable, meant that the fundamental task of the scholar was to please his patrons. There was little to be gained from ordinary people.

(3) The virtual exclusion of the rational sciences from the curricula of mainstream educational institutions (the madrassas) left no solid institutional mechanism for their propagation.

(4) The writings of all the major philosophers — Al-Kindi, Ibn Sina, Al-Razi, Ibn-Rushd, etc. — show simultaneous contempt for, and fear of, the ignorant masses. They cheerfully advocated the expediency of one truth for the masses and another for the elect. This was essential for their self-preservation and a calculated application of *taqiyya* (dissimulation) because it was not hard for fanatical mullahs to incite the masses against the philosophers. But they were also convinced that Islam mandated the study of science and philosophy. Although this was a minority viewpoint, it was still significant in the context of that society.

On the basis of these arguments, it is plausible to conclude that science was the private initiative of individual scholars with crucial support from the enlightened nobility, and with the masses being more or less out of the picture. While this appears to be the case, it must be admitted that there remains an outstanding puzzle: Muslim science lasted for nearly six centuries and this, as Sarton observed, is longer than Greek, medieval Christian, or even modern science, has lasted. How individuals could have sustained science for this immense period is indeed something that no one understands.

References

1. George Sarton, *Introduction to the History of Science, Vol. I*, (New York, Krieger, 1975), p. 17.

2. Francis Ghiles, 'What Is Wrong With Muslim Science', *Nature*, 24 March 1983.

3. For references, see S. H. Nasr, *Islamic Science – An Illustrated Study*, (Kent, World of Islam Publishing Company, 1976), p. 81.

4. Javed Ansari, 'This is a Formula for Islamic Scientific Impotence', *Arabia: The Islamic World Review*, London, 20 April 1983.

5. Ernest Renan, *l'Islamisme et la science*, (Paris, 1883), p. 17, quoted in Nikkie R. Keddie, *An Islamic Response to Imperialism*, (Berkeley, University of California Press, 1983), p. 85.

6. A. I. Sabra, 'Greek Science In Islam', *History of Science*, XXV, (1987), p. 223.

7. Jamaluddin Afghani, 'Journal des Debats', May 18, 1883, quoted in Keddie, op. cit., p. 185.

9. Religious Orthodoxy Confronts Muslim Science

History is not a science. In contrast to physics, where knowledge of the initial data determines future events, no amount of historical knowledge can help us make predictions with a degree of certainty. Causation in history — the belief that particular events were caused by particular acts — is fraught with danger because it presumes that the same cause will always lead to the same effect. On the other hand, one can also take the extreme position that the study of historical causes or explanations is worthless; that history has no lessons to teach. Acceptance of this position perforce requires that the entire accumulated experience of humankind must be rejected. Further, every single occurrence and event — whether significant or insignificant — must then be acknowledged as part of the divine design, or alternately dismissed as being purely accidental. Thereby not only the past, but even the living present, becomes incoherent and incomprehensible.

In considering the decline and ultimate ruin of science in the Islamic civilization — particularly in relation to what it may teach us about the state of science in Islam today — one could take the position that this particular historical episode is beyond analysis or simply an expression of the Divine Will. In that case, there is nothing further to talk about. On the other hand, one may wish to seek reasons for the decline. Unanimity is not to be expected: different historians, if asked to provide an answer, will fish into the same bag of facts with each one pulling out a different batch. One set of explanations will concentrate on the external factors — Mongol invasions, the sack of Baghdad, the Crusades, etc. and assign the downfall primarily to military defeat. The orthodox view will give primacy to the disappearance of Islamic values, and so on.

Rather than assign one single cause to the problem of decline I shall, instead, make an observation for which there seems to be much historical evidence. The decline of science in Islamic culture was contemporaneous with the ascendancy of an ossified religiosity, making it harder and harder for secular pursuits to exist. This does not pinpoint the orthodox reaction against science as the single cause. In particular, it does not exclude economic and political factors. But certainly, as the chorus of intolerance and blind fanaticism reached its crescendo, the secular sciences retreated further and further. Finally, when the Golden Age of the Islamic intellect ended in the 14th century, the towering edifice of Islamic science had been reduced to rubble. Thenceforth Muslim culture was to become the tenacious survival of something which had once been magnificent and new.

To get to the roots of orthodox reaction against science, we shall need to step back briefly 1,300 years into the first century of Islam.

The newly founded religion of Islam provided the Arabs with an identity, a consciousness, and a world view transcending the hitherto narrow confines of tribal and ethnic existence. In the ensuing cultural revolution, they found themselves in possession of the dazzling intellectual treasures of ancient civilizations — Greek philosophy and science, Persian literature, Indian medicine and mathematics, and certain aspects of Egyptian and Babylonian science of which even the Greeks had been unaware. These pre-Islamic sciences, which came to be known as the *ulum-al-awa'il* (knowledge of antiquity), encompassed the entire range of available knowledge — medicine, astronomy, philosophy, mathematics, natural science, the theory of music, and the occult sciences. Indeed, the *ulum-al-awa'il* was a vast storehouse of intellectual treasures. The challenge was to assimilate these elements of secular learning into the Islamic Faith. And it was soon taken up.

Exhilarated by their newly acquired mastery over Greek syllogistic logic, the early Muslim scholars were quick to use it for religious argumentation. The first notable application was to a festering dispute between the proponents of free will against those who believed in predestination. Arraigned on one side were the Qadarites who used their particular interpretation of religious doctrine, buttressed by typical Aristotelian syllogisms, to fight the battle for free will. They argued, quoting Qur'anic verses, that man could select, out of the many options open to him, the one that he wanted. This argument was not of doctrinal significance alone — it was highly political as well. The belief that one was endowed with free will and the power of decision implied, among other things, that the rule of tyrants — meaning here the Ummayad caliphs — did not have to be accepted as mere fate. As such, this was clearly a revolutionary doctrine and provided a clear early example of Islam as a potent instrument for insurrection and a rallying call against injustice. Standing on the other side of the dispute were the three sects — Jahmia, Najjaria and Ziraria, collectively known as the Jabria. The Jabria's were uncompromising fatalists and believed that every event and action was the act of God. To them, even the slaying of Imam Husain in the battle of Kerbala was an act of relentless and inexorable fate, and to condemn his murderers or mourn his death was pointless.

Because the Umayyad rulers had everything to lose, and nothing to gain from this subversive doctrine of free will, they came down heavily against the Qadarites. Their leader, Ma'bad al-Juhani, was beheaded during the reign of Marwan Ibn Abdul Malik. Over a period of time, other free willers were hanged and tortured. But the doctrine could not be suppressed. It was soon embodied in the Mu'tazila movement to which it gave birth, and which we take up next.

The Mu'tazilite Revolt Against Orthodoxy

From the bloody clashes in the streets of Basra and Baghdad between the free willers and predestinarians there emerged, ultimately, a radical school of rationalist philosophers known as the Mu'tazila (Dissenters). The impact of this philosophy on Muslim thought and society was to reverberate through the centuries.[1] The caliphs Ma'mun and Mu'tassim enforced it as state doctrine, and more than ten centuries after its birth, Mu'tazilism played a key role in shaping the ideas of Muslim reformers of the European colonial era. Its influence permeates Muslim modernist thinking even today.

It was Wasil Ibn Ata, an ex-student of Imam Hasan al Basri, who established the Mu'tazila school sometime in the early part of the 8th century. Because of his dissent from established dogma, Ibn Ata was forced to withdraw and soon thereafter established his own school. Comprising adherents who included both Shias and Sunnis, the Mu'tazila was not a separate sect although, in its subsequent development, it was to acquire some of the characteristics of one. Reacting against the rigid Jabria orthodoxy of that time, the Mu'tazila sought a reconciliation of faith with reason. This synthesis of Muslim theology with Greek logic gave birth to a theological science, *ilm-ul-kalam*, which was to form the basis of Muslim scholasticism and dominate Islamic thinking for centuries to come. This scholastic theology was, in the early days, an important means of buttressing Islamic beliefs by logical arguments and defending them from attacks by the Materialists and Manicheans.

In their quest for rational and philosophical underpinnings of the Islamic Faith, the Mu'tazilites advanced arguments based on ethics and reason, even though they naturally supported their positions using Qur'anic quotations. At times they arrived at conclusions which were entirely heretical according to orthodox opinion. Certain elements of their beliefs were particularly striking:

- The issue of free will was a dominating concern. Mu'tazilites felt very keenly the moral dilemma posed by the assertion that God deliberately misled sinners, decreed their evil deeds, and then sent them to hell for their sins. How, they asked, could a merciful and compassionate God punish someone for acts which He had commanded him to perform? The belief that predestination was a travesty of divine justice led the Mu'tazilites to claim for themselves the title of Champions of Divine Justice. Their solution of the sin-and-reward puzzle required that God be regarded as the maker of laws rather than the possessor of unlimited and arbitrary power. For the concept of Divine Judgement to be meaningful, they argued, God has given to people the power of making free unfettered choices. But the orthodox found this solution to be idolatrous: how could man be the author of his own deeds without becoming a Creator himself?

- The Mu'tazila doctrine rejected anthropomorphic representations of God popular at that time saying:

He is no body, nor object, nor volume, nor form, nor flesh, nor blood, nor person, nor substance . . . . The senses do not reach Him, nor can man describe Him by any analogy . . . . Eyes do not see Him, sight does not reach Him.[2]

These beliefs are to be contrasted with those of their opponents. Leading the movement against the Mu'tazilites was Abu al-Hasan al-Ashari, a former rationalist who turned bitterly against his past and the heresies of his former mentors. Al-Ashari's emphasis on literalism and anthropomorphic representations of God became the accepted view of orthodox Sunni Islam. Al-Ashari wrote:

We confess that God is firmly seated on His Throne . . . . We confess that God has two hands, without asking how . . . . We confess that God has two eyes, without asking how . . . . We confess that God has a face . . . . We affirm hearing and sight.[3]

By denying such attributes, and insisting on God as pure essence, the Mu'tazila were accused of denuding Him of content and making Him difficult for humans to comprehend and worship.

- Mu'tazilites had little use for the Ahadith, the traditions and sayings of the Prophet, partly because they doubted the reliability of those accounts. Claiming that reason was as important as revelation, they invented an elaborate grammatical method in the exegesis of the Qur'an to explain away those points in it which they felt were inconsistent with reason. Blasphemous as this view was to some, it paled before their assertion that the Qur'an was not eternal but was, instead, created by God (*Khalq-i-Qur'an*). They put forth numerous reasons to prove this. For example, they argued, if the Qur'an was uncreated then it must be another God, and therefore the unity of God would be violated. As another argument, they cited the fact that the Qur'an contains the speech of Moses. But Moses was a temporal creature, so how could the Qur'an be eternal?

In the early period when orthodoxy had yet to understand the power of syllogistic reasoning, Mu'tazilism had no serious ideological rival. It spread through the courts of the nobility in the Empire, into Spain, and thence Andalusia. The Caliph Mansur encouraged it without making an open commitment, but Mu'tazilism was actually enforced as the state doctrine in the reign of Mamun and Mutassim. There cannot be any doubt that Mamun was the greatest patron of philosophy and science in the entire history of Islam. His creation of the Bait-al-Hikmah (House of Wisdom) was an important milestone. In order to stock this official institute and library for research and translation, Mamun sent emissaries as far as Byzantium to seek out and purchase scientific and philosophical works.

The doctrine of rationalism was preached in mosques and madrassas, and became the distinguishing mark of the educated. The influential and intellectual classes of society — princes, courtiers, qazis, professors, doctors and traders — accepted it as their creed. The phenomenal progress in the secular sciences occurred under Mu'tazilite rulers, and most of the great Islamic scholars and scientists either openly declared their allegiance to rationalism or were heavily influenced by it.

It is important to realize that Mu'tazilism was a great revolutionary movement within Islam — not outside it or against it. But it was ultimately defeated and banished from the mainstream of Islamic dogma. Why? One might perhaps think that the Mu'tazilites — because they comprised Shia and Sunni alike — were potentially capable of ending, with the help of disciplined reasoning, the continual doctrinal feuding which had followed the end of the Rashidate caliphate. One might also like to believe that Mu'tazilism would have provided a rational basis for faith. But their eventual rejection and annihilation occurred because of a combination of two reasons.

First, the access to state power gave to the Mu'tazilites an opportunity to become corrupt and repressive. In a system wherein the caliphate was seized by intrigue or military success, the concept of participatory democracy had not existed. Repression was a normal instrument of government and could be exercised at the whim of the rulers. The Mu'tazila caliphs used it freely as well. Al-Mamun chose to persecute all such qazis, muftis, and ulema who refused to testify to the doctrine of the Qur'an's creation. A religious inquisition (Mihna) was instituted to deal with those whose loyalty to this doctrine was suspect.

The religious opposition to the Mu'tazilites was put up by conservatives like Imam Ahmed Ibn Hanbal. He was among those who were tortured for dissent, and eventually martyred. A staunch literalist, he maintained that 'every discussion about a thing which the Prophet did not discuss is an error,' and in this remained true to the bitter end. Among conservatives, he is a much venerated figure for his steadfastness and refusal to bow before the doctrine of Khalq-i-Qur'an. But not all Muslims look upon Ibn Hanbal as a hero and a saint. For example, Syed Ameer Ali, the 19th century Muslim modernist, had a different angle on this. He accuses Ibn Hanbal and other zealots of using the excesses of the Mu'tazilites as a means of manipulating the simple and backward Muslim masses into a war against rationalism:

> Ahmed Ibn Hanbal, commonly known as Imam Hanbal, made his appearance at this juncture — a red hot puritan, breathing eternal perdition to all who differed from him . . . . He denounced learning and science, and proclaimed a holy war against rationalism. The populace, carried away by his eloquence or his vehemence, took up the cry . . . . the pulpits began to fulminate fire and brimstone against the upholders of reason and the advocates of philosophy and science. The streets of Baghdad became the scenes of frequent rioting and bloodshed.[4]

The failure of rationalists to penetrate the depths of Muslim society can perhaps be gauged by the widespread sympathy enjoyed by their opponents. By many accounts, the size of the crowd which accompanied the funeral of Ahmed Ibn Hanbal is said to have exceeded 150,000 people. For those times this must have been a truly enormous figure.

There is a second, and more fundamental, reason why Mu'tazila rationalism failed to survive: it effectively gave primacy to reason over revelation, even though it asserted their mutual compatibility. Occasionally, this would lead to intolerable challenges. Nowhere is this more clearly evident than in the issue of Khalq-i-Qur'an. This doctrine posed a fundamental threat to religious dogma. In the opinion of A. J. Arberry:

> If the Koran were allowed to be created, the danger was great that it might next be allowed by those steeped in Neoplatonist thought that God's Word as revealed to Mohammed through the mediation of the archangel Gabriel shared with all created things the imperfection arising from their association with matter. The 'incomparable miracle' of the Koran must be maintained at all costs, if Revelation was not to capitulate to Reason in its very stronghold.[5]

Following the ascendancy of the conservative Sunni Caliph al-Mutawakkil, whom Syed Ameer Ali describes as a 'cruel drunken sot in league with the qazis and mullahs,' the physical extermination of Mu'tazilites, together with Shias, began in earnest. They were removed from all governmental positions, accused of heresy, subjected to torture, and summarily executed. Scholars and scientists, most of whom subscribed to rationalist beliefs, fled Baghdad for other parts of the Islamic world. Thus ended the most serious attempt to combine reason with revelation in Islam. Apart from various isolated efforts by individual 19th century Muslim reformers, the separation between the religious and secular has been complete in Islam ever since.

Orthodoxy Strikes Back

While it had fuelled the early phase of Islamic science and learning, the rationalist and secular attitude of the Hellenistic tradition was ultimately challenged by the religious orthodoxy. It soon came to be that the *ulum-al-awa'il* (knowledge of antiquity) were equated with heresy by the orthodox, and philosophy became suspect. This was not, of course, a universal attitude and, in the beginning, did not affect greatly the assimilation of secular sciences into Islamic civilization. Had it been so, Muslim science would never have been born. But with time the attitudes against secular learning hardened. By the 12th century, the conservative, anti-rationalist schools of thought had almost completely destroyed the Mu'tazila influence. So hard was this reaction, that al-Ashari is considered to be relatively moderate as compared with Ibn Hanbal, and later the Wahabis, who did not allow any form of speculation.

The most important and comprehensive work on the reaction of religious orthodoxy to the *ulum-al-awa'il* was done by the Hungarian Islamist, Ignaz Goldziher, in 1916. Drawing on a variety of original Arabic sources spanning a wide period of Islamic history, Goldziher documented the antagonism of the orthodoxy to the philosophical sciences. His work has only recently been translated from German into English. Goldziher points out that despite the extensive interest that the *ulum-al-awa'il* evoked in certain religious Islamic circles, as well as among the Abbasid caliphs, strict orthodoxy always looked with some mistrust on 'those who would abandon the science of Shafi'i and Malik, and elevate the opinion of Empedocles to the level of law in Islam.'[6] With the growing influence of narrow orthodoxy, this distrust increased in intensity and found expression in numerous ways:

- In the work of many orthodox scholars, the *ulum-al-awa'il* are pointedly referred to as the *ulum-ul-mahjura* (repudiated sciences), and are described as *hikma mashuba bi-kufr* (wisdom mixed with unbelief). The Spaniard Ibrahim Ibn Musa (d. 1398) came to the conclusion that the average orthodox theologian regarded only those sciences as worthwile that were necessary to, or useful for, religious practice (*amal*). All others were without value and only led people away from the straight path. The Hanbalite Ibn Taymiya understood ilm (knowledge) as referring to that knowledge which derives from the Prophet. Everything else he regarded either as useless or no science at all, even though it might be called by that name.[7]

- Dhahabi, a Hanbalite partisan, after lauding the erudition of a certain scholar adds, somewhat wistfully, the following remark:

  If only he had refrained from cultivating the *ulum-ul-awa'il*! These latter cause nothing but disease and ruination in religious matters. Very few of those who cultivated them have avoided such a fate.[8]

- Orthodoxy was deeply suspicious of those who had stained themselves with philosophy and discussions about the *ulum-al-awa'il*. Thus, it was a matter of considerable satisfaction when some philosopher, on his deathbed, renounced the errors of philosophy and turned his back on the intellectual leaders in whom he had confided throughout his life. It was reported with a sense of triumph that the blind scholar, Hasan Ibn Muhammad b. Naja al-Arbili (d. 1268) turned his back on philosophy. He was a Shiite philosopher, and in his house in Damascus, Muslims, Ahl-al-Kitab, and philosophers met to hear his lectures. The last thing he reportedly said before his death was: 'God the Most High is right. Ibn Sina has lied.'[9]

- In 885, all professional copyists in Baghdad were required to promise under oath to exclude from their professional activities the copying of books of philosophy. A related fact is pointed out by Tibawi.[10] Although paper was introduced into Europe by the Arabs, they shunned the European invention of printing books on it for nearly three centuries. Religious scruples regarded the mechanical reproduction of the word of God, or material connected with it, as irreverent.

- The enemies of Abd as-Sallam, a grandson of Imam Hanbal, seized upon his interest in philosophy to destroy him. During a search of his home, philosophical works such as the Rasail of the Ikhwan as-Safa were found, as well as books on witchcraft and astrology, works on the cult of stars, books of prayers addressed to the planets, etc. All of these were written in the hand of Abd-as-Sallam, who offered the lame excuse that he did not believe in these things and that he had only copied them in order to refute them. In his presence and before the assembled qazis and ulema a funeral pyre was erected in the courtyard in front of the mosque of the caliph. His books were then thrown into the fire from the platform of the mosque where the learned dignitaries had taken seats. All of this occurred before a large crowd that had gathered in front of the mosque. A man read from the contents of the books and then demanded, in the presence of Abd-as-Sallam, that those who had written these books as well as those who believed in them be cursed. The crowd complied with the request; the curses were extended to include Shaikh Abd-al-Qadir and even Imam Ahmed Ibn Hanbal, since the heretic was regarded as one of their disciples. Poetry deriding the cult of stars was recited in his presence. Abd-as-Sallam was then declared a heretic, his academic hood was taken from him, and the school of Abd-al-Qadir, in which he taught, was turned over to Ibn al-Jawzi. Later, after he had been released from prison, Abd-as-Sallam made a proper Islamic confession and renounced his earlier errors.[11]

● Geometry, perhaps because it was a characteristic part of the *ulum-al-awa'il*, disturbed the orthodox mind and geometrical figures seem to have made them particularly uneasy. In one documented case, the owner of a book containing geometric representations was condemned as a heretic. Another instance comes from a fanatic who was terrified by figures in the astronomical book of Ibn al-Haytham. He suspected them of representing 'shameful temptation, speechless calamity and blind misfortune'.[12] The abstract nature of mathematical thinking was offensive to many orthodox minds. The lexicographer Abul Husayn Ibn Faris expressed his dislike of abstraction, and criticized those non-Arab peoples

who claim to understand the essential nature of things by the use of numbers, lines and points whose relevance I cannot understand: indeed, they weaken faith and cause conditions from which we ask God's protection.[13]

● Strict orthodoxy was not very much in favour of scientific astronomy, even though some knowledge of it was necessary for determining prayer timings and the precise direction of the Qibla. Some of the assumptions of astronomy seemed to be totally outrageous. For example, when word was brought to the orthodox sultan, Khwarizm Shah, of a land of the midnight sun, he regarded the report as pure heresy (*ilhad wa qarmata*), for if such information were accurate it would put into question the very regulations which determine the times of the various prayers. Only the great Biruni, who then lived at the court of the sultan, could reassure him of the accuracy of the traveller's report.[14]

● As proof of the harmful effects of astronomy and astrology, the example of Abu Mashar al-Balkhi was often cited by those opposed to these. This famous astronomer, who had been a very pious theologian in his younger days, was on his way from Khurasan to Mecca when he chanced to visit the library of the vizier Munajjim. There

> he became engrossed in the astrological (and certainly astronomical) works to such an extent that he became a heretic, and that was the end of the Haj for him and also the end of religion and Islam.[15]

● Ibn-as-Salah (d. 1251), when asked whether it was permissible to study or teach philosophy and logic, issued the following *fatwa* in which he described philosophy as:

> the foundation of folly, the cause of all confusion, all errors and all heresy. The person who occupies himself with it becomes colourblind to the beauties of religious law, supported as it is by brilliant proofs . . . . As far as logic is concerned, it is a means of access to philosophy. Now the means of access to something bad is also bad . . . . All those who give evidence of pursuing the teachings of philosophy must be confronted with the following alternatives: either execution by the sword, or conversion to Islam, so that the land may be protected and the traces of those people and their sciences may be eradicated.[16]

● A renowned teacher of the Shafite school, Taj ad-Din as Subki (d. 1271) stated that the cultivation of logic might be allowable on condition that one first achieve mastery of the religious sciences and have a reputation as a faqih or mufti among members of the school (*madhab*). However, for persons with less background in the religious sciences, the study of logic must be considered as forbidden (*haram*).[17]

● Muslim modernists frequently identify orthodoxy as the most important cause of decline. For example, in his famous exchange with Renan, Syed Jamaluddin Afghani said:

> Al-Sayuti tells that the Caliph al-Hadi put to death in Baghdad 5,000 philosophers in order to destroy sciences in Muslim countries down to their roots. Admitting that this historian exaggerated the number of victims, it remains nonetheless established that this persecution took place, and it is a bloody stain for the history of a religion as it is for the history of a people. I could find in the past of the Christian religion analogous facts. Religions, by whatever names they are called, all resemble each other.[18]

● Ibn Khaldun, though a conservative in certain aspects of his belief, was nevertheless dismayed by the negative attitudes towards learning among the Muslims. He writes:

> When the Muslims conquered Persia and came upon an indescribably large number of books and scientific papers, Sa'd bin Abi Waqqas wrote to Umar bin

al-Khattab asking him for permission to take them and distribute them as booty among the Muslims. On that occasion, Umar wrote him: 'Throw them in the water. If what they contain is right guidance, God has given us better guidance. If it is error, God has protected us against it.[19]

Ancient orthodoxy was indeed outspoken in its opposition to the *ulum-al-awa'il* and the rational sciences, but all this did not amount to anything much and could not affect the assimilation of science into Muslim society. The turning point, however, came when the greatest and most influential of the orthodox ulema, Imam Al-Ghazzali, led the orthodox to final victory by providing them with political power. We turn next to a study of the teachings of this famous theologian.

Al-Ghazzali Routs The Rationalists

The rumblings against the secular and universalistic character of Hellenistic knowledge started, as we have seen, almost from the time of its introduction into the Islamic culture. But the confusion of competing doctrines, lack of familiarity with the techniques of logic and science, and incessant bickering, did not at first allow for a sustained and decisive attack against rationalism. It was not until the theologian Al-Ghazzali — a man who Seyyed Hossein Nasr gratefully acknowledges as having 'saved orthodoxy by depressing science' — that a coherent rebuttal of rationalist philosophy was attempted. With perspicacity, scholarship, and singlemindedness, Al-Ghazzali worked tirelessly to rid Islamic culture of the foreign intrusion of Greek thought.

Born in 1058, Abu Hamid Al-Ghazzali was introduced to the study of theology at an early age. He soon became renowned for his encyclopedic grasp of religious doctrine, and was appointed as a professor of religious sciences at the Nizamiyah University in Baghdad. Here he studied the scientific and philosophical works of the Peripatetic scholars and gained mastery over their methods. Thereafter, he underwent a deep crisis and became an ascetic. When he returned to society, it was as an inveterate opponent of all rationalist philosophers including the Materialists, Naturalists, and Theists. Ghazzali considered Aristotle to be better than most because he had effectively attacked Plato and Socrates, but still afflicted by unbelief and heresy from which he did not manage to free himself. Denouncing Muslim followers of Aristotle, Ghazzali declared that:

> We must therefore reckon as unbelievers both these philosophers themselves and their followers among the Islamic philosophers, such as Ibn-Sina, al-Farabi, and others, in transmitting the philosophy of Aristotle.[20]

The doctrines of Al-Ghazzali are voluminous and deal with every issue of importance to the medieval mind. But his views on cause and effect, reason, mathematics and logic are of special interest to us because they have been instrumental in shaping Muslim attitudes towards the sciences. In the following, we examine those of his attitudes which concern the development of science.

Ghazzali On Cause and Effect
Fire causes burning, lightning causes thunder, winds cause waves, and gravity causes bodies to fall. Such connections between an effect and its cause form the cornerstone of scientific thinking, both modern and classical. But this notion of causality is one which is specifically rejected by Asharite doctrine, and the most articulate and effective opponent of physical causality was Al-Ghazzali.

According to Al-Ghazzali, it is futile to believe that the world runs according to physical laws. God destroys, and then recreates, the world after every instant of time. Hence there cannot be continuity between one moment and the next, and one cannot suppose that a given action will definitely lead to a particular consequence. Conversely, it is false to assign a physical cause to any occurrence. In Al-Ghazzali's theology, God is directly the cause of all physical events and phenomena, and constantly intervenes in the world. Take as an example, he said, the burning of a piece of cotton by fire. The heretical Rationalist philosophers contend that it is the fire which burns the cotton. But, says Ghazzali:

> This we deny, saying: the agent of the burning is God, through His creating the black in the cotton and the disconnection of its parts, and it is God who made the cotton burn and made it ashes either through the intermediation of the angels or without intermediation. For fire is a dead body which has no action, and what is the proof that it is the agent. Indeed, the philosophers have no other proof than the observation of the occurrence of the burning, when there is contact with fire, but observation proves only a simultaneity, not a causation, and, in reality, there is no cause but God.[21]

Ghazzali on Mathematics and Science
Unlike most of the other ulema of his time, Al-Ghazzali had studied the exact sciences and was thus in a position to make an authoritative assessment of their relation to religion. His position on this issue was not one of blind opposition. None of the results of mathematics, he said, are connected with religion. Therefore, mathematics is not a forbidden subject. Nevertheless, Al-Ghazzali argued, it leads to many dangers and is very often the cause of unbelief:

> There are two drawbacks which arise from mathematics. The first is that every student of mathematics admires its precision and the clarity of its demonstrations. This leads him to believe in the philosophers and to think that all their sciences resemble this one in clarity and demonstrative power. Further, he has already heard the accounts on everybody's lips of their unbelief, their denial of God's attributes, and their contempt for revealed truth; he becomes an unbeliever merely by accepting them as authorities.[22]

The argument here is clearly that mathematics is potentially, but not necessarily, dangerous. The danger exists because those who study the subject may become inebriated with the power and beauty of precise reasoning, and so forsake belief in revelation.

But in another place, Al-Ghazzali gives a firmer opinion. He condemns mathematics with vigour and without reservation, rejecting the notion that anything good could be contained in it. Wine undoubtedly strengthens the body, he argues, but it is definitely forbidden. One could argue that the games of maisir and chess sharpen the mind, but that is no justification for pursuing them. Says Ghazzali:

> The same applies to the study of the sciences of Euclid, the Almagest, and the subtleties of arithmetic and geometry. They too render the mind more acute and strengthen the soul, and yet we refrain from them for one reason: they are among the presuppositions of the *ulum ul-awa'il* and these latter [the *awail*] include those sciences, beside arithmetic and geometry, that entail the acceptance of dangerous doctrines. Even if geometry and arithmetic do not contain notions that are harmful to religious belief, we nevertheless fear that one might be attracted through them to doctrines that are dangerous.[23]

In contrast to most of the orthodox ulema of the time, Al-Ghazzali was not, in principle, opposed to logic. However, he was forced to be somewhat equivocal on the subject as he feared being attacked as a follower of Aristotle. Thus he employed ambiguous titles for his books on logic in order to avoid using the term *mantiq*. Muhammad Ibn Tumlus, who had also written about logic, defended himself by calling upon the authority of Al-Ghazzali, saying that:

> Abu Hamid altered the titles of his books as well as the technical terms employed in them. In place of the terms ordinarily used by the representatives of that field, he used technical terms familiar to the *fuqaha* [jurists] and frequently used by the ulema of his time. This he did to protect himself and to escape what other scholars had experienced who came forward with strange and unusual things, for which they had to submit to ordeals and suffer humiliation. A merciful God protected him from these.[24]

It is somewhat paradoxical that Al-Ghazzali spearheaded the attack against free-thinkers and the proponents of logic, but in doing so had to use the weapon of his adversaries. Indeed, the stubborn ghost of Greek dialectics withstood exorcism by the greatest Asharite of all time.

Ghazzali on Abstract Knowledge

In a world view which regards revelation as source of all knowledge, the purpose of all intellectual enquiry is to support and substantiate the Divine Word. Knowledge for satisfaction of the intellect, or knowledge for obtaining recognition and reward, are impermissible. Al-Ghazzali, who was persuaded of this, sternly admonished a young scholar for his attachment to abstract knowledge saying:

O youth, how many nights have you remained awake repeating science and poring over books and have denied yourself sleep. I do not know what the purpose of it was. If it was attaining worldly ends and securing its vanities and acquiring its dignities and surpassing your contemporaries and such like, woe to you and again woe.[25]

Since science and mathematics are built on the foundation of abstract thought, and human curiosity is the fountainhead of disinterested and 'useless' enquiry, Al-Ghazzali's warning is certainly not an encouragement to study these subjects.

In the next chapter, we shall have occasion to see how some heroes of Muslim science faced these daunting obstacles to free enquiry and thought.

References

1. A. J. Arberry, *Revelation and Reason in Islam*, (London, George Allen & Unwin, 1965), *passim*; Alfred Guillaume, *Islam*, (New York, Penguin, 1954), pp. 128–42; Syed Ameer Ali, *The Spirit of Islam*, (Karachi, Pakistan Publishing House, 1976), *passim*; Majid Fakhry, *A History of Islamic Philosophy*, (New York, Columbia University Press, 1983), *passim*.

2. Arberry, op. cit. p. 23.

3. Ibid., p. 22.

4. Syed Ameer Ali, op. cit., p. 438.

5. Arberry, op. cit., p. 24.

6. Ignaz Goldziher in *Studies on Islam*, translated and edited by Merlin L. Swartz, (Oxford University Press, 1981), pp. 185–6. References to the original Arabic sources can be found therein, and are not indicated here.

7. Ibid., pp. 186–7.

8. Ibid., p. 189.

9. Ibid., p. 190.

10. A. L. Tibawi, *Islamic Education*, (London, Luzac, 1979), pp. 49–50.

11. Goldziher, op. cit., p. 192.

12. Ibid., p. 193.

13. Ibid., p. 194.

14. Ibid., pp. 196–7.

15. Ibid.

16. Ibid., p. 205.

17. Ibid., p. 207.

18. Syed Jamaluddin Afghani in 'Réponse de Jamal ad-Din al-Afghani à Renan', quoted in Nikkie R. Keddie, *An Islamic Response to Imperialism*, (Berkeley, University of California Press, 1983), p. 187.

19. Ibn Khaldun, *The Muqaddima: An Introduction to History*, (London, Routledge and Kegan Paul, 1978), p. 373.

20. W. Montgomery Watt, *The Faith and Practice of Al-Ghazzali*, (London, George Allen & Unwin, 1953), pp. 32–3.

21. Quoted by Ibn Rushd in 'Tahafut al-Tahafut', (*The Incoherence of the Incoherence*) translated by S. Van den Bergh (London, E. J. W. Gibb Memorial Series, Vol. 1), pp. 316–17.

22. W. Montgomery Watt, op. cit., p. 33.

23. *Fatihat al-Ulum*, (Cairo 1322), p. 56. Translated by Goldziher, op. cit.

24. Goldziher, op. cit., p. 201.

25. Al-Ghazzali, *Ayyuha-al-Walad*, translated by G. H. Scherer, (Beirut, The American Press, 1932), p. 57.

10. Five Great 'Heretics'

Important as military conquest was to the spreading of early Islam, it was the spectacular achievements of Muslim scholars which established the supremacy of Islamic civilization over its contemporaries. We need only recall that the Mongol invasions — which were superficially similar to the Arab conquests — produced an ephemeral empire but no civilization. Nothing but ruin and destruction remained when the Mongol hordes finally receded to their natural habitat in the Gobi desert. In contrast to this, the Islamic conquests led to a new world culture which flourished long after the military monopoly had declined.

For five centuries the flame of learning had burnt bright in Islamic civilization. To the scintillating galaxy of scholars belonged luminaries like Al-Kindi, Ibn Sina, Omar Khayyam, Ibn al-Haytham, Ibn Rushd, Ibn Khaldun, and many others. Without them the colourful tapestry of Muslim culture would have been much poorer, the claims to being a great world culture weak and unconvincing. Today, these names have become venerated symbols of past achievement. School children in Muslim countries must learn about them, history and science textbooks extol their achievements, and societies and institutes bear their names.

But for all the panegyrics and adulation, there lurks the proverbial skeleton on the closet: the great scholars of Islam were often endangered not by Mongol hordes or infidel Christians but, instead, by homegrown religious orthodoxy.

The tension between zealotry and secular learning was, as we have seen in the previous chapter, present almost from the instant at which the Hellenistic sciences were introduced into Muslim civilization. Sometimes subdued, but sometimes overt and violent, the opposition of the orthodox ulema often posed a mortal threat to those who studied science, philosophy and logic. 'The piety of theologians,' exclaimed al-Jahiz in frustration, 'consists of hastening to denounce dissidents as unbelievers.'[1] Scholars, therefore, relied on the critical support of enlightened caliphs and rulers for protection from powerful religious figures who considered their work to be heretical. But royal patronage stimulated jealousy and raised tensions because the theologians observed that a man of inferior status, the scholar, often had relatively easier access to the halls of power as well as to the Caliph. This environment placed certain important constraints on the amount and nature of intellectual and scientific activity. It made the task of taking science to the people difficult, and thus confined it to the upper crust of society. This is probably why Ibn Rushd came out with the following astonishing dictum: books written by scholars should be declared forbidden to the ordinary person by the rulers.[2]

How the luminaries of Islamic scholarship fared in their encounter with orthodoxy is the subject of this chapter.

Al-Kindi (801–873)

The founder of the Islamic Peripatetic school of philosophy and the author of 270 treaties ranging from logic and mathematics to physics and music, Abu Yusuf Yaqub Ibn Ishaq al-Kindi is known as the 'Philosopher of the Arabs' in recognition of his tireless efforts to make philosophy acceptable to theologians. He is also the only great Arab Muslim philosopher of antiquity. A thorough Mu'tazilite, he wrote that truth is universal and supreme, and that philosophy is but another form of the message which the prophets have carried. The word 'truth' for Al-Kindi had a very definite meaning. It stood for what Plato, Aristotle and other Greek sages had elucidated. The job of scholars was, in his words, 'to complete what the ancients have not fully expressed, according to the usage of our language and the custom of our times, so far as we are able.'[3]

As a rationalist, Al-Kindi proposed that certain passages from the Holy Book whose literal interpretation would be in conflict with reality should, instead, be understood as allegories to guide men of reason. Most ancient philosophers, including Al-Kindi, believed that there exist two truths: one for the stupid and uneducated masses, and the other for the cultured and the educated. Al-Kindi was of the opinion that the former were only able to appreciate simple things and so had to be enticed by the vision of houris and other physical allurements. On the other hand, the latter were given the gifts of logic and reason so that they might arrive at a deeper meaning of the Book. Al-Kindi rationalized his efforts at allegorical interpretation in this manner.

To give an example of the allegorical reasoning that Al-Kindi believed in, consider verse LV5 of the Qur'an. In this passage, the believer is told that the sun, moon, stars, mountains, trees and beasts 'bow themselves' before God. For the unsophisticated, this invokes an image wherein all creation literally bends in prayer. But Al-Kindi gave an elaborate linguistic argument that the Arabic word for 'bow' should be understood as meaning 'obey'. Thus, the naive picture of universal worship should instead be understood as the universal obedience to God's will. Carried another step forward, this becomes for him an argument for the existence of a universal law which must be obeyed by all forms of matter, animate as well as inanimate. Hence, according to Al-Kindi, something which is in apparent conflict with daily experience is transformed into something reasonable and appealing when suitably interpreted.

In the court of Al-Mamun, Al-Kindi was a star who shone bright in the foremost cultural centre of the world. His academic pursuits maintained their vigour in the subsequent reign of the rationalist Caliph al-Mutassim, and then of al-Wathiq. But then came the ascendancy of the orthodox Sunni Caliph Al-Mutawwakil, and with it the end of a long period of liberalism. It was not hard for the ulema to convince the ruler that the philosopher had very dangerous beliefs. Mutawwakil soon ordered the confiscation of the scholar's personal library, known to all Baghdad as al-Kindiyah. But that was not enough. The sixty-year-old Muslim philosopher also received fifty lashes before a large crowd which had assembled. Observers who recorded the event say the crowd roared approval with each stroke.[4]

Long before his death in 873 at the age of seventy-two, Al-Kindi had succumbed to prolonged depression and silence. Although a friend managed to retrieve his library by means of some subtle extortion, he never really recovered from the ordeal of his public flogging. Al-Kindi was the first major figure of Islamic scholarship to fall victim to the orthodox reaction against rationalism.

Al-Razi (865–925)

Famed as the greatest clinical physician of Islam, Muhammad Ibn Zakariya Al-Razi earned the title of 'Arabic Galen' and 'most brilliant genius of the Middle Ages' for his phenomenal achievements in the field of medicine. Of Persian origin, he received his medical training in Baghdad but later returned as director of a hospital somewhere near modern Teheran. He is said to have been an extraordinarily considerate physician who cared for all his patients, both rich and poor.

Although Al-Razi is best known for his writings on the life sciences, he was also a free thinker and an important philosophical figure who was even more radical than Al-Kindi in his attachment to Greek rationalism. His metaphysical system was said to be anti-prophetic in that he soft-pedalled the importance of revelation. Instead, he asserted, God created man and imparted a part of His reason to him, thereby enabling man to comprehend the material universe. Al-Razi's theory of cosmic creation required that, at the beginning, there existed only God, the soul, matter, space and time. Thereafter the physical world came into being through the intervention of God in a certain predicament of the soul, and after all souls return to their natural abode in heaven the world shall cease to exist. To be sure, this concept of cosmic destiny and transmigration of the soul was not something which fitted too well with the generally held doctrine of creation.

Al-Razi's unconventional views on religion certainly did not endear him with all Muslims. Later writers, though wondering at his erudition, condemned him for blasphemy because he openly spoke of the superiority of reason to revelation. Heterodox Ismailis, such as Nasr-i-Khusrau, also charged him with heresy. For his radical views, Al-Razi had to pay a high price: the relegation of most of his scholarly works to oblivion.

Even Al-Biruni, with the possible motive of trying to please his orthodox patron, openly denounced Al-Razi and attributed his blindness to divine retribution. It is said that the blindness resulted from the punishment meted out to him by an emir who was a member of the conservative Mansur family of Bukhara.[5] This enraged emir ordered Al-Razi be hit on the head with his book until either the book or his head broke. Thereupon Al-Razi lost both his eyesight, as well as his zest for life. When an occulist suggested remedial eye surgery, Al-Razi replied: 'I have seen enough of this world, and I do not cherish the idea of an operation for the hope of seeing more of it.' Shortly thereafter he died.

Ibn Sina (980–1037)

Abu Ali al-Husain Ibn Sina, somewhat like Norbert Wiener in modern times, was a precocious genius whose work spanned vast areas of knowledge. By the age of ten he had memorized the Qur'an to perfection, and by seventeen he was an established physician. In another year or so he had mastered the metaphysics of Aristotle. His magnum opus, *The Canon of Medicine (Al-Qanun)* remained the standard text in the field until the birth of modern medicine. But hakims in those days were not merely practitioners of medicine, and Ibn Sina is the example *par excellence* of a classic man of wisdom. A prodigious worker, his labours span the domains of philosophy and logic, as well as medicine.

Ibn Sina's dedication to Islam was steady but unconventional. The somewhat unusual nature of his commitment is borne out by the following example. During the course of his scholarly labours, he would often be beset with difficulties, in which case:

> If a problem was too great for me, I repaired to the mosque and prayed, invoking the Creator of all things until the gate that had been closed to me was opened and what had been complex became simple. Always, as night fell, I returned to my house, set the lamp before me and buried myself with reading and writing. If sleep overcame me or I felt the flesh growing weak, I had recourse to a beaker of wine, so that my energies were restored.[6]

The unconventional aspect here, needless to say, is the means of revitalization to which Ibn Sina takes recourse. It is characteristic of his distinctive personality and style.

Like his predecessor Al-Kindi, Ibn Sina was a fiercely independent-minded philosopher who insisted on the primacy of reason, although he had disputed the Mu'tazilites on various technical matters. For a time he was vizier to the emir of Hamadan. Here he got into a religious argument with strict believers of the army, and they soon called for his execution. Soldiers came to his house but, not finding him, plundered it and then called on the emir to behead him. Ibn Sina was warned in time and hid at the house of his friend Abu Said Dafdaq, where he worked on his masterpiece *Al-Qanun*.

Ibn Sina fled persecution and the wrath of rulers several times. With his books banned, and powerful enemies plotting against him, his friends counselled moderation. To this he replied: 'I prefer a short life with width to a narrow one with length,' and continued his work undaunted. Ibn Sina's attempted synthesis of religious beliefs with science and logic repeatedly earned for him the wrath of the ulema. Sensitive to allegations of heresy, he defended himself in a famous poem:

> It is not so easy and trifling to call me a heretic
> No belief in religion is firmer than mine own
> I am the unique person in the whole world if I am a heretic
> Then there is not a single Musulman anywhere in the world.[7]

But protestations notwithstanding, Ibn Sina acquired a reputation for heresy among the orthodox both in his own time as well as in later centuries. The most influential of the conservative theologians, Imam Al-Ghazzali, declared him to be an unbeliever, and specifically in 'transmitting the philosophy of Aristotle'.[8]

Like the fundamentalists of bygone ages, fundamentalists of the present day are harsh in their judgement of the great Muslim scholars and scientists. A Saudi-financed magazine based in London published an intemperate outburst:

> The story of famous Muslim scientists of the Middle Ages such as Al-Kindi, Al-Farabi, Ibn-al-Haytham and Ibn Sina shows that, aside from being Muslims, there seems to have been nothing Islamic about them or their achievements. On the contrary, their lives were distinctly unIslamic. Their achievements in medicine, chemistry, physics, mathematics, and philosophy were a natural and logical extension of Greek thought.[9]

An Indian Muslim, Mohammed Kalimur Rehman, writing in a journal of Islamic science, has similar things to say:

> Many of the philosophers were either Mu'tazilites or agnostics. Many of them practised music, astrology and magic, which are either prohibited or not encouraged by Islam . . . . Al-Razi did not believe in revelations, Al-Farabi depended on pure reason (not shariyah) for discriminating between good and bad. Al-Kindi denied divine attributes. Ibn-Sina did not believe in Maad Jismani (resurrection of the body) . . . . There was a gradual loss of Islamic values from the society.[10]

The continuity of thought between modern and ancient orthodoxy is certainly evident; one observes that the passage of centuries has not brought forgiveness for the philosophers of Islam. Note also how their achievements are rejected as 'a natural and logical extension of Greek thought'. This extremist position is remarkably similar — although the reasons for it are different — to that of many Westerners who pour scorn on Muslim achievements in the sciences. Should a non-Muslim have alleged that Muslim science is but a regurgitation of Greek science, one can safely suppose that he would be angrily challenged. But coming from supposed defenders of the faith, these insults to Muslim science and its heroes have drawn little reaction.

Ibn Rushd (1126–1198)

For his role in having forged the vital link between Aristotelian and Renaissance philosophies, Abul Walid Muhammad Ibn Rushd is by far the best known Islamic philosopher in the West. He stood in the foremost ranks of international scholars of repute. During the great philosophical and theological upheavals of medieval times, his works were frequently consigned to the fire and decried as heretical both by the Church and the orthodox Muslim ulema. Because they formed the most detailed and precise commentary on Aristotle, Ibn Rushd's writings were translated into Latin and Hebrew by European scholars. There soon appeared super-commentaries on his commentaries. Many of the writings exist only in these two languages, the original Arabic writings being long lost. This itself is a commentary on the extent to which Ibn Rushd, as a rationalist philosopher, was able to influence the mood of his times.

Like other rationalists before him, Ibn Rushd drew the ire of his opponents for suggesting that revelation must be guided by reason. In his opinion, the noblest form of worship was to study God through His works, using the faculty of the mind. He devised an elaborate scheme for the exegesis of the Qur'an, drawing upon the complex linguistic structure of the Arabic language. But it is for his rebuttal of Al-Ghazzali's arguments that Ibn Rushd is most well known.

Ibn Rushd's dispute with Al-Ghazzali, who preceded him by some 70 years, provides a fascinating view of the issues which engaged the minds of thinkers eight centuries ago. We have encountered in the previous chapter the views of Al-Ghazzali, particularly as they relate to the issue of cause and effect. In Al-Ghazzali's view everything — meaning all actions, events, physical phenomena, or whatever — is the result of continuous divine intervention. In his logic, fire burns a piece of cotton not because it is in the nature of fire to burn a substance but, instead, because of supernatural causes such as the intervention of angels.

But, for Ibn Rushd, it is patent nonsense that a multitude of angels, or other divine agents, should descend everytime a piece of cotton catches fire. Physical cause begets physical effect. One knows from daily experience that cotton put into contact with fire will burn, and it has never been seen to occur otherwise. In his famous rebuttal to Al-Ghazzali's *Tahafut al Falasifa* (*Incoherence of the Philosophers*), entitled *Tahafut-al-Tahafut* (*The Incoherence of the Incoherence*), Ibn Rushd states:

> To deny the existence of efficient causes which are observed in sensible things is sophistry . . . . Denial of cause implies the denial of knowledge, and denial of knowledge implies that nothing in the world can really be known.[11]

Ibn Rushd, as Qazi of Seville and later Cordova, became the victim of political intrigues and a target for the orthodoxy. When the Caliph Abu Yaqub died in 1184, and was succeeded by his son Abu Yusuf, Ibn Rushd soon fell out of favour. A prohibition was issued against the study of logic and science by order of the Caliph. Ibn Rushd was eventually banned from Cordova and was unceremoniously carted off to a small provincial town together with other students of philosophy. All his books, except for some strictly scientific ones, were ordered burnt. It was only towards the end of the 12th century that he was restored to favour, and returned to Marrakesh to die. Most of his writings exist today only in Hebrew and Latin, the original Arabic writings being long lost. This is an indication of the fact that, in spite of his impassioned and articulate rebuttal of Al-Ghazzali's attack on rationalism, Ibn Rushd was unable significantly to influence the trend of his times.

Ibn Khaldun (1332–1406)

The last of the intellectual giants of Muslim civilization, Abd-al-Rahman Ibn Khaldun remained a totally obscure figure until the 19th century, when he was 'discovered' by Western scholars who recognized him as a master of the science of human behaviour and a forerunner of modern anthropology. This rather astonishing neglect was, in the words of Philip Hitti, because:

> This philosopher was born at the wrong time and in the wrong place. He came too late to rouse any response among his people deep in medieval slumber, or to find a would-be translator among Europeans. He had no immediate predecessors and no successors. No school of thought could be styled Khaldunic. His meteoric career flashed across the North African firmament leaving hardly a glare behind.[12]

Remarking on his contributions as a historian and sociologist, Arnold Toynbee wrote of Ibn Khaldun that he had 'conceived and formulated a philosophy of history which is undoubtedly the greatest work of its kind that has been created in any time or place.'

In contrast to the majority of major medieval Islamic scholars, Ibn Khaldun was not a Mu'tazilite; on the contrary, he rejected the basic presuppositions of the Muslim neo-platonists such as al-Farabi and Ibn Sina. Their ontology, doctrine of emanation, and epistemology were anti-religious in his opinion. He remained violently opposed to the practice of alchemy as well.

Nevertheless, Ibn Khaldun's greatest contribution to Islamic thought was as a positivist. To him we owe the formulation of laws of social behaviour and an embryonic science of civilization. He systematically elaborated how topography, demography and economic factors act as sociological determinants. One sentence of his is particularly famous: 'The differences which are seen between the generations are only the expression of the differences which separate them in their economic life'. This sentence ought to be compared with one of Marx who said: 'The method of production in the material matters of life determines in general the social, political and intellectual processes of life.'[13] In some important ways, Ibn Khaldun had anticipated the work of European thinkers of the post-Renaissance era.

For certain orthodox ulema, in spite of his scathing criticism of the

Hellenistic inspired philosophers, Ibn Khaldun remained too much of a rationalist. In particular, it was considered outrageous that he should have applied the concept of *asabiyya* (group loyalty) to prophesy, and have stated that even a religion based on divine revelation required tribal cohesiveness for fulfilment of its mission. Arab scholars were additionally incensed by his often derogatory references to the crude behaviour of Arabs, and to the fact that he attributed most of the glories of the Golden Age to non-Arabs. For example, he wrote:

> It is a remarkable fact, that with few exceptions, most Muslim scholars both in the religious and intellectual sciences have been non-Arabs. When a scholar is of Arab origin, he is non-Arab in language and upbringing and has non-Arab teachers. This is so in spite of the fact that Islam is an Arab religion, and its founder was an Arab.[14]

Ibn Khaldun's family was from Yemen and settled in Spain. Sometimes his detractors would refer to him slightingly as 'an ignorant Berber'. In turn, he writes of the Arabs as a 'savage nation' with a propensity to plunder and destroy.

While many Muslim scholars have simply chosen to ignore Ibn Khaldun, others have lashed out at him.[15] For example:

• Sami Shawkat, a former Director General of Education in Iraq and head of a para-military youth organization, in a speech delivered in Baghdad in 1933 entitled The Profession of Death, called for the excavation of the grave of Ibn Khaldun, and preached that his books be burnt all over the Arab world.[16]

• Taha Husain, the modernist Egyptian scholar, describes Ibn Khaldun as a man with an obnoxiously inflated ego and a dishonest rationalist who merely masqueraded as a Muslim.[17]

It is a sad commentary on the state of Muslim scholarship that Ibn Khaldun remained a virtual nonentity until he was discovered by Orientalists. Now that he has their stamp of recognition, many scholars — excepting Arab racialists and the extreme orthodox — have entered into a competition to see whose encomiums are the loudest.

References

1. Hayawan, 1st ed. (Cairo, 1325), Vol. 1, p. 80, quoted by B. Lewis in *Islam in History*, (New York, The Library Press, 1973).

2. *Encyclopedia of Islam*, ed. E. J. Brill, (Leiden, 1971), Vol. 3, p. 912.

3. Abu Rida, *Rasail Al-Kindi Al-Falsafiya*, p. 97, translated by A. J. Arberry in *Revelation and Reason in Islam*, (London, George Allen & Unwin, 1957), p. 35.

4. *The Genius of Arab Civilization*, ed. J. R. Hayes, (Mass., MIT Press, 1983), p. 69.

5. Edwin P. Hoyt, *Arab Science*, (Nashville, Thomas Nelson, 1975), pp. 60–4.

6. Ibid., p. 66.

7. Quoted in S. H. Nasr, *Islamic Cosmological Doctrines*, (London, Thames & Hudson), p. 183.

8. W. Montgomery Watt, *The Faith and Practice of Al-Ghazzali*, (London, George Allen & Unwin, 1953), pp. 32–3.

9. Javed Ansari, 'This is a Formula for Isalmic Scientific Impotence', *Arabia: The Islamic World Reveiw*, 20, (April 1983), pp. 54–5.

10. M. Kaleemur Rehman, *MAAS Journal of Islamic Science*, Vol. 3, No. 1, pp. 45–56.

11. Averroes, *Tahafut al-Tahufat*, (*The Incoherence Of the Incoherence*), translated by S. Van Den Bergh, (London, E. J. W. Gibb Memorial Series, Vol. 1), p. 317.

12. Philip K. Hitti, *Makers of Arab History*, (New York, St. Martin's Press, 1968), p. 254.

13. See Ref. 2, p. 830.

14. Ibn Khaldun, *Muqadimma*, translated by F. Rosenthal, (New Jersey, Princeton University Press, 1967), Vol. 3, p. 311.

15. An account of the reaction against Ibn Khaldun can be found in Shaukat Ali, *Intellectual Foundations of Muslim Civilization*, (Lahore, United Publishers, 1977), pp. 93–191.

16. William L. Cleveland, *The Making of an Arab Nationalist*, (New Jersey, Princeton University Press, 1971), pp. 63–4.

17. Hitti, op. cit., p. 256.

11. Why Didn't the Scientific Revolution Happen in Islam?

Every great civilization writes its own history, selectively extracts data from the past, and then proves to its satisfaction that its greatness has no peer or rival. The dominant civilization of our times, the West, has also defined a vision of cultural and intellectual history wherein the development of science is presented as the unilinear and inexorable march of Greco-Roman ideas into the European Renaissance period. It is only over the last few decades that there has been some widening of perspective, and beginnings of a realization that the roots of science are to be found in highly diverse cultural and temporal locations. Principally because of the work of historians of science like Sarton and Needham, the role of other major civilizations — particularly the Islamic, Chinese and Hindu — can no longer be peremptorily dismissed as before.

Given the fact that, at the peak of their glory, all the major civilizations had made creditable advances in human knowledge, it becomes a viable hypothesis that any one of them could have fathered the Scientific Revolution. But the historical fact is that it was in the West where modern science began. Why the West? For sociologists like Max Weber — whose work profoundly influenced Western perspectives on Oriental civilizations — the reason is to be found in the superiority of the collective European mind. Weber had gone so far as to suggest that Europeans are genetically endowed with comparatively greater amounts of rationality, thereby allowing for the speedier development of a rational capitalist ethic.

Such racialist arguments are not worthy of serious discussion. For one thing, the rapid growth of scientific culture in many non-European countries today provides an obvious refutation of the claim that the European mind has a monopoly on scientific thought. But there are still many questions left to answer and debate. In particular, why did the Scientific Revolution not take place within Islamic civilization between say, the 9th and the 13th centuries? This question is not absurd. A Martian visiting planet Earth in 1100 AD would have concluded that the Arabs were by far the most advanced civilization.

Five centuries of Islamic scientific and intellectual leadership could have, but did not, lead to the emergence of a modern, universal system of modern science. Obviously, the explanations one puts forth must necessarily be speculative. There is no laboratory in which to observe how the germs of scientific progress, when injected into different social environments, respond to different nutrients and conditions. But even if the internal complexity of human society and the diverse nature of external influences upon it preclude the isolation of a single factor, the arguments and partial attempts at explanation can be interesting, rewarding and perhaps important. This brings before us matters whose domains range from philosophy and law, to economics and politics. Hard though these questions may be, they are not irrelevant; some of the forces which retarded scientific development in Muslim societies in the past are operative today as well.

In seeking to answer the question which forms the title of this chapter, it appears fruitful to consider five distinct sets of causes:

- Those related to matters of attitude and philosophy;
- Those deriving from a certain concept of education;
- Those which are the consequence of the particular nature of Islamic law;
- Those which can be traced to the non-existence, or weakness, of certain socio-economic formations such as autonomous cities and trade guilds;
- Those deriving from the particular character of politics in Islam.

It can be argued that these causes are not independent; each does influence the other. For example, attitudes and philosophies are shaped by the level of sophistication of productive forces in a society — it is an obvious fact that people living in cities think and behave very differently from those in villages. But the reverse is also true. The successful assimilation of new productive forces into the economic structure of society does demand certain attitudinal requirements as a prerequisite. Similarly, education necessarily reflects existing beliefs, but can also be a vehicle of change. So, rather than engage in an extensive debate of which is the cause and which the effect, we shall be satisfied by identifying what appear to be plausible and logical explanations.

Reasons of Attitude and Philosophy

The acquisition of positive, rational knowledge — or, what is more or less the same thing, the pursuit of science — is determined to a great degree by the overall idea system which prevails at a given time in society. Overall idea systems — by which is meant beliefs, attitudes, social mores, general assumptions, and specific religious and ideological positions — are of the most profound importance in human history. Julian Huxley compared them to skeletons in biological evolution: they provide the framework for the life that animates and clothes them, and in large measure determine the way it shall be lived.

The notion of rationality — which is so crucial to science — exists within every idea system although the importance assigned to it may vary. What does rationality mean? The 19th century philosopher Nietzsche gave a succinct definition: rationality is a matrix of connections which assigns cause to effect. Looking for the roots of rationality, Nietzsche delved deep into the psychobiological roots of epistemology. He argued that rationality is an inescapable consequence of what he calls man's 'will to power'. Buried in the human psyche, he argued, is a deeply seated — and possibly inexplicable — urge to have control over the events of the outer world. This 'will to power' is the psychological mainspring of all creative activity. Rationality is essential for the sublimation of this urge because without it there can be no chance for any human control over events or conscious social change. Stripped of the 'will to power', humans become mere buoys that float on the waves.

Armed with this, we can proceed to ask the question: what impels one society to nurture science to a degree which is greater or lesser than in another society? If science is viewed as a consequence of man's 'will to power', then the answer is to be found precisely in the fact that societies, like individuals, differ greatly in the extent to which they possess this inherent drive. One would expect that the search for causal connections — rationality — will become less intense once it is admitted that God's will forms part of the matrix of connections. That is, the greater is divine intervention in the affairs of the outside world and the smaller the influence of mortal will on the Divine Will, the less scope there is for any exercise of the 'will to power'. If divine intervention is complete, then curiosity, imagination, and ambition become superfluous. A society oriented towards fatalism, or one in which an interventionist deity forms part of the matrix of causal connections, is bound to produce fewer individuals inclined to probe the unknown with the tools of science.

In the heyday of its intellectual and scientific development, Islamic society was not a fatalistic society. The fierce debates between those believing in free will (the Qadarites) and the predestinarians (the Jabrias) were generally resolved in favour of the former. But the gradual hegemony of fatalistic Asharite doctrines mortally weakened the 'will to power' of Islamic society and led to a withering away of its scientific spirit. Asharite dogma insisted on the denial of any connection between cause and effect — and therefore repudiated rational thought. It also rejected secondary causality, the notion that God is ultimately responsible for everything but only through the laws He has made for the world.

The anti-science nature of the Asharites is evident from their belief that any kind of prediction is impossible. Even a speeding arrow may or may not reach its destination, they said, because at each moment along its path God destroys the world and then creates it afresh at the next moment. Where the arrow will be at the next moment, given that it was at a particular spot at an earlier moment, cannot be predicted because it is God alone who knows how the world is to be recreated. We have also encountered the views of Al-Ghazzali — who was the most influential of the Asharites — in detail in an earlier chapter. In fervently denying the existence of causal connections, he went so far as to say, as we saw, that a piece of cotton does not burn merely because fire was put to it but, instead, because God intervenes either directly or through his angels. Al-Ghazzali ends one of his arguments on the subject saying: 'And this refutes the claim of those who profess that fire is the agent of burning, bread the agent of satiety, medicine the agent of health, and so on.'[1] The eventual preponderance of such fatalistic attitudes, the denial of independent judgement, and rejection of the Greek rationalizing culture, made it harder for any important intellectual advance to occur, much less allow for a Scientific Revolution.

A second factor which discouraged learning for learning's sake was the increasingly utilitarian character of post Golden Age Islamic society. Utilitarianism — the notion that the only desirable things are those which are useful — was not an obsession of Islamic society in the early days of its intellectual development. When, for example, Caliph al-Mamun created the Bait-ul-Hikmah in Baghdad and sent emissaries far and wide to seek manuscripts on matters of learning and science, the basic motive was altruistic rather than materialistic. Indeed, the possibility of material reward in the form of improved or new technology was virtually non-existent because the relation of ancient science to ancient technology was far removed from the one that obtains today. Although there are exceptions to which one may point, like alchemy and medicine, knowledge was not principally valued for utilitarian ends. But eventually the notion that the only useful knowledge is practical knowledge, and the inevitable denigration of theoretical knowledge, permeated throughout Islamic society. This was coincident with a growing rigidity of dogma and a closing of the doors of theological enquiry.

We can witness the lack of interest in 'useless' theoretical knowledge among Muslims beginning around the 14th century, and continuing well into our own times. Even Ibn Khaldun, the most celebrated thinker of the Muslim Middle Ages, showed only mild curiosity about goings-on elsewhere in the world:

> We learn by report that in the lands of the Franks on the north shores of the sea, philosophical sciences are much in demand, their principles are being revived, the circles for teaching them are numerous, and the number of students seeking to learn them is increasing.[2]

But Ibn Khaldun did not see this as an alarming development or an occasion for trying to emulate the Franks. On the contrary, he remained bitterly opposed to the study of philosophy as well as alchemy. His attitudes reflect the mood of his time, which had lost the spirit of free enquiry.

The same lack of curiosity was shown by subsequent generations of Muslims. We see this in the attitude of the Turkish Ottomans who, in the 16th century, had established an extensive and magnificent empire. Ottoman rulers did recognize the utility of some recent technological inventions of the West and they even appropriated some of these. But they were not inclined to allow advances in thought or to recognize that technology was a consequence of scientific thinking. This was observed, for example, by Ghiselin de Busbecq, ambassador of the Holy Roman Empire in Istanbul, in a letter dated 1560 in which he wrote that:

> No nation has shown less reluctance to adopt the useful invention of others; for example, they have appropriated to their own use large and small cannons and

many other of our discoveries. They have, however, never been able to bring themselves to print books and set up public clocks. They hold that their scriptures, that is, their sacred books, would no longer be scriptures if they were printed; and if they established public clocks, they think that the authority of their muezzins and their ancient rites would suffer diminution.[3]

The general lack of interest among Ottoman Muslims in the recently discovered wonders of science is also reflected in an embassy report by Mustafa Hatti Efendi, who went on a mission to Vienna in 1748. While he was there, the Turkish entourage was invited by the Emperor to visit an observatory, where various strange devices and objects were kept. Efendi and his group were not impressed:

> The third contrivance consisted of small glass bottles which we saw them strike against stone and wood without breaking them. Then they put fragments of flint in the bottles, whereupon these finger-thick bottles, which had withstood the impact of stone, dissolved like flour. When we asked the meaning of this, they said that when glass was cooled in cold water straight from the fire, it became like this. We ascribe this preposterous answer to Frankish trickery.[4]

The utilitarian spirit was also shared by the Mughuls who ruled over India from 1480 until the victory of the British in 1757. In the reign of Akbar there had been a marked enthusiasm for useful technology. Right-angled gearing, distillation of alcohol and perfumes, lenses for spectacles and telescopes, water cooling using saltpetre, etc. made their appearance in India in Akbar's time. Around the middle of the 17th century, large numbers of ships resembling the modern ships of the European imperial fleets were built in India. But for all this, and the undisputed magnificence of Mughal architecture, history does not credit them with significant intellectual achievements such as the establishment of universities, observatories, or encouragement of positivistic thought.

Utilitarianism — and a thinly veiled anti-intellectualism — are, of course, to be found aplenty in modern times as well. For example, the science adviser to the late President Zia, Mr M. A. Kazi, minced no words on the subject:

> In Islam there is no science for the sake of science and there is no knowledge for the sake of knowledge. Everything is for an end, which is using scientific knowledge for the good of humanity at large.[5]

The Saudis, for their part, have made no secret of their liking for the comforts provided by the wonders of modern technology, and for their dislike for theoretical, scientific knowledge. There is little doubt that they fear the liberating effect it has on the minds of men, and the dangers it holds in store for a rigidly hierarchical and dynastic society where the leaders derive their legitimacy by appeal to divine sanction.

The present dominance of utilitarian values in Muslim society does not augur well for the development of science. When people are determined to care for nothing except what is directly and obviously useful, they become incapable of developing abstract thought and creating the intellectual apparatus for science which, by necessity, must be far removed from what is obviously visible or useful. An Iranian physicist succinctly states the case:

Only true spiritual societies have been able to develop science . . . . It is inherent in a utilitarian society that it is unsympathetic to true spiritual values . . . . A nation which has no great philosophers will never have any great scientists. Heidegger says that the philosopher is a man who is always capable of wonder. This also characterizes the scientist. The utilitarian man is not capable of wonder. Hence, it is doubtful whether he can develop science.[6]

The Role of Muslim Education

The ultimate values and goals to which a society aspires are to be found in the manner by which it educates its young. It is here where one faces squarely the question of whether the society values transformation and change, or whether it prefers the existing order or the past instead.

It is useful to enumerate clearly the distinctions between traditional religious and modern secular education. For they define two radically different models

	Traditional Education	*Modern Education*
(1)	Other-worldly orientation	Modern orientation
(2)	Aims at socialization into Islam	Aims at the development of individuality
(3)	Curricula unchanged since medieval times	Curricula respond to changes in subject
(4)	Knowledge is revealed and unchallengeable	Knowledge is obtained through empirical and deductive processes
(5)	Knowledge is acquired because of a divine command	Knowledge is needed as a problem-solving tool
(6)	Questioning of precepts and assumptions not welcomed	Questioning of precepts and assumptions welcomed
(7)	Teaching style basically authoritarian	Teaching style involves student participation
(8)	Memorization is crucial	Internalization of key concepts is crucial
(9)	Mind set of student is passive-receptive	Mind set of student is active-positivistic
(10)	Education is largely undifferentiated	Education can get very specialized

of educational philosophy and have two radically different sets of goals and methods. In the jargon of social scientists, these are called ideal types.[7] The contrast will be made between a pure, hence theoretical, version of traditional religious education and a corresponding pure version of modern education. The table on the previous page encapsulates the differences.

While the notion of ideal types is necessarily an abstraction, the above archetypes effectively distinguish between the two fundamentally different approaches to education. It also suggests that the rote nature of education in contemporary Muslim societies can be traced to attitudes inherited from traditional education, wherein knowledge is something to be acquired rather than discovered, and in which the attitude of mind is passive and receptive rather than creative and inquisitive. The social conditioning of an authoritarian traditional environment has, as an inescapable consequence, that all knowledge comes to be viewed as unchangeable and all books tend to be memorized or venerated to some degree. The concept of secular knowledge as a problem-solving tool which evolves over time is alien to traditional thought.

Because the teacher derived his power and authority from unchallengeable sources, the style of traditional teaching was inevitably authoritarian. In Moghul India, as in village schools even today, the teacher, muallim, or ustad, sat facing his students arranged in rows in a semi-circle before him. At the end of a dictation or commentary on a text, he would rise with the words: 'And Allah knows best'. Thereafter, the students would reverently kiss his right hand and disperse.

The static, rote-centred concept of education has roots which can be traced back into history, beginning with the Nizammiyah curriculum devised in the 11th century. This curriculum was faithfully passed on to subsequent generations, and adopted in unchanged form in Mughul India. The emphasis was largely on memorization of the Qur'an and Hadith. Ibn Khaldun, in a comparative study of education in Muslim lands of the 14th century, pointed out that only in Muslim Spain and Persia were subjects such as poetry, grammar and arithmetic included in the syllabi. Elsewhere, subjects unrelated to the Qur'an were regarded as being too secular to teach to children. The pupil would copy a verse on to his tablet, memorize it, and then erase it to make space for the subsequent verse. One old book recorded that during the Abbasid period, school pupils used to have Qur'anic reading half the morning and, except for some recreation, writing for the remainder of the day. On Tuesday afternoons and Thursday mornings, the boys corrected what they had written.

Traditional education, with its emphasis on perfect memorization, created its own standards of excellence and role models. Among those who are quoted is Muhammad ibn-Ziyad al-Arabi of al-Kufah, who died at Samarra in 840 AD, and who is said to have met with a hundred pupils.[8] He dictated to them for ten years, during which time nobody ever saw a manuscript in his hand because he had such a prodigious memory. As another example, one 9th century author says with great awe that: 'Murarraj had a better memory than other people. He caught a passage from me and remembered it all night long, repeating it the next day, although it was about fifty pages long.' Yet another story is told about a scholar who went from Baghdad to Sijistan to give a course of lectures. In order to avoid carrying books, he memorized the traditions to which he wished to refer. The story was that, although he quoted 30,000 traditions about the Prophet, the persons checking his lectures were unable to find more than three mistakes.

Following the end of the Golden Age of Islam around the 13th century, Muslim education simply ceased to change. The curriculum was so restricted in scope that even Aurangzeb, the arch-conservative Mughal emperor, felt compelled to direct harsh words to his erstwhile teacher:

> What did you teach me? You told me that the land of Franks is a small island where the greatest king had previously been the ruler of Portugal, then the king of Holland and now the king of England. You told me about the kings of France and Spain that they are like our petty rulers . . . . Glory be to God! What a knowledge of geography and history you displayed! Was it not your duty to instruct me in the characteristics of the nations of the world — the products of these countries, their military power, their methods of warfare, their customs, ways of government and political policies?
>
> You never considered what academic training is requisite for a prince. All you thought necessary for me was that I become an expert in grammar and learn subjects suitable for a judge or a jurist.[9]

What Aurangzeb was pointing out was the narrow scope of learning, which more or less excluded general knowledge and the natural sciences. Religious learning, with grammar and literature as the supporting instruments, totally dominated education. The private curriculum of Shah Waliullah (d. 1761) was relatively wider in scope and included some amount of mathematics, astronomy and medicine. But secular learning always remained a low priority among Muslims of the sub-continent. Moreover, even where some degree of free enquiry and experimentation was permitted, the implications of that were firmly limited to the world of inert matter and not allowed to intrude into religious and cultural domains.

This state of affairs persisted until the beginning of the 19th century when the British sought to introduce 'European science', and a system of modern management and accounting into the schools of the sub-continent. The two major communities, the Hindus and Muslims, reacted differently to this decision. The Hindus welcomed it enthusiastically, and pressed the British to give more opportunities for secular education and establish more colleges and schools.

The Muslims, on the other hand, looked upon the British decision with suspicion and resentment. In part this was because the British had forcibly put an end to centuries of Muslim rule in India. Hence, 'European science' was seen as a ruse of the enemy for subverting the Islamic religion and culture. The resistance to science was heightened by the characteristic arrogance of the imperialists who openly ridiculed past Muslim achievements in science. For example, in a speech on 2nd February 1835, Lord Macaulay derisively referred to:

[Muslim] medical doctrines which would disgrace an English farrier, astronomy which would move laughter in girls at an English boarding house school, history abounding with kings thirty feet high and reigns thirty thousand years long, and geography made of seas of treacle and seas of butter.[10]

A combination of hurt, pride, defiance and conservatism led the Muslims to reject modern learning. The ulema were particularly hostile and, after Macaulay's decision in 1835 to introduce modern education throughout India, a petition was signed by 8,000 ulema in Calcutta asking the government to exempt Muslims.[11] It is said that the Education Bill was partly responsible for the bloody events of 1857. Parents kept their children away from schools, preferring either to keep them at home or send them to madrassahs. Social pressure, including threats and derision, was applied against the small number of parents who defied the ban. Used to the bygone glories of the Mughal era, Muslims considered most intellectual work, including accountancy and bookkeeping, as fit for low-caste Hindus only. This was the bleak environment in which Syed Ahmed Khan started the battle for Muslim educational reform, a battle which he won but only partly.

To conclude, rote learning and authoritarianism are the inevitable products of traditional learning, and such learning is natural for a society in equilibrium. But when society evolves towards greater complexity, it cannot rigidly adhere to the simplicity of past patterns and must search for solutions which satisfy the needs of progress while maintaining some level of historical and cultural continuity. The inability of the traditional system of education to respond adequately to a changing world may well have been the most critical factor which denied to Muslims the chance of spearheading the Scientific Revolution.

The Role of Muslim Law

The Scientific and Industrial Revolution of post-Renaissance Europe was not a creation of philosophers and thinkers alone; it was a very complex economic and social phenomenon as well. Advances in technology certainly gave rise to powerful new means of production, but it was the European bourgeoisie which harnessed the technical progress and ultimately brought about the metamorphosis of a feudal society into a modern capitalist one. The bourgeoisie, following Marx, can be defined as a class capable of coordinating the means of production and of bringing about fundamental structural transformations by making innovations and investments. Marx, while recognizing the vital role that the bourgeoisie played in transforming society, also identified it as the exploiter and natural enemy of the working class.

Asking why the Scientific Revolution did not occur in Islam is practically equivalent to asking why Islam did not produce a powerful bourgeois class. It has been argued, particularly by Weber and his followers, that the nature and practice of Islamic Law was instrumental in discouraging the emergence of a bourgeoisie and nascent capitalism. We shall now explore this claim.

The Weberian argument goes something like this. The existence of a bourgeois class makes essential the existence of a legal system which can resolve disputes over property rights, contractual obligations, banking and financial transactions, etc. Legal judgements should be derivable from rational laws as opposed to arbitrary ones, and the scope of these laws should be broad enough to cover the wide range of problems and cases which occur in a complex economic environment. New laws are needed for new situations, and these must be consistent in spirit with the existing laws. Legal rationality is a prerequisite for modern capitalism; without a coherent and comprehensive legal system, the economic system would soon fall to pieces.

The secular and rationalized legal framework needed for the emergence of capitalism, the argument continues, is incompatible with the nature of Islamic law. The latter is inseparable from ethics and religious belief, and as such is not rooted in clearly definable principles. It derives entirely from the revelations and traditions of the Prophet. The legal activity of a qazi (judge) amounts to discovering a sacred legal tradition and holding it to be applicable to the case in hand. In Islam, claim the Weberians, there is no law-making, only law-finding. The absence of a sharp distinction between Islamic ethics and law means that a coherent legal system cannot put at the service of the bourgeoisie in order to protect private property within a comprehensive, rational system. And so, Weber argued that because:

> religious courts had jurisdiction over land cases, capitalistic exploitation of the land was impossible, as, for instance, in Tunisia . . . . The whole situation is typical of the way in which theocratic judicial administration has interfered and must necessarily interfere with the operation of a rational economic system.[12]

In strictly formal and textual terms, Weberians are probably right in arguing that the Islamic Shariat is hostile to important elements of capitalism, and this did block the emergence of institutional banking along the lines the Europeans were then developing. It is also true that the Shariat is an almost immutable set of rules which cannot be changed according to the times. As a matter of fact, the four legal schools operative among Sunnis today have been unchanged from the time that they were founded, respectively, by Malik Ibn Anas (d. 795), Abu Hanifa (d. 767), Mohammed Ibn Idris al-Shafi'i (d. 820), and Ahmad Ibn Hanbal (d. 855). The differences between them stem entirely from the different weights they attach to various Qur'anic verses and the degree of validity which is assigned to various Prophetic traditions. Between these schools, all major problems of Islamic jurisprudence had been resolved by the end of the 11th century. With this the doors of *ijtihad* were formally closed.

But the actual impact of the Shariat in determining the direction of economic development in Muslim society cannot simply be inferred from formal arguments. In actual practice, various injunctions of the Shariat have been effectively bypassed by Muslims throughout the ages whenever important economic or political interests have been at stake. The French Islamist, Maxime Rodinson, argues that, for example, the Islamic prohibition on lending money at interest had never stopped the practice of usury on a large scale in Muslim society. The practical effect of the ban was to create ingenious methods of circumvention. These methods have a name in Arabic: *hiyal*, meaning ruses, or wiles. Entire books, dating back to the 9th century, are devoted to expounding various forms of *hiyal*. Rodinson's book *Islam and Capitalism* contains a fascinating account of the past and present practice of circumvention.

Exponents of the Shariat argue that it is all-encompassing; international trade, joint stock companies, loans from foreign donors, principles of taxation, etc. involve issues of Islamic law. But the fact is that these have not even been seriously raised or debated, much less resolved. In consequence, one finds that all Islamic countries have definite rules governing essentially economic matters which derive from secular, universalistic legal principles. It could be argued, for example, that Islamic law should bar Islamic countries from accepting loans with interest from non-Islamic or Islamic countries. But in practice the Shariat has not influenced the attitudes on this issue. In their domestic policies too, modern Islamic states pay only lip service to the Shariat. For example, the insistence of certain fundamentalists that all depictions of the human face be banned has not prevented the modern state from imposing the requirement that citizens possess identification cards with pictures, or led to a ban on television broadcasting. The need of the state to impose its control over the population is clearly the dominant force.

One can identify numerous other instances where even religious authorities transparently violate the Shariat — in spirit if not in letter. One example is the overwhelming approval by the local ulema of the heroin trade in the deeply religious area of Pakistan's Frontier province. The religious arguments given to legitimize trade in this narcotic are entirely specious. Clearly, material interests are capable of overpowering moral, ethical and religious considerations.

To conclude, although the development of capitalism in Islamic lands would have been favoured by a relatively fixed set of codified rules based on rational principles, there is no compelling evidence that in actual practice the Shariat alone prevented the Muslim world from developing along this road. Our search for the causes of non-development of a modern industrial Islamic culture cannot therefore end here.

Economic Causes

When Muslim lands were invaded and colonized by imperial powers in the 18th century, Muslim society was in a state of frozen medievalism. There was no Islamic bourgeoisie which could use advances in technology to bring about the transformation from a feudal society to a capitalist one. In spite of this, it is sometimes claimed that India and Egypt were on the point of arriving at a capitalist socio-economic formation when the onset of colonial rule interrupted their natural development. Such claims cannot, of course, be rejected out of hand. But two important elements militated against the growth of an indigenous bourgeois class — the existence of an urban ruling class based on a stable system of extraction from the peasantry, and the absence of autonomous cities and trade guilds which played such an important role in the development of European capitalism.

These two factors will be examined more closely below.

Extractive Economy

Whether the case be that of Arab lands under the Ottomans or Indian under the Mughals, Islamic civilization has been very definitely urban based. Villagers have had little cultural contact with the city civilization aside from selling produce to city dwellers, and they lived a remote and backward existence in an entirely self-enclosed world. Caliphs and kings appointed local governors and officials who ensured that peasants would continue to supply revenue and food. Even in conditions of famine, the city would be better off than the village.

The parasitic dependence of the city on the villages, and the assured supply of food and revenue, substantially reduced the incentive for technological advances in production. In this pre-capitalist society, the aim of production was immediate consumption, albeit regulated by traditions and the prevalent hierarchical structure. The aim was not the improvement or development of new productive forces. The stability of this system of extraction may explain why Indian society under the Mughals, though brilliant in many respects, remained essentially medieval. A noted scholar of the history of science in India, Irfan Habib of Aligarh Muslim University, first raises and then answers the question of why Mughal nobles and learned men showed so little urge to obtain knowledge of mechanical devices:

> An explanation may lie in the economic position of the Mughal nobility. The Mughal ruling class was based on an internally stable system of extraction of agrarian surplus, its transfer to towns through sale of foodstuffs and raw materials, and the existence in the towns of a large urban population offering craft-goods and services of all kinds. So long as an internal agrarian crisis did not break out, the Mughal ruling class had little scarcity of resources and little sense of deprivation in not obtaining the mechanical toys from Europe. Only in war weaponry was this need felt; and this could be met by importing European guns as well as gunners.[13]

Habib also explores the possibility that the fairly sizeable amount of merchant capital which existed could have been a source for investing in new technology, and hence that, left to itself, capitalist development in Indian society would have soon followed. But the conclusion is negative:

> Workshops or karkhanas owned by them also existed. But . . . . these were set up mainly when the raw material was too expensive to be given out to the artisans at home. The tools apparently remained those of the artisan. Thus there was no development of even primitive machine-capital, which might in time have attracted larger investment for the installation of technological improvements. There is the possibility too that the merchants earning

excessively large profits out of the commerce in commodities and luxuries for a very small ruling class possessed of immense wealth had little inclination to invest in devices that were irrelevant to the established commercially rewarding trades. In essence, then, we come back to our major thesis that the agrarian exploitation pursued successfully by the Mughal Empire made its economy immune, by and large, to the temptations of imitating European technology until it was too late.[14]

Autonomous Institutions

In his analysis of the rise of European capitalism, Weber argued that the autonomous European city was important to the growth of a free associational life, as well as the development of trade and professional guilds, and hence was instrumental in the emergence of a unified social and legal community. Most European cities in the middle ages were legally autonomous, maintained garrisons, and were internally cohesive in the face of external challenges. This was made possible because these social institutions were not set within a rigid, lasting patrimonial order. Weber credited the particular nature of Christianity for stimulating this growth in social order, but his arguments in support of this contention are not very convincing. Nevertheless, the importance of autonomous social institutions does seem to have a logical bearing on the development of capitalism.

In this context, the tradition of Islamic city life appears to have been rather different as compared to European cities. In Muslim lands, cities were externally controlled by the ruling dynasties and trade, transport and military life dominated by them. External control meant that municipal institutions either did not develop, or had little effective role in governing the life of the city. Therefore, instead of being an integrated whole, the city in Arab lands as well as Mughal India was a collection of heterogeneous self-contained cells which regulated mosques and other community facilities. Affiliation to a particular group or sect was an important part of the social consciousness. Elements of this structure are visible today as well.

While the fragmented nature of city life did not allow for the development of corporate institutions, Islamic craft guilds were quite similar to those in European cities.[15] As a matter of fact, guilds or corporations are known to have existed in Islamic society as far back as the 9th century. They included professions ranging from jewellers, doctors, teachers, water carriers, carpenters, and even prostitutes and thieves. However, the degree of control over the guilds by the external authorities was considerably greater. Perhaps the major motivation was to prevent the guilds from emerging as focal points of resistance to taxation. So, the guilds were in fact created and controlled by the state which determined norms of work, organization, training, the type and quality of product, and the prices at which finished goods could be sold. It is perhaps indicative of the extent of control that in 1807 strict orders were issued to the cobblers of Istanbul not to make boots, shoes and slippers with pointed toes as these were contrary to ancient tradition.[16] It seems to be the case that:

Islamic guilds were not, therefore, organizations created by workmen to protect themselves and their craft; they were organizations created by the state to supervise the craft and workmen and above all to protect the state from autonomous institutions.[17]

Extrapolating from the European experience, one can surmise that the existence of autonomous institutions would have stimulated the growth of industry in Islamic lands and allowed it to maintain the lead which it possessed over the rest of the world until the 14th century. At that time, industry in Islamic lands consisted mainly of paper making in Iraq, Syria, North Africa and Spain; and production of textiles, clothes, carpets, shoes, etc. In Spain there was open-cast mining of iron ore and copper, ship-building, and metal-working. Unfortunately metal and machine industries did not exist and industrial goods from Islamic lands could not compete with the already industrializing West. Although some of the ancient crafts such as glassmaking, metal-working etc. did retain their fine quality, by the beginning of the 18th century the symmetry which had once existed between East and West had been totally lost.

Political Factors

In 1258, when the Mongol marauder Halaku Khan sacked Baghdad, he had the reigning Caliph kicked to death and the Abbasid Caliphate was abolished. Chroniclers of the times say that 800,000 corpses were heaped up on the streets of the city. Irrigation works were destroyed, and conditions of famine arose. What had once been the centre of Islamic culture and civilization was now no more.

But it is important to note, disastrous as they were, the Mongol depredations came at a time when Islamic civilization had already entered a state of decline. The caliphs had lost their power to secular sultans, and the institution of the caliphate had been tottering at the time it was abolished. Further, though the damage inflicted by the invasions was considerable, their effect was localized to Iraq and, to a lesser extent, Syria. The Muslim civilization in Spain and the Maghreb was unaffected. Moreover, the marauders gradually converted to Islam and began a new period of cultural and economic development. One cannot, therefore, blame external political factors alone. Rather there were elements internal to the society which played a very important role in arresting its economic, political and intellectual evolution.

The fact that a powerful Islamic capitalist bourgeoisie did not emerge, and the weakness of autonomous institutions like cities and trade guilds, was closely connected with the fact that the caliphate in Islam — setting aside the case of the first four pious caliphs — was not determined by institutionalized, well-defined procedures which would ensure continuity of policy or encourage alternate centres of power. In principle, as in Al-Mawardi's theory of the caliphate, the caliph was supposed to conform to high ideals of piety and justice. But, in practice, the reins of government could be seized by intriguers, or those who wielded the greatest power. The divorce of ethical ideals from the exercise of temporal power by caliphs was recognized by Al-Ghazzali:

> An evil-doing and barbarous sultan, so long as he is supported by military force, so that he can only with difficulty be deposed and that attempt to depose him would cause unendurable strife, must of necessity be left in possession, and obedience must be rendered to him, exactly as obedience must be rendered to emirs . . . . Government in these days is a consequence solely of military power, and whoever he may be to whom the holder of military power gives his allegiance, that person is the caliph.[18]

In comparing Islamic political history to that of Europe, one is immediately confronted by the radically different way in which religion entered the sphere of politics. The Christian Church was an all-powerful institution which commanded the total allegiance of its subjects and which, from the centre of the papacy in Rome, made and unmade kingships as far away as England and France. The tyranny exercised by the Church left no room for dissent. The inquisitions it instituted against suspected heretics form one of the most dreadful chapters of human history. Only after the Lutheran Reformation was its authority tempered.

In contrast to this, Islam had no Church and no formal centre of tyrannical religious authority. Thus the level of persecution of Islamic scholars and thinkers was much less than in Europe; there is nothing like the Inquisition in Islamic history. One can credit this fact to the nature of Islamic belief, which admits a greater freedom of interpretation of doctrine. But this freedom also led to the absence of a central political–religious authority which could resolve or mediate disputes. Usurpers could seize state power and claim religious leadership, they could turn disputes over territory or power into an occasion for *jehad* (holy war), or they could mobilize religious sentiments of the masses to suppress minority or unorthodox religious groups. The process of splintering into new sects was also aided by the absence of a centralized Church. Paradoxically, a superior moral position — the right of the individual to interpret doctrine without the aid of priests — appears to have led to a systemic organizational weakness which proved fatal to Islamic political and economic — not to speak of scientific and technological — power in the long run.

References

1. Averroes, *Tahafut Al-Tahafut (The Incoherence of the Incoherence)*, translated by S. Van den Bergh (London: Luzac and Co., 1954), I, p. 318.

2. Ibn Khaldun, quoted in *The Arabs* by Peter Mansfield, (Harmondsworth, Penguin Books, 1987), p. 102.

3. Quoted in B. Lewis, *The Muslim Discovery of Europe*, (New York, W. W. Norton, 1982), pp. 232–3.

4. Ibid., p. 232.

5. M. A. Kazi in 'Knowledge For What?', (Proceedings of the Seminar on the Islamization of Knowledge, Islamic University, Islamabad, 1982), p. 69.

6. Mohammad Hussein Saffouri in *Islamic Cultural Identity and Scientific-Technological Development*, Klaus Gottstein (ed.), (Baden-Baden, Nomos, 1986), p. 92.

7. An informative discussion on the past and present of Muslim education can be found in *Modernization of Muslim Education*, (Lahore, Islamic Book Service, 1983).

8. *Muslim Education in Medieval Times*, Bayard Dodge, (Washington D.C., The Middle East Institute, 1962), p. 11.

9. S. M. Ikram, *Rud-i-Kawthar*, (Karachi, 1958), pp. 424–6, quoted in *Islam* by Fazlur Rehman, (London, Weidenfeld and Nicolson, 1966), p. 187.

10. H. Sharp, *Selections from Educational Records: Part I (1781–1839)* (Calcutta, Government Printing, 1920), p. 110.

11. Maulana Hali, *Hayat-e-Javed*, (Lahore, 1957), p. 447.

12. Max Weber, *Economy and Society*, (Vol. 2, New York, G. Roth and C. Wittich 1968), p. 823.

13. Irfan Habib, 'Changes in Technology in Medieval India', paper presented at the Symposium on Technology and Society, Indian History Congress, Waltair, 1979.

14. Ibid.

15. Bryan S. Turner, *Weber and Islam* (London, Routledge and Kegan Paul, 1974), pp. 100–106.

16. H. A. R. Gibb and H. Bowen, *Islamic Society and the West*, (London, 1950), Vol. 1, p. 283.

17. Turner, op. cit., p. 103.

18. Al-Ghazzali in *Ihya II 124* (Cairo, 1352), quoted in *Studies on the Civilization of Islam*, by Hamilton Gibb (New Jersey, Princeton University Press, 1962), pp. 142–3.

12. Some Thoughts for the Future

Muslim society, bullied by the military might of the West, pushed into retrograde positions by reactionary internal forces, torn by bitter rivalries and enmities, disappointed by its historical fate, and culturally wedded to the past, is in dire need of educational, social and political reform if science and human dignity are to flourish.

Militant Islamic movements have sprung up all across the globe, a manifestation both of the perceived need for reform and of the sense of bitter anger and frustration which pervades the Muslim world today. The motivations for the resurgence are diverse. One category of movements, such as in Palestine and Kashmir, is centred around protest against socio-political injustice. Another kind, of which Iran under Imam Khomenei is the prime example, found in Islam an ideology of revolutionary mobilization and emerged as a consequence of the excesses of secular elites. A third category, represented by the Jamaat-e-Islami of Pakistan and Ikhwan-ul-Muslimeen of Egypt, has roots in a segment of the expanding middle class which seeks power but cannot be politically fully accommodated in the present systems based on patronage and fedual power. And finally, there is an international movement, based primarily in the Western countries, of immigrants who seek, through participation in Islamic movements, a sense of community and psychological security in an environment which is culturally alienating and economically difficult.

Leaders of the resurgence hold the West principally to blame for the present state of the Muslim world. The corruption introduced by Western ideas and culture, and the diabolical connivance of the superpowers today, are emphasized as being the cause of underdevelopment in Islamic countries. The solution is stated to lie in following a truly Islamic path, and rejection of all that is perceived as Western — Western science, Western rationalism and Western democracy. Supporters see in the resurgence a significance which outstrips even that of the French Revolution, which was a landmark victory for the intellectual and physical liberation of the French people.

But there is deep cause for worry because, in the fight against injustice and domination, it is the orthodoxy alone which has been successful in translating popular resentments into political gains. Fundamentalist movements have come to dominate intellectual discourse in key Muslim countries and the

Muslim modernist movement, which emphasizes Islam's compatibility with science and rationalism, has lost its cultural and ideological hegemony. The modernist has been effectively banished from the political and cultural scene and the modern educational system, which was nascent 50 years ago, has visibly collapsed in key Islamic countries. Orthodoxy has arrogated to itself the task of guiding the destiny of Muslims. But their prescription for society is an invitation to catastrophe and possibly to a new Dark Age for Muslims. Rejection of colonialism has become an excuse to justify a blind backtracking into the past and an hysterical rejection of knowledge and rationality. This can only worsen the highly skewed balance of power in the world today. The truth is that one part of humanity has been cut off from contact with the processes of rational and scientific thought. This has automatically endowed another part of humanity with the attributes of power.

Instead of the orthodox programme, what is needed is a framework for thought and action, based upon science and reason, but in harmony with the inherited cultures of the Muslim peoples.

First, we need to renounce the notion that there exists a simple and unique solution for all the dilemmas of society, or that a repertoire of every possible problem and its solution is to be found somewhere in tradition. The fact is that a modern society faces highly complex issues and choices in almost every sphere of activity. Many issues have simply no precedent in the past. To name but a few: pollution versus demands for industrial expansion, increased efficiency through automation versus employment, quality versus quantity in education, international banking and trade, corporate law, and so on. Complex societies have complex problems which may have only complex remedies. No remedy is likely to be perfect. In such circumstances, one seeks a quantitative, rather than qualitative, measure of success. Absoluteness is thereby lost and issues become murky and grey, instead of black and white.

Because the rules of a modern society are not absolute, they can be changed in the light of accumulated experience to alleviate excesses and mistakes. Reform is not instantaneous, but proceeds by degrees. In contrast, the dogmatist dreams of reforming all of society in one holistic sweep and believes that he has in his possession a unique, unalterable blueprint. This quest for a utopia leads to authoritarianism, intolerance and violence because, once the end goal has been defined, no one is allowed to criticize or change it. The insufferable arrogance of those who claim to be in sole possession of religious truth is the cause of immense misery and suffering. Very often, the targets of utopian violence are actually members belonging to the same faith.

Therefore, instead of planning for utopia, it makes much more sense to attempt a partial and piecemeal solution to the problems right in front of us and to deal with them in a systematic, logical and realistic way. The realization that an all-encompassing solution is not available requires a high degree of social, as well as individual, maturity. But it is only a mature society which can possess intellectual and religious tolerance, and which can provide basic liberties to its citizens.

Second, we must fight against the tendency to confuse modernization with Westernization. The two have come to be viewed as synonymous, but it is not necessary to be Western in order to be modern, or to pose a dichotomy between modernity and tradition. One can find in the history of Islamic culture — in the works of Ibn Sina, Ibn Rushd, Al-Razi and many others — an insistence on a rational creed, and hence the seeds of the modern approach to life. Modern man does not deny spirituality. But he is oriented towards the present and future rather than the past, is open to fresh experiences and new ideas, accepts reason and calculability instead of fate, has a large inventory of knowledge and facts at his disposal, relies on planning and organization, is willing to accept the right of others to their opinions, and believes in individual merit and rights. In order to function, organized societies need modern people — people who can relate cause to effect, can resolve conflicts without the use of violence, know how to use available public services, can spend their money efficiently, and use their leisure time usefully.

Modernity is a goal to be struggled for; it is intrinsic to man's rational nature and not a colonial import. To encourage the growth of modern attitudes in a population, it is by no means necessary to induce in it consumer greed for Western products. Imitation of foreign patterns of consumption has certainly not promoted a rational ethic. On the contrary, it has often had the effect of degrading cultural identity and increasing wastage of resources. As one example, bottle feeding of infants is common Western practice and is therefore thought to be a very modern thing which should be imitated. But, given its high cost relative to income, and the dangers of insufficient sterilization in typical Third World environments, bottle feeding is often not the choice which makes optimal use of available resources. Hence it is not truly modern, although it is Western.

Modernity and science go together in our age, and science is the supreme expression of man's rationality. But we need to recall that in the colonized countries, science first came to be known to people by its products rather than as a system of ideas. Even today, trapped in the network of Western trade, science in the peripheral countries continues to be identified with weapons, aircraft, television, and so on. Similarly, the hi-tech electronics industry, located in the havens of South East Asia and using a cheaply bought repressed labour force of peasant origin, has made little contribution towards appreciation of the scientific method. Even the elites in developing countries know nothing about the development of calculus or electromagnetism and why, without these theoretical tools, the modern products of science would have been impossible. Indeed, appreciation and internalization of science cannot occur without the simultaneous development of a rational, modern and egalitarian system of education. At present, there is insufficient realization of the need for this. To invest resources in education is necessary, but far from enough — the content of education is even more important. The end goal of education in a modern society is to produce persons capable of critical thought, who believe in the power of reason, and who have internalized concepts and values crucial to the functioning of organized society.

Third, a truce needs to be declared in the continuing opposition to modern science as an epistemological enterprise, although debate on its utilitarian goals must continue and even be sharpened. Many great scientists, and enlightened leaders of the religious establishment, have affirmed that there can be no real opposition between true religion and science, and that one is indeed the complement of the other. The religious element in man's soul — his ability to wonder and reflect — is something to be recognized and cultivated. Science can be used to enhance the moral values of life because it insists upon searching for the truth. At its deepest level, it does create a feeling of reverence because an advance of knowledge brings us face to face with the mystery of our own being.

But, while recognizing that religion and science are complementary and not contradictory to each other, a clear demarcation betwen the spheres of the spiritual and the worldly is necessary. Secular and religious knowledge have historically come to be closely intermingled in Islam, a fact that was regarded as unfortunate and contrary to true Islam by modern Islamic rationalists, such as Syed Ahmed Khan. The mission of the rationalists was to disentangle the two and to reduce the bewildering proliferation of verbiage and confusion on almost every issue. To take just one example, enormous confusion surrounds the definition of *ilm* (knowledge). Franz Rosenthal lists 107 definitions, and a 16th century Arab scholar has given 316. Muslim scholars have yet to give a definitive view on how to relate the various specializations of modern knowledge to the original Qur'anic interpretations of *ilm*.

In order to separate the domains of religion and science, it must be recognized that science is reason organized for understanding the material universe. Religion, on the other hand, is a reasoned and reasonable abdication of reason with regard to those questions which lie outside the reach of science, such as 'why does the universe exist?' or 'what is the prupose of life?'. Modern science is equally consistent with religion and atheism; this openness implies a high degree of freedom of interpretation. There is no conflict unless the domains are caused to overlap, as when theologians insist on giving answers to questions which are only amenable to a scientific treatment. There has to be a realization that changes in religion do not amount to a denial of religion. An alteration in scientific outlook — let us say the supercession of classical mechanics by quantum mechanics — is generally viewed as a victory for science. But an alteration in religious outlook — let us say acceptance of the Great Flood as a symbolic rather than literal truth — is usually looked on as a defeat for religion. Yet, either both are defeats or both are victories — not for partial activities such as religion or science, but for humanity.

While science must be vigorously pursued both for development and for enlightenment of the mind, one must be clear that science is not a replacement for religion and that it does not constitute a code of morality. Science provides a unique framework and paradigm for calculating and quantifying; but it knows nothing about justice, beauty, or feeling. The emotional void in a technological culture, the unbridled pursuit of weapons of destruction, the callous destruction of the environment in the name of progress, and the imbalances induced by science in the economic and social progress of humanity, are the consequences of a unilinear vision of progress which consecrates and elevates science to the level of an ethic and a morality. This delusion must be opposed as vigorously as rationality must be fought for. But the battleground for the skewed outlook on science is primarily in the West, while the struggle for rationality is in the East.

Fourth, it needs to be recognised that there is no law of nature confining scientific and technological progress to the developed nations of the West. Science and technology are not at the will or service of Western political and national interests, but are universal. There is no reason to accept the inequalities within and between nations as natural or ordained by Providence. These inequalities can be, and must be, mitigated. After all, peoples everywhere in the world have basically equal capabilities and should have the same rights.

What this demands is that the structures of domination have to be dismantled — structures that permit not only the suppression and denigration of one nation by another, but also of one segment of society by another. The latter is a highly visible reality in most developing countries, where one witnesses the modernization of tyrannical military–bureaucratic elites, but not the modernization of people. True progress towards modernity requires that mass participation in planning and execution be encouraged wherever this is an available option. To rely on the people is an expression of respect for cultural heritage, for it is only they who are the bearers of culture and tradition. At the same time, one must be cautious and bear in mind that all traditions are not positive and do not necessarily lead towards forward development.

One can be optimistic about the triumph of reason even at a time when it appears to have fallen into disfavour. Reason may well be a small force, yet it is constant and works always in one direction. In contrast, the forces of unreason destroy one another in futile strife. Historically, humankind has not gone forward as one united body; on the contrary, each advance has come after a protracted struggle between the forces of reason and unreason, between those who seek more light and those who are afraid of it. The enrichment of life, the uplift of human dignity, the liberation of the creative spirit and the vindication of freedom — this is the struggle ahead of us.

In closing, I wish to emphasize that this book has not sought to seek a judgement of the Islamic Faith on the basis of the scientific underdevelopment of Muslim countries. Such a commentary would be quite unwarranted for three reasons. First, there is an overwhelming consensus among Muslims that Islam, in its truest form, is presently not being practised anywhere in the world. Hence, in this view, no connection between present realities and the true Islamic idea is permissible. Secondly, there exist various interpretations of the faith which allow for a separation between the worldly and the other-worldly, and hence for compatibility with scientific thought. Thirdly, and finally, the material success of the adherents of a given religion obviously says nothing about the goodness or truth of that religion.

The last point is an important one. To appreciate it, we need only recall that when Buddhism first reached Japan in the 6th century AD, the government, being in doubt as to the truth of the new religion, ordered one of the courtiers to adopt it on an experimental basis. If he prospered more than others, the religion was to be adopted universally. Otherwise it would be politely returned to wherever it came from. But this utterly simplistic criterion of worldly success has certainly not gained wide acceptance. To conclude: the truth of Islam as a faith is not be be judged by either the accomplishments, or the failures, of its adherents.

Appendix
They Call It Islamic Science*

There has emerged, in recent years, a remarkable new manifestation of orthodox religiosity which is, in essence, an attempt to extend the scope of Islamization in Pakistan beyond the sphere of social concerns and into the domain of natural phenomena. They call it Islamic science.

Rising like a phoenix from the ashes of a long gone medieval age, this new 'science' seeks to establish that every scientific fact and phenomenon known today was anticipated 1,400 years ago and that all scientific predictions may, in fact, be based on the study of the Holy Book. Once again, as in medieval times, theology is being crowned as the Queen of Sciences. Generous support for this vision of science comes from certain Muslim states, patronage of important personages, and what appears to be a limitless supply of funds from individuals and organizations. These have brought into existence something which is being offered as the Islamic alternative to the challenge of modern Western science. Ordinary secular science, according to proponents of the new Islamic science, has no business being here in the Land of the Pure. Together with various other foul products of godless secular civilizations — such as capitalism or socialism or democracy — modern science also needs to be unceremoniously shipped back to the West, where it supposedly belongs.

The Scientific Miracles Conference

I had the privilege of recently observing at close range the new Islamic Science. The occasion was provided by the international conference on Scientific Miracles of Qu'ran and Sunnah, inaugurated by President General Mohammed Zia-ul-Haq in Islamabad on October 18, 1987. This large-scale affair, with hundreds of delegates from various Muslim countries, had been jointly organized by the International Islamic University in Islamabad together with the Organization of Scientific Miracles in Mecca. The magnificence of the arrangements was beyond dispute, but luckily the burden on Pakistani taxpayers was said to be limited. About half the total conference expenses —

---

* This appendix is an extended version of my article originally published in the January 1988 issue of the Karachi monthly *Herald* and has been reproduced with permission.

around 66 lakh rupees ($400,000) — were borne by the brotherly government of Saudi Arabia which often subsidizes such excellent causes. Lest it be thought that this conference was a freak occurrence, I should mention that it had been preceded by two others of a similar nature some months ago in Karachi, as well as many earlier ones. New ones are doubtlessly being planned, and will also take their due place in history.

The Scientific Miracles Conference provided me with a fascinating glimpse into the concerns and issues which the new Islamic science addresses. While the reader is urged to study for himself the published version of scholarly papers read at all such conferences, the following shortlist of rather suggestively titled papers presented at the Scientific Miracles Conference by itself speaks volumes:

(1) Chemical Composition of Milk in relation to Verse 66 of Surat An-Nahl of The Holy Qur'an.

(2) Description of Man at High Altitude in Qur'an.

(3) Cumulonimbus Clouds Description in Qur'an.

(4) Have You Observed the Fire?

(5) Revelation of Some Modern Oceanographic Phenomena in Holy Qur'an.

Sixty-five other papers of a similar nature were also presented by the pious, bearded participants. Serious discussions supplemented the formal paper reading sessions. As a mere onlooker I felt out of my depth, finding even the titles of some sessions to be incomprehensible. For example, one of these was advertised as Panel Discussion on Things Known Only To Allah, scheduled for sometime in the evening after prayers. I was unable to attend, but subsequently have often wondered what secrets the panelists were privy to.

The Amazing Conclusions of Islamic Science

The achievements of modern science are said to be difficult to understand. Perhaps so. But achievements of the new Islamic science are even harder to comprehend. Nevertheless, the reader is urged to ponder upon certain remarkable results presented at these various Islamic science conferences and then to draw for himself whatever conclusion he pleases. A selection follows:

● Dr Mohammed Muttalib, who teaches earth sciences at the famous Al-Azhar University in Egypt, presented an extremely erudite paper on the relation of geological facts and phenomena to Qur'anic verses.[1] For the ordinary type of scientist this paper was not particularly easy to understand — and frankly it still eludes me. Mountains have roots in the earth, said the good doctor, and Allah made them act like pegs which tether a tent to the ground and keep it from blowing away. Without mountains, he emphasized, the earth's rotation would cause everything simply to fly apart. It would be totally catastrophic — no mountains, no earth.

I must admit finding this conclusion a little odd. The learned author, it appears, was genuinely unaware of a phenomenon which Mr Newton was fond of calling gravity. Ordinary physics, which most of us know at least a bit about, tells us that on earth the force of gravity considerably exceeds the centrifugal force. Were the opposite true, we would all be sent whizzing into space with each of us being his own spacecraft. Hence, says the usual run-of-the-mill physics, even if all the mountains on earth were bulldozed flat the earth would still not disintegrate. Of course, no one advocates that such a thing should be done — it would be an aesthetic and ecological tragedy to do away with mountains. But the point is that mountains as tent pegs may make an excellent metaphor, but has no factual significance. However, if the universe runs according to Dr Muttalib's extraordinary physics and not ordinary physics, then, of course, my critique of the doctor's thesis is without foundation.

● Another paper, also presented at the Scientific Miracles Conference, dealt with a matter of doctrinal importance in a manner which, to say the least, was extraordinary. Engineer Abdal Fequi of Egypt, drawing on his experience with armour piercing anti-tank ammunition gained during service in the Egyptian army in 1976, gave very impressive evidence that Allah intends us to use *empty* copper shells in order to destroy such men and jinns as may dare to venture in spaceships into forbidden regions of the heavens.[2] Now, why empty copper shells instead of ones filled with explosives? This pious engineer argues — very persuasively in his opinion — that an empty cone allows for the buildup of a destructive shock wave much more effectively than a solid cone. Because Divine Wisdom is perfect in all respects — including the selection of materials for heavenly missiles — therefore, empty copper shells must be the Lord's choice.

This is all very well, except for one small thing which should not be taken as a disparagement. Knowledgeable people in the armament business say that copper shells are going out of fashion and the industry is going gung-ho on a certain new molybdenum alloy which contains the explosive charge better. So here is a puzzle: are the heavenly missiles really going to be made of old-fashioned copper, or is it going to be molybdenum instead? A difficult question indeed!

● *Munafiqat* (hypocrisy) is certainly an endemic problem in our society. While many will acknowledge this, there are very few amongst us who are either talented or brave enough to apply mathematical methods to this problem. But at the International Seminar on Qur'an and Science, organized in June 1986 by the Pakistan Association of Scientists and Scientific Professions, one intrepid scientist presented a bold new scientific theory of *munafiqat*.[3]

Dr Arshad Ali Beg, a senior scientist at the PCSIR (Pakistan Council for Scientific and Industrial Research) has a mathematical formula by which, he says, the degree of *munafiqat* in a society can be calculated. The work of this Islamic scientist rests on an analogy between polarizing forces acting on molecules in a liquid and corresponding forces acting on individuals in a society. So, everything happens through chemical reactions such as:

Infidels + Teaching of the Prophet $\longrightarrow$ Religious Society.

Skipping the details, which the reader can find in his paper, let me quickly come to his conclusions: Western society is calculated to have a *munafiqat* value of 22, while Spain and Portugal have a value of only fourteen. It is a bit of a mystery that no *munafiqat* values are given for Pakistani society which, it is sometimes alleged, is run by crooks and *munafiqs*. But for all that, the reader will surely admit the novelty of Dr Beg's work and forgive minor omissions.

- It appears that a recent convert to the new Islamic science is the chairman of Pakistan's Space Organization, SUPARCO, which is the Pakistani equivalent of NASA in the US. In a paper read at the Karachi Qur'an and Science Conference, Mr Salim Mehmud proposed that an explanation for the Holy Prophet's *Mairaj* (ascension to heaven) be sought in Einstein's theory of relativity.[4] As every believer knows, the Ascension took almost no time — it is even said the chain hanging from the Prophet's door was still swinging when he returned from his meeting with God. The apparently short duration has been often interpreted — and most recently in a slick film produced by the International Islamic University — as an example of relativistic time dilation. The phenomenon of time dilation is well known to physicists: moving clocks appear to run slow.

Unfortunately, there is a slight problem with this explanation. The theory of relativity actually says precisely the opposite of what the chairman sahib thinks it says. Alas, every textbook on relativity unequivocally states that more time will elapse for a person who stays at rest, than for another who goes and comes back from a long journey at high speed. One wishes that the honourable chairman had taken some time off to study the principle of relativity properly before enthusiastically proposing it as a solution of theological mysteries. Quite possibly, our country's feeble little space programme would be better off if more attention were paid to research in mundane space science instead of spiritual dynamics.

- Published quarterly from Islamabad under the rather weighty title *Science and Technology in the Islamic World,* this journal is an important advocate and means of propagation of the new Islamic science. On its editorial board are the heavyweights of the Pakistani science establishment — the men who decide the fate of science in Pakistan through their policy decisions, funding of projects, establishment of new institutions, and so on. Here is a small sample of the articles which they have apparently deemed fit for publication, and which have actually appeared in this journal in recent issues:

(1) Some Qur'anic *Ayaat* Containing References to Science and Technology;

(2) Symmetry of Universe and the Qur'anic Principle of Creation in Pairs;

(3) Some Ahadith Containing References to Jihad;

(4) The Monograms of Two Popular Pakistani Banks and Their Probable Significance;

(5) Dichotomy of *Insan* (Man) and Jinn & their Destiny.

The concerns of this high-powered journal evidently have little to do with conventional science and technology. But what it loses in conventionality, it makes up for in pure novelty. Take, for example, the last mentioned paper above, authored by Dr Safdar Jang Rajput, a senior scientist with DESTO (the Defence Science & Technology Organization).[5]

The starting point is what every reader surely knows — God made jinns out of fire at the time that He made man out of clay (or black mud, say some). For Dr Rajput, these fiery spirits are a living reality and clearly something with which he is deeply preoccupied. They even form the subject of his research. A summary of his principal results in jinnology, published in the above quoted article, is as follows:

(1) It is highly probable that the origin of jinns is methane gas, together with other saturated hydro-carbons, because these yield a smokeless flame upon burning. This conclusion is predicated on the known fact that God made jinns out of fire, together with the known fact that no jinn emitting smoke has ever been seen.

(2) The virginity and beauty of the houris of heaven is another known truth Add to this the fact that they were created for being used. Because the users can be either men or jinns, it follows that both men and jinns are similar and isogenotypes. QED.

(3) After protracted debate, the final conclusion on the nature of jinns is the following: 'I cannot help but say that the jinns are the white races.'[6]

Dr Rajput is by no means the only highly placed Pakistani scientist for whom jinns are so profoundly important. A senior director of the Pakistan Atomic Energy Commission, Mr Bashiruddin Mahmood, in 1980 had recommended that jinns, being fiery creatures, ought to be tapped as a free source of energy. By this means, a final solution to Pakistan's energy problems would be found. [See letters attached to this appendix for a debate on this issue.]

- Incredible as it may sound, a German delegate to the Islamic Science Conference held in Islamabad in 1983 claimed to have calculated the Angle of God using mathematical topology. He states the angle to be pi/N, where pi = 3.1415927 . . . and N is not defined. The reader of this book has a right to be sceptical. Can anyone even think of calculating such a bizarre thing? To allay any doubts, I suggest that the reader refer to page 82 of the Islamic Science Conference Abstracts published by Pakistan's Ministry of Science & Technology (1983). At that point, the only thing to distrust will be one's own eyes. The reader may also confirm that this lunatic was fully hosted and supported at the expense of the Pakistan government. Why, one may ask, was this man not challenged for his blasphemy? There appear to be two reasons. For one, his blatherings (at least the published ones) are so incoherent that probably no one had a clue what he was saying. And, for another, he wasn't the only guy tripping high.

Is This Science?

A person educated outside a strict orthodox environment is likely to see such papers as the incoherent babbling of defective minds. He may even suggest the services of some good psychiatrist. Other critics may angrily denounce this new so-called Islamic science as unscientific. But this criticism could be unfair. Science can mean one thing to one set of people, and something quite different to another set. To end this confusion, it is necessary first to clearly define modern science, and then see what is being called Islamic science these days.

Modern science is a set of definite rules by which one seeks a rational comprehension of the physical universe. It derives its awesome power and authority entirely from a method that combines observation and inference. All scientific knowledge is constructed on the objective base of our sense experiences. This objectivity is made possible because experiment and logical consistency are the sole arbiters of truth — of no consequence is the scientist's mood or moral character, his political beliefs or nationality, or even his status in the world of science. On this last point, consider, for example, that Einstein was never taken too seriously when he (wrongly) set out to criticize quantum mechanics — this in spite of the fact that he was acknowledged as the greatest living physicist of the time.

Whether or not one likes it, it is indisputably true that modern science is completely secular in character. There is no appeal to divine authority for verification of scientific facts; the existence of such authority is neither affirmed nor denied. However, individual scientists are sometimes deeply religious and struck by the purpose, order and precision of the universe. One need only recall that the men considered to be the founders of modern science, Galileo and Newton, were generally very religious subscribers to the beliefs and practices of the Christian Church. Nevertheless, science and religion went their separate ways after the great divide was heralded by the Copernican revolution in the 17th century.

Here is an example from modern times which vividly illustrates the above point. In 1979, the Nobel Prize for Physics was awarded to Abdus Salam, Steven Weinberg, and Sheldon Glashow for having discovered the fundamental theory uniting two basic forces of nature — the 'weak' and the 'electromagnetic'. Known as the Salam–Weinberg theory, it represents one of the most profound discoveries of this century. But look at the beliefs of its discoverers! Salam quotes profusely from the Qur'an, prays regularly, and even makes some of his wellwishers uncomfortable by his zealousness and devotion to the Ahmedi sect, to which he belongs. This sect was excommunicated from Islam in 1974, and legally Salam is not considered a Muslim in Pakistan. But this appears to have only strengthened his resolve. On the other hand, Weinberg is Jewish by birth. But he is an avowed atheist for whom the universe is an existentialist reality devoid of sense and purpose. An enormous ideological gulf separated these two brilliant physicists. And yet they both arrived at precisely the same theory of physics more or less simultaneously!

Falsifiability: A Criterion for Science

How can one separate true science from non-science? Alternatively, what entitles a particular set of propositions to be called a scientific theory? This is not altogether a settled matter, but one persuasive answer is to be found in the principle of falsifiability, enunciated in clear terms by the English philosopher of science, Sir Karl Popper.[7] If we are to call this or that a scientific theory, says Popper, then it is absolutely necessary that the theory make predictions which can be checked for correctness against observation and experiment. If the theory makes no testable prediction, then there is no way to prove that it is wrong. Any unfalsifiable theory is simply not a scientific theory. This does not mean that it is bad or wrong or whatever, but merely that it is not to be considered a theory of science. Of course, many good things — maybe the best things in life — have probably nothing to do with science at all.

This falsifiability principle can be illustrated, to give one example, with Aristotle's theory of the natural place. Aristotle believed that a stone falls to the earth because the earth is the stone's mother, and the stone wishes to fall into its mother's lap — which is obviously the most natural place for the stone to be. Now we can ask two questions about this. First, is this a scientific theory? Second, was Aristotle right or wrong? As for the first question, the answer is No. Aristotle's theory does not tell us how a stone's speed increases with time, whether lighter or heavier objects fall at different speeds, and so on. It explains why bodies fall, but makes no predictions which we could actually check against experiment. Because there is no way to prove it false, therefore it is definitely not a scientific theory. As for the question of being right or wrong, the answer is surprising: nobody knows. The reader may feel quite sure of his answer. But can he prove that a stone has no affection for Mother Earth?

So now let's apply the criterion of falsifiability to various theories of the new Islamic science. A number of such theories were described earlier, and the reader is invited to apply the criterion to those as well. But here are some more.

- Look at Figure 2. It contains a formula by which you can calculate the total *sawab* (reward) earned for *namaz*, as a function of the number of people praying alongside you. The author of this formula is Dr M. M. Qureshi, a leading member of the Pakistani scientific establishment, ex-chairman of the PCSIR, ex-chairman of the physics department at Quaid-e-Azam University, Pakistan's representative to various international bodies, and so on. Is the doctor sahib correct? Nobody can really say; we shall have to wait for the Day of Judgement to find out. But the theory is definitely not one of science: no experiment can be devised to prove that this doctor's formulae and graph are wrong.

Figure 2: The Quantity of *Sawab* (Divine Reward) Earned by Prayer

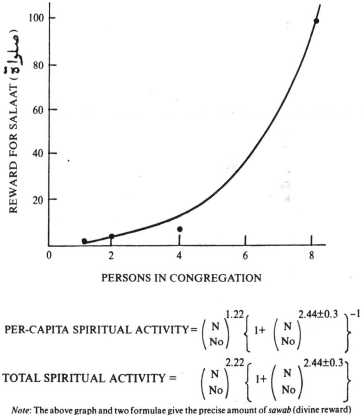

$$\text{PER-CAPITA SPIRITUAL ACTIVITY} = \left(\frac{N}{N_o}\right)^{1.22}\left\{1+\left(\frac{N}{N_o}\right)^{2.44\pm0.3}\right\}^{-1}$$

$$\text{TOTAL SPIRITUAL ACTIVITY} = \left(\frac{N}{N_o}\right)^{2.22}\left\{1+\left(\frac{N}{N_o}\right)^{2.44\pm0.3}\right\}$$

Note: The above graph and two formulae give the precise amount of *sawab* (divine reward) earned for praying as a function of the number of people praying in the congregation.
Source: Islamic Science Conference Proceedings 1983, Volume 2, page 255.

• Now look at Figure 3. A senior director of the Pakistan Atomic Energy Commission, who has been entrusted with designing major parts of a nuclear reactor theorizes in his book entitled *Mechanics of the Doomsday and Life After Death* how the universe transits from the World of Spirits to the Final Day. He shows that this is closely similar to the establishment of a magnetic field in a current-carrying conductor with subsequent radiation of waves from an aerial. Application of Popper's criterion to this example is left as an exercise for the reader. [Note: the diagram reproduced here contains an inadvertent mistake, but this has not been removed. Please see the exchange of letters attached to this appendix where this mistake is the subject of some acrimony.]

Figure 3: The Universe: Its Beginning and Its End

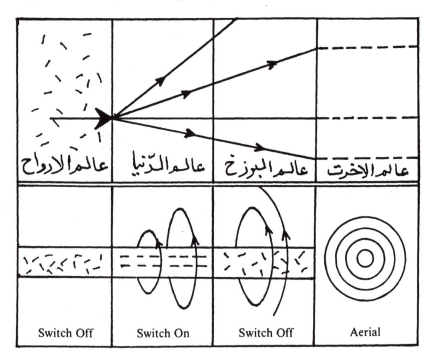

Note: An Islamic scientist describes his conception of how the universe began and will end, making an analogy with the passage of electricity in a wire. At the beginning there was disorder in the World of Spirits, just as electrons are disordered in a conductor. Then . . . . And finally, the soul is radiated into the Final World just like an electron radiates off electromagnetic waves.

Source: Mechanics of the Doomsday and Life After Death, by S. Bashiruddin Mahmood, published by the Holy Qur'an Research Foundation, Islamabad.

What Islamic Science Actually Is

Let me now try to resolve what the new Islamic science actually is. There will be no disagreement, even from its advocates, that its purpose is basically religious. Observe, for instance, that the 70 papers accepted for the Scientific Miracles Conference had first been refereed by bearded theologians of the International Islamic University at Islamabad for their theological correctness. But no panel of scientists was asked to referee any paper for its *scientific* correctness.

It is evident that neither the premises, nor the conclusions, of the new Islamic science are the least bit in doubt. It seeks to reaffirm what is already known, not search into the unknown. No new mathematical principles are sought, no experiments will be designed for its verification, and no new devices or machines will ever be built on account of it. The new Islamic science, like Creationism in the West, is a reaction against modern science. It is not a new direction of science.

And how Islamic is Islamic science anyway?

It is a perilous proposition in these terms to argue that one thing is more or less Islamic than another. The demon of fanaticism sleeps slightly, and always sword in hand. It is easily awakened by the sound of arguments on this subject. The imprimatur of the ulema is not to be taken lightly.

But it remains a worrying thought that a person who tries to write a mathematical formula for *munafiqat* reduces a religious concept to an object of cheap ridicule. The work of that German lunatic who calculated the Angle of God at the 1983 Islamic Science Conference has already been discussed. Was that a service to Islam? And what should be said of that highly placed Pakistani scientist who advocates using fiery jinns as fuel, and hence solving Pakistan's energy crisis?

In truth the new Islamic science is nothing but a fraudulent use of the word science. It seeks to capitalize on the science practised by the early Muslims. But it shares none of qualities which immortalized the achievements of scientists in Islam's Golden Age. If they were alive today, the great men of Islamic scholarship — like Ibn Sina, Omar Khayyam, Ibn al-Haytham, and others — would probably be deeply embarrassed to see what is being called Islamic science. These scholars, while deeply committed Muslims, practised science of an essentially secular kind. Mouthing empty platitudes was not their business, nor did they try to find mathematical equivalents of *munafiqat* or *sawab*. Instead, they discovered important physical laws and created new concepts. Today we remember Nasir-ud-Din-al-Tusi for his trigonometry, Omar Khayyam for his solution of cubic equations, Jabir Ibn Hayyan for the ingenuity of his chemical apparatus, Al-Jazari for his intricate machines, and so on. Their science dealt with reality. This is why their place in world history is secure. And this is also why orthodoxy never forgave them, and to this day denounces them as heretics and unbelievers. It is an almost forgotten fact today that these heroes of Muslim culture were most often threatened not by infidel Christians and Mongol hordes but, instead, by a virulent anti-science section of the orthodox Muslim ulema.

Its Political Roots

What, then, really lies at the root of the new phenomenon which goes under the name of Islamic science? What political forces sustain it, and to which social classes does it appeal the most? Will the phenomenon survive, or is it a bubble about to burst? These are difficult questions and require much thought. In lieu of a comprehensive analysis, all I can do here is make some observations.

First, the new Islamic science has been fathered by the global resurgence of orthodoxy in Muslim countries; it is not peculiar to Pakistan by any means. Egypt, Saudi Arabia and Malaysia are also particularly active centres. However, it is not confined by national boundaries and is particularly to be found amongst immigrants settled in the West. It evidently provides a form of psychological defence against the continuous battering by modern science in its many manifestations. For this reason, one must not expect the phenomenon to disappear in the decades to come.

Next, we note that the proponents of this bizarre science are not the traditional ulema but, instead, holders of high-level degrees in scientific fields. Most of them have studied in the West, although almost none of them have any significant professional achievements to their credit. Islamic science provides a refuge from the challenge of doing difficult science. This suggests that Islamic science may have relatively little to do with a revival of the Faith. While this return to a medieval Dark Ages way of thinking does have a few genuine adherents — mostly in the educated middle classes — by and large it is a game which is being played for personal profit and advancement. Charlatans and incompetents among scientists are assured of being in good favour with the authorities if they sing the right tune. Appointments, promotions, travel money, etc. form the stakes. Of no small importance is the Saudi factor; this infinite reservoir of hard cash has worked wonders.

At its root, the new Islamic science, at least in my own country, originates from the historic compromise between the orthodox ulema and those who govern Pakistan in the name of Islam. For the ulema, Islamic science permits an extension of the domain of religious law into the area of natural phenomena, and thus a means of challenging the growing dominance of secular science. For the ruling elite, however, it is part of a calculated and cynical manipulation of religious sentiment. Without state patronage there would be no Islamic science.

But the state is only a half willing partner. It is true that top government functionaries finance its activities and give grandiose speeches at its major meetings and conferences. But privately they scoff at the very idea of Islamizing science. They accept the superiority of modern analytical methods; get their medical problems treated by doctors rather than traditional hakims; and invariably send their children to English medium schools rather than Urdu medium schools or madrassahs. The fact that Pakistani universities have, with official connivance, succumbed to rule by fundamentalist students is not liked. But the cost is bearable to the rulers because, once their children are old enough, they can be sent to American universities.

In private, Pakistani military officers and bureaucrats view the mullah as an object to be both ridiculed and feared. Ridiculed, because he is seen as an anachronism rooted in a medieval world, with worries and concerns hopelessly irrelevant to modern times. And feared because, should his sanction disappear, the legitimacy of ruling this land in the name of Islam will evaporate.

****

A Response

The above article elicited outrage from at least one of the Islamic scientists mentioned in it. It seems but fair to give his point of view here, and my own subsequent reply.

This with reference to the article 'They Call It Islamic Science' by Pervez Hoodbhoy in your January '88 issue. Through this article the writer has done a great injustice not only to the undersigned (and various other authors working on the Holy Qur'an and Sunnah of the last Prophet of God (PBUH) with reference to modern developments of knowledge) but also to your esteemed readers. He has distorted and misquoted facts from my book and tried to make a mockery of a very serious topic.

For example, if you refer to Box 2 [see Figure 3 above] of his article, it is a distorted version of Diagram No. 25 from my book *Mechanics of the Doomsday and Life after Death*, published by the Holy Qur'an research foundation. To prove his point of view, Mr Hoodbhoy has changed the original text. He writes: 'An Islamic scientist describes his conception of how the universe began and will end, making an analogy to the passage of electricity in a wire . . . and finally the soul radiates off into the final world just as an electron radiates off electromagnetic waves.'
Your readers should know that Mr Hoodbhoy has cheated them by presenting something which is not in the book. I would like to reproduce the exact copy of the page which has been falsified by Mr Hoodbhoy. This figure shows graphically the Islamic concept of the *soul* and *not* the 'conception of how the universe began and will end', as wrongly stated by Mr Hoodbhoy. The electrical analogy of the switching on or off of the electrical current shown in this diagram is with reference to the phenomenon of human life, and does not refer to the start and end of the universe as he has falsely stated.
Thus Mr Hoodbhoy is guilty of dishonest reporting, with no regard even for an elementary level of morality. But this is not all: he has not spared even some other respected personalities. For example, Mr Hoodbhoy has mockingly referred to the paper of the SUPARCO chairman, Salim Mahmood, about the science of cosmology, stating that the chairman sahib has proposed an explanation of the Holy Prophet's *mairaj* (ascension to heaven) be based on Einstein's theory of relativity, and then distorting the

actual text of the relevant paragraph to support his thesis.

Anyone who compares the two texts will be able to see clearly the difference between what was said by the SUPARCO chairman and how it has been interpreted by Mr Hoodbhoy. What Mr Mahmood is actually arguing is that present scientific knowledge is still incapable of explaining such miraculous events. Not only is Mr Hoodbhoy dishonest in his report, he also has the cheek to make derogatory remarks about Mr Mahmood and the government department he is heading.

And as if this were not enough, Mr Hoodbhoy has also referred to a paper by engineer Abdal Fequi of Egypt on earth sciences, presented at the International Conference on Scientific Miracles of Qur'an and Sunnah. The text of the paper has no relationship with what Mr Hoodbhoy maintains has been said in it. He has also made a mockery of the conference and its organizers, where this and seventy other papers were represented by various learned personalities and scientists.

One can disagree with a philosophy, but no one has the right to make fun or cast aspersions on personalities or cheat the general public by misreporting. Mr Hoodbhoy has gone so far as to call people working on Islam and science 'lunatics'. This is crossing all limits of decency. But should one expect any honesty or decency from anti-Islamic forces?

S. Bashiruddin Mahmood
Chairman, Holy Qur'an Research Foundation
Islamabad

My Reply to Mr Mahmood

After reading Mr Bashiruddin Mahmood's response to my article, I plead guilty to a monstrous error and humbly beseech the reader of this magazine for his forgiveness. In truth, the word 'universe' was inadvertently substituted for the word 'soul'. If any reader was misled by this, then I apologize. By confusing one absurdity for another, I made a mistake fully as serious as forgetting to cross a 't' or dot an 'i'.

On the substance of the matter I feel quite unrepentant. Mr Mahmood says his analogy of the passage of electric current through a wire with the transformation of the soul is based on Islam. That may well be his understanding of Islam, but it certainly is not mine. Nowhere in the Holy Qur'an, or in any of the Ahadith, have I seen mention of electrons, magnetic fields, electromagnetic waves, and aerials. Mr Mahmood's bizarre speculations have, so far as I can see, no basis in Islamic texts. As such they represent a grotesque caricature of a religious idea. Let him be warned that good Muslims do not like their religion to be made fun of, or used for nonsensical purposes.

Mr Mahmood comes to the defence of SUPARCO chairman Salim Mahmood, claiming that the chairman had made no attempt to link the Holy

Prophet's *mairaj* (ascension) with Einstein's relativity.

This is false, and what I had said is correct. The text of the chairman's speech, which Mr Mahmood offers as vindication of his point, is on the contrary an explicit attempt to connect the mystery of the ascension with relativity. That text betrays a certain incoherence and dislocation of thought, but even after repeatedly reading it, I can find no reason to believe that my understanding was at fault.

As for Mr Fequi and his research on the nature of divine missiles, the reader is welcome to look at his published paper, which is available from the Islamic University. I do not see how there can be any question of inaccuracy — I simply wrote down in my article what is present in that paper.

In closing, I should like to remind the reader of this magazine that Mr Bashiruddin Mahmood, chairman of the Holy Qur'an Research Foundation, is known for far more than making electromagnetic analogies of the human soul. His real fame derives from a published paper wherein he suggests that jinns, whom God made out of fire, should be used as a source of energy in a world beset by an energy problem.

I am pleased to be the target of Mr Mahmood's vilification, because this means my article successfully hit a nerve-centre of obscurantist nonsense. Though he alleges it, I had no intention of calling all those who work on Islam and science either frauds or lunatics. Far from it. But can it be denied that people of this type are busy scrambling these days to get on to the bandwagon which they call Islamic science?

Dr Pervez Hoodbhoy
Department of Physics
Quaid-e-Azam University
Islamabad

****

The heated controversy over the claims of 'Islamic Science' was picked up by a few international newspapers and magazines. In particular, the *Wall Street Journal* came out with a special investigative article on the subject of Islamic Science, published on the front page of the issue of 13 September 1988. A portion of that article, which is of especial interest in view of the exchange reproduced above, is given below:

> Across town in a quiet neighbourhood, S. Bashiruddin Mahmood, director of the Holy Quran Research Foundation, has become a sort of eminence grise in Pakistan. By day, Mr Mahmood, a nuclear engineer, designs leak-detection systems for nuclear plants. By night he concocts Islamic theories.
>
> Those who dare criticize such attempts say that in 1983, Mr Mahmood turned up at an Islamic science conference and read a paper saying that djinns — Koranic creatures made of fire — could be harnessed to solve

energy shortages. Mr Mahmood denies that he said it. 'Absolute nonsense',
he insists during a chat.

What then did he say?

Choosing his words carefully, Mr Mahmood explains that djinns are
made out of energy, and that King Solomon figured out how to put them to
work for him.

'I think that if we develop our souls we can develop communication with
them', he says.

Mr Mahmood isn't surprised that some people frown on his Islamic cause.
'Every new idea has its opponents', he says, 'But there is no reason for this
controversy on Islam and science because there is no conflict between Islam
and science.'

References

1. Mohammed Mutallib, 'Geology In The Light of Quranic Verse', presented at
the First International Conference on Scientific Miracles of Qur'an and Sunnah,
1987, available in published form from the International Islamic University
Islamabad.

2. Muhammad Abd Alkader Al Fequi, 'Views on the Scientific Miraculous
Aspect of the Holy Qur'an in Relation to the Earth Sciences', presented at the
Scientific Miracles Conference, op. cit.

3. M. Arshad Ali Beg, 'Qur'an and Scientific Interpretation of *Munafiqat*',
published in proceedings of the International Seminar on Qur'an & Science,
(Karachi, Pakistan Association of Scientists and Scientific Professions, 26 June
1986), pp. 46–55.

4. Salim Mahmood, *Elm-e-Falkiat*, published in proceedings of International
Seminar on Quran & Science, (Karachi, Pakistan Association of Scientists and
Scientific Professions, 17 June 1987), p. 42.

5. Safdar Jang Rajput, 'Dichotomy of *Insan* and Jinn & Their Destiny', published
in *Science and Technology in the Islamic World*, Vol. 3, No. 1, (Islamabad, Jan.–
March 1985), pp. 28–48.

6. Ibid., p. 35.

7. K. R. Popper, *The Logic of Scientific Discovery*, (London, Hutchinson, 1968),
passim.

Index

Zed Books Ltd

is a publisher whose international and Third World lists span:

- **Women's Studies**
- **Development**
- **Environment**
- **Current Affairs**
- **International Relations**
- **Children's Studies**
- **Labour Studies**
- **Cultural Studies**
- **Human Rights**
- **Indigenous Peoples**
- **Health**

We also specialize in Area Studies where we have extensive lists in African Studies, Asian Studies, Caribbean and Latin American Studies, Middle East Studies, and Pacific Studies.

For further information about books available from Zed Books, please write to: Catalogue Enquiries, Zed Books Ltd, 57 Caledonian Road, London N1 9BU. Our books are available from distributors in many countries (for full details, see our catalogues), including:

In the USA
Humanities Press International, Inc., 165 First Avenue, Atlantic Highlands, New Jersey 07716.
Tel: (201) 872 1441;
Fax: (201) 872 0717.

In Canada
DEC, 229 College Street, Toronto, Ontario M5T 1R4.
Tel: (416) 971 7051.

In Australia
Wild and Woolley Ltd, 16 Darghan Street, Glebe, NSW 2037.

In India
Bibliomania, C-236 Defence Colony, New Delhi 110 024.

In Southern Africa
David Philip Publisher (Pty) Ltd, PO Box 408, Claremont 7735, South Africa.